Indigenous London

THE HENRY ROE CLOUD SERIES ON AMERICAN INDIANS AND MODERNITY

Named in honor of the pioneering Winnebago educational reformer and first known American Indian graduate of Yale College, Henry Roe Cloud (class of 1910), this series showcases emergent and leading scholarship in the field of American Indian Studies. The series draws upon multiple disciplinary perspectives and organizes them around the place of Native Americans in the development of American and European modernity, emphasizing the shared, relational ties between indigenous and Euro-American societies. It seeks to broaden current historic, literary, and cultural approaches to American Studies by foregrounding the fraught but generative sites of inquiry provided by the study of indigenous communities.

Series Editors

NED BLACKHAWK
Professor of History and American Studies, Yale University

KATE W. SHANLEY
Native American Studies, University of Montana

Indigenous London

Native Travelers at the Heart of Empire

Coll Thrush

Yale
UNIVERSITY PRESS
NEW HAVEN AND LONDON

Published with assistance from the Mary Cady Tew Memorial Fund.

Yale University Press books may be purchased in quantity for educational, business, or promotional use. For information, please e-mail sales.press@yale.edu (U.S. office) or sales@yaleup.co.uk (U.K. office).

Set in Fournier MT type by Integrated Publishing Solutions.
Printed in the United States of America.

ISBN 978-0-300-20630-2
Library of Congress Control Number: 2016933934
A catalogue record for this book is available from the British Library.

This paper meets the requirements of ANSI/NISO Z39.48-1992 (Permanence of Paper).

10 9 8 7 6 5 4 3 2 1

In memory of those who did not return

It is in the nature of the city to encompass everything.

—Peter Ackroyd, *London: The Biography,* 2001

Contents

Acknowledgments

This book has its origins in a conversation with my former husband, a Londoner by birth, back in 2007. My first book, *Native Seattle: Histories from the Crossing-Over Place*, had just been published, and was receiving good press. But London always called. Every time I'd been there, I'd wondered why I hadn't chosen British history as my field of expertise; the city is a powerfully alluring place and text. So when Simon half-jokingly asked, "Why don't you write a book like *Native Seattle* about London, so you could go there on your research grants?" I at first laughed. Who was I, after all, to write about London? But within about five minutes, I realized, *That's it. That's the next book.* What would it be like to take the central concept of *Native Seattle*—reframing the history of a city through Indigenous experience—to the center of empire? That is the project here, so my first acknowledgment is to Simon Martin.

My second acknowledgment is that I write from occupied territory. With the exception of several sojourns in London and elsewhere, the vast majority of this book was produced in Vancouver, which stands on Indigenous land. More specifically, the University of British Columbia (UBC) is a guest of the Musqueam Nation, which has inhabited this space for thousands of years, since time immemorial. I wish to honor the graciousness and hospitality that I, like many of my colleagues, have received in this, their traditional, ancestral and unceded territory.

I also want to acknowledge my own embeddedness in this story. For me, London is a place of ancestry. My forebears, at least on one side of my family, called the city home. Some appear in genealogical records from the sixteenth century, others emigrated from there to the Jamestown Colony at the beginning of the seventeenth century, and still others were married at St. Martin-in-the-Fields in the eighteenth century. In that, like in writing from Indigenous territory, I myself am entangled in the history herein. This has always informed my relationship with the city, so I acknowledge that place and its people in addition to the place where most of the book was written.

It is out of this history, and the recognition of my inherent settler privilege, that *Indigenous London*'s intellectual and political agendas arise. This book is not about "giving voice" to Indigenous people—they already had (and have) it. Nor is it about "making space"—they already were making (and continue to make) it. Instead, it is a project primarily concerned with the kinds of projects outlined by Māori scholar and activist Linda Tuhiwai Smith. In her canonical work *Decolonizing Methodologies*, Smith sets out twenty-five kinds of research initiatives that can serve the interests of Indigenous peoples and communities. No single work can do all twenty-five. But *Indigenous London*, I think, at least partially satisfies Smith's call to Indigenize history by centering "landscapes, images, languages, themes, metaphors and stories" from the broader Indigenous world. I also have endeavored to practice what she calls "decolonizing reading." As Smith describes, such reading is a way "to locate a different sort of origin story, the origins of imperial policies and practices, the origins of the imperial visions, the origins of ideas and values." Those creation stories were often born in the crucible of the empire's capital.

At the same time, a project on the scale of this book simply cannot meet the expectations for community-engaged research that Smith and others call for and which have become the norm in much of the field of Indigenous studies. In an ideal world, I would have spent great amounts of time working in descendant communities, being directed by those communities' own research initiatives, and developing relationships that might lead to other projects. But when a book covers more than five hundred years and engages the history of some forty distinct Indigenous peoples, such deep engagement is impossible. Doing ethical Indigenous research and doing global Indigenous history are, necessarily, at odds with each other. My response to this problem has been to rely on the good graces and outstanding scholarship of friends and colleagues, many with expertise on, with, and/or from within the communities whose stories appear in this book and on the time periods with which I was concerned. Without their insights, I would have made some rather embarrassing mistakes, and the end result would be a much inferior work. And so I wish to thank Margery Fee, Josh Reid, Kelly McDonough, Lisa Brooks, Heather Miyano Kopelson, Mary Fuller, Kelly Wisecup, Jenny Pulsipher, Paul Irish, Grisham Langton, J. Kēhaulani Kauanui, Marie Alohalani Brown, Kuʻualoha Hoʻomanuwanui, Jacob Pollock, Jenny Thigpen, Alice Te Punga Somerville, Alyssa Mt. Pleasant, Brendan Hokowhitu, David Gaertner, Lynne Fitzhugh, Boyd Cothran, Laura Peers, and Joe Genetin-Pilawa, among others too numerous to name here. I also wish to thank the individuals that I interviewed and spoke with for the final chapter of the book: Peter Morin, Esther Jessop, and Maia Nuku. Jace Weaver and Daniel Heath Justice warrant special thanks for their support all along the way.

No academic project is ever done entirely by the person whose name appears on the cover, so I also want to express my gratitude to the many undergraduate and graduate students who have worked for me as research assistants over the years. Meredith McInnis, Reina Mistry, Adair Harper, Jennifer Robinson, Eric Wright, Geoff Bil, Laura Madokoro, Clara Wong, and Mark Werner each contributed to the project in crucial ways. I also wish to share my deep thanks to my colleagues and friends with whom I had regular writing dates: Carla Nappi, Thomas Stingl, Hugh Leschot, and Laura Ishiguro.

There are many others to whom I am indebted. In particular, I wish to thank my hosts from various visits to campuses across North America and Great Britain: Tony McCulloch, Jacqueline Fear-Segal, J. B. Shanks, David Stirrup, Sarah Pearsall, Pekka Hämäläinen, Josh Reid, Ned Blackhawk, Henrika Kuklick, Jeani O'Brien, Caroline Dodds Pennock, Annis May Timpson, and many others.

For most of my time in London, Annie Southerst and Belinda Evans (and their dachshunds Lola and Scout) provided a home away from home in Stoke Newington, and Sally Labern did the same for a short while in Stratford. Enormous gratitude goes to Sophie Mayer, who offered companionship and poetic consultation in London. Sven Klinge also deserves special mention as my "man on the ground" in London, whose knowledge of the detritus of empire within the London landscape, especially as it relates to

Indigenous and other travelers, far outweighs my own. Sven was also particularly helpful in "ground truthing" the self-guided tours at the end of *Indigenous London*.

I also want to thank the institutions that supported this project: the Huntington Library in San Marino, California; the British Library in London (particularly Carole Holden, Philip Hatfield, and Philip Davies); the Institute for Historical Research at the University of London; UBC's Hampton Grant program; and the Social Sciences and Humanities Research Council of Canada.

Next to last, I wish to offer my sincerest thanks to the editors and staff at Yale University Press. Laura Davulis, my editor during the bulk of this work, lent her sharp eye and even sharper sense of humor; Chris Rogers, upon taking over for Laura, proved to be a wonderful advocate for the project; Henry Roe Cloud Series editor Ned Blackhawk has never ceased to be an important mentor, advocate, and friend; and Eva Skewes, Phillip King, and Kate Davis helped keep the editorial process running smoothly.

And lastly, my husband Oren, who has reassured me throughout the often fraught process of writing, held down the fort during my long sojourns away from home, and generally made space within our relationship for the work that needed doing. The burdens of any writer's spouse are often heavy ones, and Oren bore them gracefully and with fierce reminders that I could in fact do this. Love is a powerful space for creation, and *Indigenous London* is proof of that.

Thank you all.

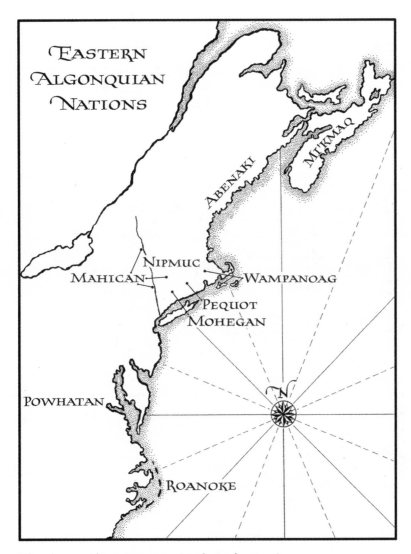

Selected eastern Algonquian nations. (Map by Jocelyn Curry)

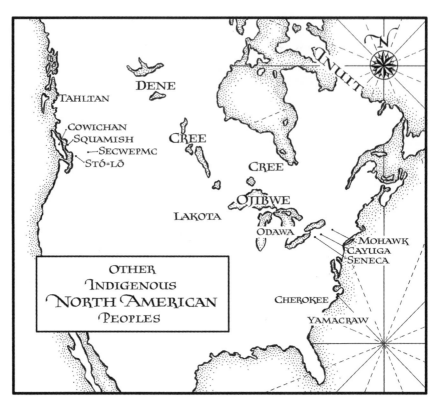

Other North American Indigenous nations from which travelers came. (Map by Jocelyn Curry)

Selected iwi (tribes) of Aotearoa (New Zealand). (Map by Jocelyn Curry)

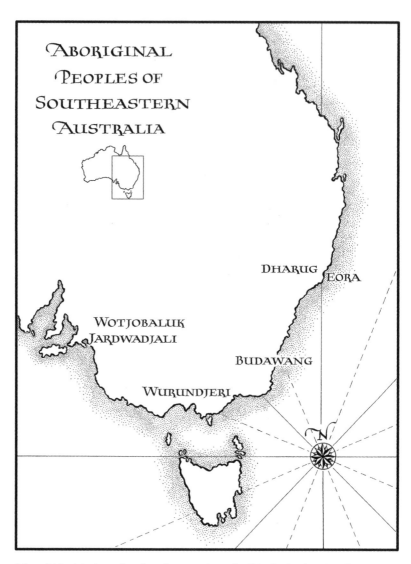

Selected Aboriginal peoples of southeastern Australia. (Map by Jocelyn Curry)

Indigenous London

1. The Unhidden City

Imagining Indigenous Londons

> The notion of a "hidden history" appeals to me though more, I suspect,
> on grounds of alliteration than on anything more substantial. In reality
> the immensity of London's history is not so much hidden as forgotten.
> —Richard Tames, 2006

> Settler colonialism is an inherited silence where you know memories
> are supposed to be.
> —Maya Mikdashi (Ojibwe), 2013

At the dawn of the sixteenth century, Westminster Palace dominated the
north bank of the Thames just downstream from the River Tyburn. Near
the palace, the gothic spires of St. Stephen's Chapel, surrounded by clois-
ters and vicars' houses, must have been reflected from time to time in the
Thames: glory to the Christian God and to the king's power twinned in the
slack stillness of a once pagan river. The heart of the palace was Westminster Hall, the fourteenth-century work of master architect Henry Yevele and
master carpenter Hugh Herland. White stags cavorted around the cornices,
angels and shields stared down from the hammer beams, and statues of dead
kings guarded niches around the walls. The rest of the ancient palace is long
gone, but Westminster Hall, witness to countless intrigues and assertions of
will and might, remains one of the oldest visible sites of power in London.[1]

Sometime between September 1501 and September 1502, something
entirely unexpected and unprecedented took place there:

> This yere also were browgth unto the kyng iij men takyn In the
> Newe ffound Ile land, that beffore I spak of In wylliam purchas

tyme beyng mayer, These were clothid In bestys skynnys and ete Rawe fflesh and spak such speech that noo man cowde undyrstand theym, and In theyr demeanure lyke to bruyt bestis whom the kyng kept a tyme afftyr, Of the whych upon (ij) yeris passis (afftir) I sawe ij of theym apparaylyd afftyr Inglysh men In westmynstyr paleys, which at that tyme I cowde not discern ffrom Inglysh men tyll I was lernyd what men they were, But as ffor spech I hard noon of them uttyr oon word.[2]

This year were brought unto the King three men taken in the New Found Island, that before I spoke of in William Purchase's time being mayor. These were clothed in beasts' skins and ate raw flesh and spoke such speech that no man could understand them, and in their demeanor like to brute beasts, whom the King kept a time after. Of the which upon two years passed after, I saw two of them appareled after Englishman in Westminster Palace, which at that time I could not discern from English men until I was learned what men they were. But as for speech, I heard none of them utter one word.

The only evidence of a visitation by strangers seemingly from another world, this lone archival fragment tells us very little. The "Newe ffounde Ile land" could mean anywhere in the lands to the west across the Atlantic; this is only ten years after Columbus, after all. But the passage also offers hints as to the identity of these foreigners. The reference to raw flesh suggests that the visitors were Inuit, people for whom uncooked meat was the sole source of crucial vitamins in their far northern homeland. We also know that two of them survived in London for two years, that they were guests of Henry VII, and that at some point they had traded in their caribou-and-sealskin parkas for hose and doublets.

But beyond that, their presence is a mystery. How did they get there? Did they come willingly or as captives? And what happened to them? Among the scant records of the explorations of the Italian explorer Giovanni Caboto (John Cabot), leader of some of the first English expeditions into the northwestern Atlantic, there is no mention of such men. Historian Peter E. Pope argues convincingly that Bristol merchants and their Azorean colleagues were a more likely source, having received royal patents to "occupy, possess, and subdue" anything they should find, and having received rewards "in consideracion of the true service which they have doon unto us to our singler pleasure as Capitaignes into the newe founde lande."[3] But these three strangers do not appear in those records, either. As for what became of them, we might infer that the third man died sometime during those two years; it is possible the other two died later. Certainly, there is no evidence that any of them returned home, alive or dead. One run-on passage in archaic English, recorded in a chronicle nearly eight decades later, is all there is. Sandwiched between news of great feasts and of beheadings at the Tower, the account might just as well sit in the middle of an empty page, largely silent, barely uttering "oon word."

Thus begins Indigenous London.

This book is not about the ancient indigenous peoples of Britain who settled the lands on either side of the Thames beginning hundreds of millennia ago. It is not about Paleolithic hunters following herds of aurochs and elk across an "English Channel" that did not yet exist; it is not about Neolithic farmers who raised great henges; and it is not about the Celtic Catuvellauni, who worshiped at wells and groves and threw offerings of shields, swords, and heads into the Thames. The languages of these peoples likely gave us the names for both the city and its river, although no one knows for sure. As much as they might have shaped the city in ephemeral but fundamental ways, as much as their lives are in a way London's creation story, this book is not about them.

Instead, this book is a history of London framed through the experiences of Indigenous people who traveled there, willingly or otherwise, from places that became Canada, the United States, New Zealand, and Australia.[4] They were Māori war chiefs and Mohawk diplomats. They were Eora explorers and Seneca athletes. They were Hawaiian royalty and Mohegan missionaries. As this first chapter shows, they were also mysterious Inuit visitors, celebrated and vilified Ojibwe performers, compelling Mohawk writers, and savvy Salish political leaders. Most of all, they were people who experienced London's empire firsthand, both in their home territories and in the empire's heart. The stories of these men, women, and children, few in number but with cultural and political impacts far outweighing their head count, are offered here as a new kind of London story. It is a deeply human story, simultaneously intimate in its scope and global in its reach.[5]

When I first embarked on this work, I thought I would be uncovering a "hidden history." Like Richard Tames, I was attracted to the alliteration of the phrase, but there was more to it than that. London, by its very nature, suggests hidden-ness. Amid the closes, mews, and lanes of the city, the deep past is ever present in the form of Roman walls, medieval churches, Tudor pubs, and other artifacts. In the city of the twenty-first century, when seemingly placeless finance and capital shape the global city and draw our attention away from the emplaced past, other times and worlds still seem possible: London within, under, or just behind the one we can see.

"I love a little bit of secret history," Samuel Johnson famously wrote, and the search for hidden Londons has been a pastime and preoccupation throughout the city's modern history. For all of the official histories of kings and queens, admirals and rebellions, London's story has nearly as often been told as one of secret realms, forgotten lives, and hidden geographies. In the early nineteenth century, for instance, Thomas De Quincey described the city's clandestine territories of addiction and obsession in his *Confessions of an English Opium-Eater* (1822), as he compulsively sought escape from everyday life through drugs and sex. Three decades later, reformer and campaigner Henry Mayhew exposed for all to see the unseen lives of the destitute in the city; his *London Labour and the London Poor* shocked the city with its sympathetic, if highly sentimentalized, accounts of impoverishment and desperation in the backstreets and decrepit neighborhoods where the polite classes never ventured. Mayhew's London, at least for those who did not live there, had been a profoundly hidden place. No doubt inspired by such accounts, the editor of *The Daily Telegraph* wrote in 1859 that "London is an amalgam of worlds within worlds, and the occurrences of every day convince us that there is not one of these worlds but has its special mysteries and its generic crimes." He was correct. London in the nineteenth century was replete with seemingly hidden worlds, exposed to the urban imagination through fiction, exposé, and the muckraking press. These were the worlds of Oliver Twist and Jack the Ripper, of slumming flaneurs crossing urban boundaries of class and status, of Oscar Wilde's homosexual underworld and the occult spaces of Arthur Machen's *The Great God Pan*.[6]

In the early twentieth century, this trend of discovering and documenting hidden Londons continued. Fictionist P. L. Travers and realist Jack London each contributed to the tradition, offering magical chimney sweeps dancing over the rooftop world alongside Mary Poppins and grim East End workhouses and bunkhouses inhabited by the working and unworking impoverished. In the latter parts of the century, writers drew on what had become a time-honored practice, creating a self-conscious—and in the words of Iain Sinclair, "shamanic"—landscape of the occulted city. Peter Ackroyd's encyclopedic knowledge of nooks, crannies, and hidden persistences limned a biography of London that confounded simplistic narratives of inexorable progress into a history-free future. Will Self's explorations on the Thames foreshore and beyond lauded the practice of walking and wandering through the remnants of the past. Sinclair's own exegeses on abandoned rooms in the East End, Olympics-related transformations in Hackney, and ley lines across the entire city inspired a leftist psychogeographical revolution in the urban imaginary, in which capital and power struggled with unruly and unconquered yesterdays.[7] Meanwhile, fantasy and speculative-fiction authors such as J. K. Rowling, Neil Gaiman, and China Miéville each added their own fantastical landscapes within the city's official one. Diagon Alley and Platform 9¾ at King's Cross, Night's Bridges and an angel named Islington, and malevolent squid cults with their sights set on collections of the Natural History Museum were but more examples of Londons-within-London.[8]

Such accounts of other Londons gesture toward the irreducible survivals of past landscapes in a place that constantly unearths its own history; such is the very nature of a city. As Timothy Morton has written, "The streets beneath the streets, the Roman Wall, the boarded-up houses, the unexploded bombs, are records of everything that happened to London. London's history is its form. Form is memory."[9] Neither frozen in amber nor free to escape into a future without consequences, the conversation between past, present, and future is literally built into the landscape of an ancient place like London. From histories of the Underground to accounts by urban explorers entering the city's sewers and crypts, from compendia of obscure folklore to catalogs of nearly forgotten ghost stories, London provokes a predilection with the hidden.[10] And this is not a matter simply of the city's intelligentsia and professional historians; just as influentially, popular tourist guides, wildly successful walking tours, and urban travel narratives are also in on this story making. Just count the number of them with "Hidden," "Secret," or "Other" in the title.[11]

And so, with *Indigenous London*, I thought I would be adding to the canon of secret Londons through the inscription of another fugitive layer, another arcane and invisible text in the palimpsest that is the urban landscape. I thought I would be discovering something no one had thought of before: a heretofore invisible Indigenous version of the urban past. But I was wrong. As Maya Mikdashi suggests, the challenge of colonialism—as of history more generally—is one of memory as much as it is of what actually happened. The problem of London's Indigenous history is an enforced silence, not the hidden-ness of past events. The people in this book, it turns out, did not need discovering. Indigenous people never do.

In the middle of the nineteenth century, the Egyptian Hall stood prominently amid the bustle and wealth of Piccadilly. Built in 1812, it promised "Fifteen Thousand Natural and Foreign Curiosities, Antiquities, and Productions of the Fine Arts." These included everything from unicorn horns and anatomical abnormalities to objects brought to England by Captain James Cook. With its facade of papyrus columns and caryatids, it became one of the city's most popular show venues; visitors might examine Napoleonic artifacts one year, a reconstructed Theban temple the next. They thrilled to elaborate panoramas in one season, and in another marveled at Théodore Géricault's *The Raft of the Medusa*. The spectacles at the Egyptian could also be human ones: a group of Sami reindeer herders, conjoined twins, or P. T. Barnum's protégé Charles Sherwood Stratton, better known as Tom Thumb.

Few events at the Egyptian Hall, however, could compare with what took place there one night in 1843. All around the main exhibition hall, dozens of painted portraits covered the walls; their subjects were women and men from distant lands, with names like Kee-món-saw and La-dóo-ke-a. Most of them had painted faces and wore feathers and skins. Along with the paintings, the room was adorned with artifacts that had belonged to the people in the portraits: spears, dresses, bows, drums, and even human scalps. No exhibition had ever brought together such a range of material related to the Indigenous peoples of North America.[12]

The Ojibwe performers who accompanied George Catlin in 1843, painted in oil by Catlin sometime in the 1860s. (Courtesy of the National Gallery of Art, Washington)

Then, on that night in 1843, the paintings seemed to come alive. Six men emerged onto a raised stage. Drums began to pound, and the six began singing, their voices unlike anything that had ever been heard in Piccadilly. The audience immediately reacted. Some surged forward toward the stage, while several women "screamed quite as loud as the Indians did, as they were making a rush for the door." After each song, the audience erupted into applause and stomped its feet wildly until the room was positively electric. Then, when the last song had ended and the applause had died down, a lone white man stepped forward and invited questions. The room erupted again, with hand upon hand shoved into the air, waving to get the man's attention. Their queries were often ignorant, to say the least. Had the Indians been captured with pits or with lassos? Did they eat the scalps they took from their enemies? Why had they traveled by ship when Europe and America were connected? On it went until the hall's owner forced the night to end. Women who hadn't fled ran up to the dancers and kissed them, stepping away with paint-stained faces. The debut of the "Ojibbeway Indians" had been a resounding success.[13]

The white man at the center of this spectacle was the American George Catlin, who had made a career by displaying paintings made during long sojourns in the central and western parts of North America. The performers, meanwhile, were Ojibwe men from the north shore of Lake Huron.[14] They included their leader Gwiiwizens (The Boy), seventy-five years in age, a veteran of the War of 1812 and an adroit observer of his audiences: he understood immediately, for example, what the wild foot stomping signified. Other members were military leaders, warriors, and medicine men, and in addition to the men, the group included three women who stayed backstage during the performances. Last, there was the translator, Cadotte, the son of a French trader.[15]

From the moment of their arrival in Manchester, the streets had been filled with cries of "Indians! Indians!" and London was no different after their first appearance at Euston Station. "The announcement of the arrival of the Ojibbeways which had been made in the public papers . . . brought a flood of applicants for private interviews with them," wrote Catlin, self-servingly, in his published account of the group. Such was the demand that Catlin eventually had to shut the doors to their lodgings in George Street in Marylebone and prevent all public visitors; he also took them out of the city several times "for their health." Not all opinions were positive, though: upon first meeting her new lodgers, the group's hostess quailed, saying that she "did not expect such wild, black-looking savages from the Indies."[16]

All of this is to say that the Ojibwe visitors of 1843 were far from hidden. Indeed, they were some of the most visible people in the city during their time there. Even before the arrival of The Boy and his fellow performers in 1843, George Catlin's exhibition of paintings and artifacts had elicited widespread commentary from the London press. While some coverage was unabashedly racist—*The Times* called the show "horribly illustrative of savage life" and reminiscent of "the most abhorrent and execrable cruelties"— most accounts lauded Catlin's display. *The Atlas* noted that "their existence is a miracle, and the artist may be proud of the fire and spirit, the truth and energy, yes, and the freedom and power with which he has, under such circumstances, conveyed to canvas the vivid impress of the ancient nobles of the forest and the prairie." *The London Saturday Journal* was perhaps the most effusive. "In visiting," the anonymous reporter noted, "the town-bred admirer of the freedom and grandeur of 'savage life' might find somewhat, at first sight, to feed his sentimental fancies . . . and make an unfledged adventurer long to dash away." One paper, *The Quarterly Review*, even went so far as to offer a critique of British and white colonialism, lamenting "the melancholy fate which has befallen the Indian race, and which overhangs the remnant of these victims to our power."[17]

With the arrival of The Boy and his group, such feelings intensified, often for the worse. When Cadotte fell in love with, and eventually married, a young English woman named Sarah Haynes, fears of miscegenation produced a flood of negative responses. Catlin, for his part, wrote that he "did not feel authorized to countenance a union of that kind." The popular press went further. Balladeers produced two songs, "The London Lass and the Ojibbeway Indian" and "The Ojibbeway Indians and Love," which made prurient hay from the Cadotte-Haynes marriage. They described the Ojibwes as wearing "a dirty clout" with "a great bone ring run through their snout" and decried the ways in which women from Hampstead had been drawn to the men's "jiggo jiggem hanging down" and had fallen in love "with those great Indian blacks."[18]

The most strident condemnation of Indigenous performers in the city, though, came from one of its most famous residents: Charles Dickens. Having seen firsthand the performances of The Boy's group, the renowned author and journalist was having none of the romantic claptrap. In an excoriating column in *Household Words,* he described Catlin's colleagues as "wretched creatures, very low in the scale." The so-called noble savage, he wrote, was "something highly desirable to be civilised off the face of the earth . . . cruel, false, thievish, murderous; addicted more or less to grease, entrails, and beastly customs; a wild animal with the questionable gift of boasting; a conceited, tiresome, bloodthirsty monotonous humbug." Even worse than the performers themselves, though, were the fawning press and public. "It is not the miserable nature of the noble savage that is the new thing," Dickens complained; "it is the whimpering over him with maudlin admiration . . . and the drawing of any comparison of advantage between the blemishes of civilisation and the tenor of his swinish life." Dickens also damned any shred of noble savagery that might exist in the hearts of Londoners: "It is my opinion that if we retained in us anything of the noble savage, we could not get rid of it too soon."[19]

To focus solely on this heady combination of spectacle and racism, however, would be to miss a simple fact: The Boy, Cadotte, and the others could look back. Just as they were visible to the city, so was the city visible to them—and they had opinions about it. Upon their arrival in the coal smoke–enshrouded city, for example, the performers of 1843 declared, "the prairies must be on fire again." They were also deeply disturbed by London's houses, so enormous and with no one standing at their windows. They wondered about the crimes men had committed that led to them wearing sandwich boards, marveled at the wealthy people who rode in carriages among the city's poor, expressed concern about public drunkenness, and paid special attention to a pair of South Asian immigrants seen sweeping the streets. When the group was taken to see Isambard Kingdom Brunel's famed Thames Tunnel, they were shocked to learn that they were under the river and that ships moved over their heads. They called it the Great Medicine Cave and, on leaving, performed a ritual dance at its entrance. In these and many other instances, The Boy, Cadotte, and the others cast an Ojibwe gaze on London, finding it wanting and wondrous at the same time.[20]

More than having just opinions of the city, however, the Ojibwe performers of 1843 also had diplomatic goals. When the Duke of Cambridge agreed to introduce them to Queen Victoria during a meeting at the concert rooms in Hanover Square, they canceled performances in order to prepare spiritually for the audience. On the same day that they arrived at Buckingham Palace, The Boy recounted his people's alliance with the Crown and with the famed Shawnee leader Tecumseh during the war against the Americans, using the language of kinship—Indian children, Great White Mother—to further cement the reciprocal relations between the two nations. Then the group performed a dance in the receiving rooms, asserting their own cultural authority deep within the spaces of British power.[21]

In this, "Catlin's Ojibbeways" were part of a larger history in which Ojibwe men and women traveled to London to assert their territorial sovereignty against the encroachment of settlers. The first came several years before The Boy and his fellow performers. The Methodist minister Gakiiwegwanabi, more commonly known by his English name Peter Jones, made trips to Britain in 1831, 1837, and 1845, each time presenting a petition to the queen protesting the subdivision and sale to whites of his people's lands along the Credit River near Toronto, Canada. Also in the 1840s, Gaagige-gaabaw, or George Copway, an Ojibwe missionary and author, traveled to Britain and Europe on a speaking and fund-raising tour. Two years after the visit of The Boy's troupe, George Henry, or Maungwadaus, the half brother of Gakiiwegwanabi and a chief at Credit River, brought his family and other Ojibwes from Walpole Island in far southeastern Ontario. They performed every day at the Egyptian, just like their predecessors, and were sponsored by George Catlin himself. Then, in 1859, Gakiiwegwanabi's niece Naaniibawikwe (Catherine Sutton), who had first traveled to England in 1837 with her uncle, returned to petition the queen yet again over the Credit River lands. This two-decade pattern of travel to London, much of it within a single family, shows how the city mattered to Ojibwe people.[22]

Each of these people was fully aware of their visibility. Gakiiwegwa-nabi, for example, was acutely cognizant that he was something of a spectacle:

> Ever since I came to London, my presence . . . created no little ex-citement, and brought out many to the meetings. The English people are desperately fond of new things, and when anything novel is an-nounced to the public it is always sure to bring a large congregation. . . . They ask more questions than I am able to answer, or they throw questions one top of the other, so I can get no time to answer before another is brought forth.[23]

Maungwadaus, for his part, seemed to relish in the attention, noting that the war chief of his group "shot a buck in the Park, through the heart, and fell down dead three hundred yards, before four thousand ladies and gentlemen. This was done to amuse them." And Naaniibawikwe also knew the power of being a visible Indian in London; she gave a powerful speech at a meeting-house in Gracechurch Street that, according to one observer, "struck a chord that vibrated near the heart."[24]

Like The Boy and his performers, each of these Ojibwe visitors also had things to say about the city. Gakiiwegwanabi took the opportunity, for example, to sit on the Coronation Chair while visiting Westminster Abbey. "I can now say that I, a poor Indian from the woods of Canada," he later wrote, "sat in the King's and Queen's great crowning chairs," an act that was both ironic and deeply symbolic. Gaagigegaabaw, meanwhile, offered more-direct critiques of the city:

> Oxford, Holborn and Cheap-side seemed to me literally crammed and suffocating. Old houses, settled at the corners, but looking as if, had they ever been going to fall they would have tumbled long before. Antique and odd-looking edifices, smutty walls, and narrow, worn-out pavements, were among the first objects that presented themselves to my view. And this is London!

The House of Commons, Gaagegigaabaw wrote, was "more like a giant coffin than anything else," and without gaslight, the fuggy darkness of the streets meant that a man "must accustom himself to walking by faith, or feeling." Maungwadaus, for his part, cast London society in terms that related to his home territories: the city's endless crowds were "like musketoes . . . in the summer season"; elite women talking ceaselessly at dinner were "like ravens feasting on venison"; and drunken military officers at the same meal had noses like ripe strawberries and voices like bullfrogs.[25]

Whatever their opinions of the city, the land question remained central. Gakiiwegwanabi had presented wampum during at least one of his sojourns in the city—white beads for good feelings, black for troubled hearts—but, as his repeated visits suggest, he failed to secure rights to the Credit River lands. Although they received an audience with the queen, the 1843 performers do not appear to have been able to present a formal petition over their lands on Lake Huron. Naaniibawikwe, despite her successes at public speaking and the clear affection between her and the queen, had her aims thwarted when the sovereign and her functionaries turned the authority over Credit River to the provincial authorities. And for some, the costs were even greater: seven of Maungwadaus's group, including his wife and three of his children, died during their tour of Britain and France.[26]

Whatever the outcome of journeys, this small stream of Ojibwe visitors in the middle of the nineteenth century illustrates the fact that Indigenous London was far from hidden. Indeed, Ojibwe London was highly visible. Gakiiwegwanabi, Gaagegigabaaw, and the others are there in the archives. Imagining Ojibwe London means speaking back to the supposed silence that is part of the narrative estrangement of Indigenous and urban histories. It is not an act of discovery; rather, it is an act of *recovery*, of acknowledging the deep entanglements of London's places, people, and histories with Indigenous places, people, and histories, and vice versa.

London might seem an unlikely place to find Indigenous history. Indeed, urban spaces in general are typically seen, both by the general public and by most scholars and policy makers, as spaces in which Indigenous people have little presence and even less significance. This is the result of one of the most powerful narratives in global history: that of historical progress from savagery to civilization. This teleology has its own long history, going back to at least classical Greece and Rome, whose leading thinkers cast the wilderness and city and their respective peoples as antonyms to each other. Picked up again in the Renaissance and Enlightenment by Europe's intellectual elite, such ideas helped make sense of encounters with heretofore-unknown societies, such as those in the Americas or the Pacific. Always, the city served as the ultimate avatar of civilization, while Indigenous peoples were its foil, whether savage or noble in their difference. This is what I call the narrative estrangement of urban and Indigenous histories: the deeply held notion that urban and Indigenous histories, like urban places and Indigenous peoples, have little to do with each other except as mutually exclusive opposites. It is perhaps the most unchallenged aspect of the ways in which history, from the local to the global, has been articulated in the West.

This is History writ large: History as measuring stick, History as human classification, History as, ultimately, a bludgeon. At its core, the narrative estrangement of the urban from the Indigenous has reflected a broader perceived estrangement of Indigenous people from modernity, framed in binaries such as civilized versus savage, rational versus irrational, or historical versus timeless. These binaries have in turn undergirded hundreds of years of racist colonial policies. They have justified the dispossession of land through doctrines of discovery and of *terra nullius,* which proclaimed that "savages" did not use the land in ways that led to civilized progress (and toward, it should be noted, the ultimate endpoint: the city). This estrangement has also served as a foundation for policies of genocide, both physical and cultural: either Indigenous peoples must give way to civilized conquest, or the survivors must be assimilated through programs such as residential schools and stolen generations. The estrangement has so shaped the ways in which we think about the past, present, and future that it is often impossible to imagine a story line in which Indigenous peoples not only survive into the present but are active participants in its making.

Cities have been central to this, both as primary technologies of the colonial dispossession of Indigenous lands—there is no better way to expropriate territory than to build a city—and as spaces imagined as free of Indigenous bodies, minds, and histories. Meanwhile, Indigenous people who remain in or move to urban places are all too often portrayed, if at all, as somehow out of place, and that out-of-place-ness is all too easily transformed into absence. The result is a blindness read back onto the past from the present, an inherited silence where history should be.

In recent years, however, a host of writers, academic and otherwise, have begun to challenge the narrative estrangement of urban and Indigenous histories by writing the city as Indigenous space. This is especially true in Canada, the United States, New Zealand, and Australia, where the majority of Indigenous people now reside not on reserves or reservations but in urban places. These scholars examine the ways in which town-making was in itself a form of colonial incursion; they recover the ways in which Indigenous labor and knowledge contributed to city life, particularly in the early years of settlement; they speak back to urban dispossession and narrative exclusion by showing the ways in which Indigenous communities have persisted, reconstituted, or even invented themselves in urban spaces despite challenges ranging from poverty, addiction, and discrimination to legal disenfranchisement and the very idea that they should not exist. Urban Indigenous life, one of the major grounds of Indigenous resurgence in the late twentieth and early twenty-first centuries, is one of the best examples of what Ojibwe writer Gerald Vizenor calls survivance: not just mere survival, but powerful resistance.[27]

Indigenous London builds on this growing scholarship to offer an extended intervention into the narrative estrangement of urban and Indigenous histories. It assumes that Indigenous people around the world, far from being passive victims or metaphorical foils, have in fact actively engaged with and helped create the world we call modern, including its great urban centers.

It illustrates this by telling the stories of Indigenous children, women, and men who made long journeys from their homelands to the metropolis at the heart of an empire (and who sometimes made it home again). Like those of the Inuit, Ojibwe, Mohawk, and Salish travelers described in this opening chapter, the stories of Indigenous visitors throughout the rest of *Indigenous London* offer new insights into the city's history.

I make two claims in particular about the deep connections between London and its Indigenous history. First, I argue that London has been entangled with Indigenous territories, resources, knowledges, and lives from the very beginning of its experiments with colonization. From Roanoke informants teaching a sixteenth-century natural philosopher about their homeland to insistence upon relations with the British Crown in Canadian Indigenous activist circles in the twenty-first century, London was drawn into Indigenous worlds. This entanglement was often material. Historians such as Julie Flavell and Peter Mancall have written eloquently about the ways in which the stuff of the Americas—tobacco in the Strand, deerskins in the docklands, beaver hats in shop fronts—transformed the city in the seventeenth and eighteenth centuries.[28] Meanwhile, Cherokee scholar Jace Weaver has argued for something he calls a "red Atlantic," in which Indigenous travelers and intellectuals from the Americas shaped a transoceanic culture of encounter, engagement, and generative power.[29] Such things connected the places and spaces of London to the spaces and places of Indigenous polities and personhoods, not just across the Atlantic but, eventually, around the world. As Miles Ogborn has written, any good history of a place like London "must be one that appreciates both the particularities of location and the connections to other spaces and other places. . . . Modernity," he continues, "was not simply born in London, but London was transformed by modernity as its positions in the regional, national, and global geographies that tied it in various ways to other places were reconfigured."[30] In other words, as historian Catherine Hall has argued, London was not just actor but acted-upon, not just the center but also the periphery.[31]

Second, and emerging from this entanglement, I argue that the urban spaces of London have been one of the grounds of settler colonialism. By "settler colonialism," I mean the practices of dispossession, of which city building was only one, that marginalized Indigenous peoples and established societies of majority European descent in places such as Australia, Canada, New Zealand, and the United States. As Lorenzo Veracini has shown, settler colonialism required both the physical and narrative removal of Indigenous populations. While increasingly sovereign settler states, such as the United States and New Zealand, often led the way in such efforts, these practices of dispossession ultimately had their origins in political, military, and ideological proclivities and prerogatives that were born in London. As home to the Crown, for example, London was the space in which decisions were taken that rippled across the world to Indigenous territories.[32]

Theoretical interventions aside, I am first and foremost interested in recovering the lived experiences of Indigenous people who found themselves, intentionally or otherwise, in the city beginning in the early sixteenth century. All too often, Indigenous people in urban places have been cast as powerless victims or powerful metaphors rather than as real people with agency and humanity. The stories herein emphasize both these things in an effort to answer the historian's most basic question: What was it like? I also hope, though, to move beyond a simple account of social experience to offer a new and disorienting perspective on one of the world's most well known cities. In his influential book *Indians in Unexpected Places*, Dakota scholar Philip J. Deloria describes the ways in which we expect only certain kinds of stories about Indigenous people: that they belong in the past, that they have culture rather than history, and that they have little place in the modern world except as noble, exotic, pathetic, or laughable anomalies. There is little room among such expectations for Indigenous people in urban places. And Indigenous people in London are perhaps the most unexpected of all.[33]

In the years around the turn of the twentieth century, the private drawing room was as much a place of performance as the Egyptian Theatre had been in the middle of the nineteenth century. Lavishly furnished and beautifully lit, decked out with pianoforte and flowers, such spaces were the territory of formality and gossip, pleasure and edification. For the aristocratic, cultural, and political elite who could afford them, drawing rooms were the loci of everyday, cultured life and places of social power.

In 1894, a newcomer to London appeared in one of these rooms. At the Mayfair home of Henrietta Vyner Robinson—Lady Ripon and the wife of

Tekahionwake, or E. Pauline Johnson, the Mohawk poet and performer who captivated audiences in 1894 and 1906. (Image HP025606, courtesy of the Royal British Columbia Museum, B.C. Archives)

the former viceroy of India—the woman from far away recited poems and short stories of the people and places of her homeland. Not long after, she appeared in the fashionable Hanover Square drawing room of Charles Aidé, a publisher and author and a leading light of London's demimonde. The visitor had two names: one was E. Pauline Johnson; the other was Tekahionwake, "Double Life." She was a member of the Mohawk Nation and came from the Six Nations reserve in Ontario and had made a career for herself in Canada as a poet and performer of Indigenous-inspired stories. In all, she would make two visits to London.[34]

The first visit, in 1894, saw her living on Portland Road in a room she decorated with white and purple wampum, her buckskin costumes, and a ceremonial mask hung above the fireplace. She quickly became something of a sensation, receiving for her performances not only money but complimentary tickets to shows featuring the most popular actors of the day: Lillie Langtry, Henry Irving, Ellen Terry. While performances at aristocratic homes like that of Lady Ripon were a common feature of her sojourn, Tekahionwake preferred those of London's intellectual circles. "I have met all sorts of Lords and things," she would write, "and found them for the most part interesting, but I much prefer *thinking* London to *aristocratic* London." In "thinking London," she also presented wampum to the eminent artist Sir Frederick Leighton, president of the Royal Academy, and spent time at the St. John's Wood home of the painter Lawrence Alma-Tadema. One of the most important relationships she established was with the publisher John Lane, in whose Albany Street home she performed her material, and who would go on to publish her collection *The White Wampum* soon after she returned to Canada.[35]

Nearly twenty years later, Tekahionwake returned to London. This time, she resided in the more lavish St. James's Square, and while many of her old friends seemed to have lost interest in her as a performer, she did finally find a promoter and soon after, a patron in the form of Lord Strathcona, the high commissioner for Canada. Her career reached new heights; she performed at the Steinway Theatre and in Dominion Day celebrations, enjoyed tea on the terrace of the House of Commons, and was received at the home of novelist and parliamentarian Sir Gilbert Parker, whose Carlton House Terrace residence had also seen visits by Mark Twain, J. M. Barrie, and Arthur Conan Doyle. Meanwhile, several of her works, including an essay called "A Pagan in St Paul's," appeared in the London press. And often, her written work and performances reminded her readers and listeners that her people had once been important political, economic, and military allies to the British.[36]

During Tekahionwake's time in London, she also recorded her opinions of the city. "London," she wrote, "looks a strange place to the Red Indian whose eyes still see the myriad forest trees, even as they gaze across the Strand, and whose feet still feel the clinging moccasin even among the scores of clicking heels that hurry along the thoroughfares of this camping-ground of the paleface." She also cast the city in specifically Indigenous terms: she linked London's tall stone buildings with skyward-stretching Saskatchewan tipi poles; she compared the stone of those buildings to the ceremonial stone pipes and corn-pounders of her people; she described the singing of a boy's choir in relation to the singing of Mohawk priests; and she imagined the fires of the longhouse as she gazed at altar candles at St. Paul's Cathedral. And she could be quite critical of the city, describing it as "fetid" and smothering. And as would be the case for Indigenous visitors throughout London's history, she was appalled by London's poverty, writing that "With slums like this in the heart of London, they'll *dare* to send missionaries to our Indians in Canada!" It would be in this filthy city, though, that she would make one of the most important friendships of her life, a relationship that began with a simple greeting in the Chinook Jargon, a trading creole made up of several European and Indigenous languages: "Klahowya, tillicums!" ("Greetings, friends!").[37]

The four men to whom she spoke these words had arrived at the infernally busy Euston Station in 1906, from an even more distant place: the west coast of Canada. They included Ispaymilt from the Cowichan Nation, whose territories rested on the eastern coast of Vancouver Island, and Basil David, a Secwepmc from the Bonaparte Reserve in British Columbia's interior. The party also included Simon Pierre, a translator from the Katzie Reserve of the Stó:lō people east of Vancouver. But the man who would become the most famous member of the group was S7aplek, a leader from the Squamish Nation, whose territory ranges from what is now the city of Vancouver north into the mountains.[38] S7aplek carried the ancestral name Capilano—given to him by Squamish elders specifically for the journey—which linked him to a leader who had greeted the first Europeans to arrive in Squamish territory in the late eighteenth century. S7aplek was obviously the leader of the delegation; in a photo snapped at the train station that appeared in a local paper, he wore regalia that denoted his right to speak for the Indigenous people of British Columbia: a bright sash from the upper Fraser River, buckskin and fox fur from the northern interior, and his own mountain-goat wool blanket that symbolized his important place among his people.[39]

S7aplek (second from right) and his three compatriots at Euston Station in 1906, pictured in the *London Daily News* on August 3, 1906.

The four men had traveled from a deeply contested place. In the early decades of the twentieth century, First Nations people in British Columbia had begun to build political coalitions in response to the widespread taking of land by settlers, done without the benefit of legal processes such as treaties. The delegation that arrived in London in 1906 emerged out of this process, building on kinship and other connections that had already existed between the Cowichan, Secwepmc, Squamish, and Stó:lō peoples, all of whom were related as part of a larger coastal and interior Salish world. Out of these connections came the idea of sending community leaders to meet with the Crown and circumvent provincial and federal authorities. Not surprisingly, this made Indian Affairs officials nervous, particularly because none of the Indigenous participants seemed willing to share their plans with the outsiders. Colonial officials did have some sense of what might be afoot; S7aplek recalled, "the white men told me, not to come to the great King . . . because he did not like his dusky children. We would never come back to our people alive, they said." But he and the others remained tight-lipped about the plan, even until their departure from Vancouver's Canadian Pacific Railroad station, which involved dozens of Indigenous leaders and thousands of onlookers.[40]

It was only when the train pulled out of the station, with S7aplek and his colleagues on board, that their formal petition was unveiled to the public and to a deeply embarrassed colonial government. It drew attention to the fact that the Indigenous title to most of British Columbia had never been extinguished. It also appealed to the honor of the Crown. "The Dominion government is made up of men elected by white people who are living on our lands," it said, "and, of course, we can get no redress from that quarter. We have no vote. If we had it might be different, but as it is we are at the mercy of those that have the vote, and alas! they have no mercy."[41] In the end, it would be the delegates' time in London, not in Victoria or elsewhere in British Columbia, that would animate this adroitly worded expression of Indigenous authority over traditional territories that had been home since time immemorial.

Before meeting the king, however, Ispaymilt and his three colleagues had to meet the city. Immediately after their arrival, the foursome was taken to their lodgings in officers' barracks at Buckingham Gate. From there, a Vancouver expatriate showed them around the city. They saw the London Zoo, where a stranger asked if he might clip some of S7aplek's hair for his "pilatory" collection. To a Squamish man, for whom hair, like any body part, was a source of personal spiritual power, such a request caused deep offense. "He make too free and ask too much," was the response. Indeed, the noise and hectic pace of the city could easily overwhelm the visitors; Basil David in particular seems to have suffered, thrashing and crying out in his sleep from nightmares involving motorcars and traffic.[42]

While the press focused on the visitors' exotic appearances and their aspirations to "civilization," the men themselves focused on diplomacy. "We talk with the King," S7aplek recounted, "and at the end he shake my right hand hard and with his left hand pat my left shoulder three times . . . and say 'Chief we see this matter righted but it may take a long time, five years perhaps.' "[43] However, Canadian officials had been working to undermine the delegation's efforts. Men representing British Columbia had been running interference, doing their best to prevent the three leaders, through the translation of Simon Pierre, from presenting their grievances at the source of the empire's power. While these attempts appear to have been fruitless—the visitors were perhaps too much of a spectacle to avoid—Canadian officials had managed to achieve one element of their agenda: limiting the Indigenous leaders' time in the presence of the king to only fifteen minutes. Nevertheless, the four travelers were hopeful. S7aplek told a *Daily Mirror* reporter, "We are carrying back glorious memories. We have seen the King and Queen, we have visited your wonderful Abbey, and everybody has treated us kindly. When we reach home we shall tell our camp all about it, and won't we open their eyes!"[44]

And just before they departed London for their homelands, the four men again met with Tekahionwake. There was clearly a deep connection between her and the group. Nothing illustrates this more than the fact that three years later, the Mohawk writer moved to Vancouver. As S7aplek put it, she "came into the west and into their hearts at the same time." There, she began a collaboration that would last the remainder of her life. She worked with S7aplek (who continued to use the name Joe Capilano) and his wife Líxwelut (Mary Agnes) to collect and publish traditional Squamish stories about important places in the landscape around Vancouver.[45] Published in 1911 as *The Legends of Vancouver*, the suite of tales included one that highlighted the connections between London and its far-flung colonial city. In it, two Squamish sisters were warned about the impending arrival of a war party from the Tsimshian people of the northern British Columbia coast. In response, they invited the Tsimshian to a potlatch feast, an enormously important ceremony that cemented political, social, cultural, and economic relations, which had the effect of turning the visitors into friends and allies. The story was remembered through the presence of two tall mountains, known as The Two Sisters, which rise over Vancouver's urban landscape. To settlers, however, the peaks are known as The Lions, named after Edwin Henry Landseer's famous statues at the base of Nelson's Column in Trafalgar Square.[46]

S7aplek died in 1910, and three years later, Tekahionwake died of breast cancer. Their joined lives, however, spoke to the ways in which London was entangled with both Mohawk and Salish histories. Tekahionwake had sought audiences in the imperial capital, to great success. In doing so, she capitalized on notions of the "noble savage" that had been so popular in the city, and indeed were cast against the city as an antonym—and perhaps even balm—to urban modernity. Her fame, then, relied in no small part on the relationship between urban and Indigenous histories.[47] And as her path crossed with that of S7aplek and his compatriots, and as other Mohawk people followed her to Vancouver, Mohawk and Squamish and other histories intersected, all because of a seemingly random encounter at the heart of empire. Meanwhile, the name S7aplek remains an important one in the Squamish Nation, with the man who carries it today holding the right to sing a song created specifically for and about the 1906 delegation.

Last, the British Columbia leaders' experiences in London can tell us something about the city itself. During their visit to Westminster Abbey, they encountered the Stone of Scone and the shrine of Edward the Confessor. As historian Keith Carlson has argued, the four visitors, for whom stones could be ancestors and sources of spiritual and political authority and for whom ancestral names could carry power across the generations, such sights would have been legible according to Indigenous ways of knowing. The stone under the Coronation Chair would have made immediate sense, and the centuries between Edward the Confessor and Edward VII likely constituted, in their minds, a short distance indeed. But this moment of encounter also tells us something about the city: at the height of its imperial modernity, an ancient block of sandstone and a set of 840-year-old bones still emanated power that served as the basis of sacred political authority. Perhaps this was a city that was not entirely modern after all.[48]

It is not just that Indigenous histories in and of the city are unexpected; it is also the case that they, and histories of the city more generally, are enmeshed with each other. *Indigenous London* is thus organized around what I call "domains of entanglement." Each chapter focuses on one relatively abstract way in which urban and Indigenous histories are linked at nearly global scales: knowledge, disorder, reason, ritual, discipline, and memory. Each is a field of engagement between urban and Indigenous peoples and places, simultaneously speaking to broad, almost existential categories of human experience and to concrete, intimate encounters in one particular city. Each chapter then uses a particular set of travelers to illustrate the workings of the domain in question, just as this introduction uses the story of Inuit, Ojibwe, Mohawk, and Salish visitors to offer arguments about the presence of Indigenous visitors from the very beginnings of London's exploration of the "new world," about the visibility of such visitors, and about the entanglement of urban and various Indigenous histories. Perhaps most important, though, *Indigenous London* is as much about the city as it is about Indigenous travelers. Identifying Indigenous histories of the spaces of the city challenges the absence that others have assumed or the hidden-ness that I had expected, and moves not just toward the limning of presence, but further on to substance: to the idea that Indigenous people in London were not just there, but that they mattered to the city's history, just as the city mattered to their individual and collective histories. These journeys were far more than what anthropologist James Clifford has called "an indigenous detour"; rather, they were central to the fashioning of a global and transnational colonial world.[49]

There are key patterns among the urban and Indigenous stories that are told in this book. Despite the diversity of Indigenous peoples included herein, there are in fact common threads of Indigenous urban experience. Most of the travelers were men. They were also typically close to the sites of power and the people who inhabited them during their time in the city—not just in being shown places like Westminster Abbey, but by meeting with aristocrats, royals, eminent thinkers, religious leaders, and other figures of political and social prominence and influence. Meanwhile, Indigenous travelers, when we know their attitudes toward London, expressed two particularly strong critiques of the city. First, they were shocked by its ecology—smog, filth, and the inability of Londoners to feed themselves through subsistence practices such as hunting—and second, they were each deeply disturbed by the city's profound inequalities of wealth. These critiques matched closely key debates among Londoners themselves, highlighting how Indigenous people were able to identify some of the most pressing urban issues of their day. In short, Indigenous travelers were intellectual contemporaries of some of the great urban critics and commentators throughout London's history.

Last, the defense of Indigenous lands is central to their stories. Whether in the form of an activist Mohegan missionary bucking his religious superiors to pursue a land-claims case in the eighteenth century, or of Māori chiefs seeking British military alliance and matériel to expand their territories in the nineteenth century, London became the ground not just of settler colonialism, but of Indigenous resistance and survival. As Antoinette Burton has argued, such perspectives and experiences were more than simple critique; rather, they were dissent: against the violence of colonial policies, against narratives of primitivism or savagery, and against the very notion that they had no place in the metropole.[50]

Indigenous London, meanwhile, ignores some of the city's most important London stories. The Great Fire of 1666, for example, does not appear
here, despite its centrality to the story of the city. Nor do the great epidemics of the early modern and Victorian city. Even though epidemic diseases,
with their origins in the urban "Old World," decimated Indigenous peoples
throughout the Americas and the Pacific—and killed quite a few Indigenous visitors—the urban policies and practices that addressed such ecologies
rarely intersected with those visitors' journeys. The great nineteenth-century
remakings of sewer visionary Joseph Bazalgette and bridge maker Brunel,
meanwhile, have little that is substantive to say about Indigenous travelers,
even as they reshaped the landscape through which such travelers moved and
as they highlighted the modernity against which Indigenous peoples were
often set as foils. These and other engineering schemes had little relationship
to Indigenous visitations except as spectacles that were meant to cow the visitors into submission to civilization. Finally, the twentieth century's trends
toward decolonization and diaspora have been of relatively small import to
Indigenous peoples. The Inuit, Ojibwe, Mohawk, and Salish peoples, for example, have continued to be marginalized in their traditional territories even
as Canada has been freed from Britain's direct imperial control.

Nonetheless, while London's Indigenous history might not intersect
with every dynamic of the city's past, many of the metropolis's key stories—
from Tudor mercantile power and Georgian social unrest to Victorian reform
and the rise of Edwardian suburbia—are central to *Indigenous London.* Each
of these key London stories, in fact, begin to look different when considered
alongside those of Indigenous travelers to the city. Indeed, that is the point
of *Indigenous London:* to re- or disorient the city's story, casting it in its own
imperial light and even, perhaps, Indigenizing it.

To Indigenize London, though, is to begin to come to terms with the
undeniably human costs of empire. All too often, Indigenous people have
been portrayed, especially in urban places, as little more than metaphors: as
foils for modernity, as exotic spectacles, or as doomed relics. One of the main
goals of *Indigenous London* is to move beyond the purely symbolic to insist
on the personhood of Indigenous children, women, and men who came to
the city, willingly or otherwise, and to wherever possible restore their agency
to the heart of the story. But that same emphasis on agency can all too easily

mask the pain and trauma that are also at the center of the story. To move toward a reckoning with that pain and trauma, this book includes six interludes that attempt to sidestep a traditional scholarly approach by insisting on the affective. Offered in the form of free-verse poetry built in part out of archival fragments represented in italics, each of the interludes focuses on an object—a mirror, a debtor's petition, a pair of statues, a lost museum, a hat factory, and a notebook—to refract the intimacies of encounter in a way that is not so much about academic arguments as it is about the soul of the matter. They are examples of what anthropologist Renato Rosaldo has called "antropoesía," or "verse with an ethnographic sensibility," and are meant to bring a kind of transhistorical immediacy to a book that might at first glance seem to be primarily about the past.[51] Through the use of the present tense, unfettered play with language, and juxtapositions of archival materials, the interludes ask the reader to be present, even if only for a few moments, with the human consequences of the larger story of Indigenous London. Those consequences continue to resonate into the twenty-first century, in no small part because they remain attached to the objects that are the subject of each interlude. In this way, the very fabric of the city itself holds history, holds clues to Indigenous lives, holds the entanglement of urbanity and Indigeneity.

Palace. Theater. Drawing room. Train station. Shrine. These are just some of the spaces of Indigenous history in London, to which we might add other sites: parks, taverns, zoos, armories, hospitals, prisons, and the very streets themselves. Each is implicated and imbricated in the networks of empire, along which ideas such as the noble savage and the civilized city, things like wampum and cathedrals, and people like Ispaymilt and The Boy traveled and even occasionally encountered one another. The "New ffounde Ile land," the lands around the Great Lakes, and the city of Vancouver are also tied up in London's history.

In this way, Indigenous London is not unlike the other histories within the city—ones that have been not so much hidden as they have been largely ignored by London's elite. These are the so-called "subaltern" cities, the Londons of immigrants and others outside the structures of power and the imaginary of civic selfhood, whose lives bind London to other, often far-flung places. Historians have mapped out these other cities—Jewish, Irish, Asian, Black—within Anglo London, with the result that the history of the city has been profoundly transformed in recent years, appearing not as a linear progression of great Anglo civic leaders and an inexorable march toward a postimperial postmodernity, but as a site of deep contestation and conflict, and a mosaic of diverse peoples that have been central to the city's fashioning. As China Miéville has written, "diasporas have sustained us."[52]

These other, unhidden Londons have a long history as well. In the middle of the nineteenth century, William Wordsworth could see them; the astute observer of civic life perceived London's panoply of ethnic diversity as one of the city's defining traits. While writing his famous *Prelude* in the 1840s, Wordsworth cast his gaze upon the streets and thoroughfares of London and found a dazzling and dizzying array of humanity that included visitors, immigrants, and Londoners of almost countless stripes. And when he finally published *The Prelude* in 1850, he counted Indigenous visitors among the throngs:

> Among the crowd, conspicuous less or more
> As we proceed, all specimens of man
> Through all the colours which the sun bestows,
> And every character of form and face:
> The Swede, the Russian; from the genial south
> The Frenchman and the Spaniard; *from remote*
> *America, the hunter Indian;* Moors,
> Malays, Lascars, the Tartar and Chinese,
> And negro ladies in white muslin gowns.[53]

No doubt inspired by The Boy and the Ojibwe performers of 1843 (and no doubt aware of Charles Dickens's tirade against them), Wordsworth's "hunter Indian" appeared as just one more piece of the human mosaic of what was by then the world's most powerful imperial city. There they were, more than metaphor, more than anomaly. It turns out that, from the sixteenth century and into the twentieth, Inuit, Ojibwe, Mohawk, and Salish Londons, like those of the other Indigenous travelers whose stories follow, mattered to the city. And they were never hidden at all.

A Devil's Looking Glass, circa 1576

Dr. Dee's Mirror
Obsidian
Mexica, 15th–16th century A.D.
Diameter: 18.400 cm
M&ME 1966, 10-1, 1
Enlightenment: Religion

Earth, spit up the black drink from the Underworld,
pour *itztli*, hot black glass, out onto yourself.
Black glass waits in craters and on smoking slopes; it waits for the people.

Origins:
Brutus, descended from Aphrodite, kills his king-father with an errant arrow.
Exiled over the sea, he comes to an island where he pits tribes against each other.
When he dies, he is buried in a great hill where a White Tower is built.
There, along the flowing waters, a great city grows.

Origins:
The people, emerged from The Place of Seven Caves, led by Hummingbird of the Left,
leave Aztlán, Land of the White Heron, for the shore of a distant lake far to the south.
When they arrive, an eagle, cactus-perching and serpent-bearing, awaits them.
There, in the standing waters, a great city grows.

You will cut your hands to ribbons, taking the black stone.
In the mountains above the great valley,
you will collect great shards of the earth's black offering
and carry it down from places with names like Zacualtipan and Jilotepeque.
You will carry it into your cities;
it will cut your hands and your captives' arteries to ribbons.

The obsidian scrying mirror of Mexica origin that once belonged to
John Dee, the astrologer and mathematician who coined the phrase
"the British Empire." (© The Trustees of the British Museum, all
rights reserved)

Listen to the stories:
The god Tezcatlipoca, the Black Smoking Mirror, also known as Mountain Heart,
sacrifices his foot to a sea monster's jaws, then makes the world from her body.
He rules the north and night, jaguars and hurricanes, temptation and war.
His signs are heron feathers, quetzal feathers, vulture,
flint knives, obsidian mirrors, and copal smoke.

Listen to the stories:
Arthur joins the nation together, stretches his dominion to Ireland and America.
Brendan, with his coracle of saints, feasts atop a sea monster on the way to America.
Madoc, escaping war, disappears with his blue eyes into America.
Their signs are calfskin and quill, tallow and ink black.

Use pieces of it to give teeth to your *macuahuitl,* your fanged sword.
Use its blackness to pierce your tongue and penis and thank the gods.
Make ear spools, make labrets, cut meat,
polish it with bat droppings into dark mirrors.

Children are born in Tenochtitlan, are schooled to give praise to the Smoking Mirror.
O master, O our lord, O lord of the near, of the nigh,
O night, O wind: thou knowest the things with the trees, the rocks.
And thou knowest of things within us.
Thou hearest us from within, what we say, what we think, our minds, our hearts.
Smoke and mist arise before thee.

A child is born near the Tower, is schooled to give praise
to God, maps, mathematics, and the mysteries of alchemy.
John Dee prays to the angels, and this is their answer:
Unto this Doctrine belongeth the perfect knowledge.
In these keys which we deliver, are the mysteries and secret beings and effects
of all things moving, and moved within the world.
These calls touch all parts of the world.

Prophecies and knowledge of the world abound.
Pulled up in nets: gray birds with mirrored heads.
Seen in mirrors: armies of two-headed monsters and great dogs.
Across the sky: a comet, perhaps a returning serpent.
Moctezuma awaits more signs.

Prophecies and knowledge of the world abound.
Dee calls to the angels of the West from his sweetwood table:
Patax for curing disease, Iipo for transformation,
Leaoc for finding precious stones, and Nlrx for secrets discovered.
He calls to the fire-beings *whose wings are of wormwood, and of the marrow of salt,*
who have setled their feete in the West.

Tenochtitlan falls.
A great flood of gold and souls overspills the lake edge
and runnels and crashes across the Atlantic:
to Madrid, Málaga, Seville, the Vatican.

The Mexica on scholars:
The wise man: a light, a torch, a stout torch that does not smoke . . .
his are the black and red ink, his are the illuminated manuscripts,
he studies the illuminated manuscripts. He himself is writing and wisdom.
He is the path, the true way for others. He puts a mirror before others;
he makes them prudent, cautious; he causes a face to appear in them.

Dee's house, the scholar's house, is filled with paper and braziers.
To Mortlake come the great explorers of the day: Frobisher, Gilbert, Raleigh.
He reads their stars, assays their false gold, instructs them in navigation.
Angels, wonders, marvels, kinds of men: natural philosophy.
The greatest library in Europe, historians will later claim.
Elizabeth Regina pays visits, gazes into mirrors.

Along with the souls and gold, the mirror made of itztli
travels the Atlantic, comes ashore in Spain
and makes its way via a courtier's trunk to a royal palace in Prague.

No scholar works alone.
Dee hires men with the ability to peer into surfaces and see past them,
to divine messages from divine spirits, to be his *colloquium of angels.*
Edward Kelley is either the greatest of these or the greatest of charlatans.
Rumors fly of necromancy.

Dee and Kelley travel to Prague.
The mirror returns with them to London.

The Mexica say:
They knew and remembered all of the things that their ancestors
had done and left in their annals, from more than a thousand years back
before the Spaniards came to this land.
The great texts of the Mexica are destroyed,
sometimes by the Mexica themselves: burn or be burned.
We are crushed to the ground. We lie in ruins.
There is nothing but grief and suffering in Mexico and Tlaltelolco
where once we saw beauty and valor.
For Torquemada, Zumárraga, Cortés: the great victory.

Dee returns to a library emptied by a mob.
Fire, crashing, tearing of vellum, sundering of bindings, dispersal of the great works.
Thus ended Mortlake, where seven spiritual ministers *fell down like dross of Metal;*
where seven more *clasped together and fell down in a thick smoke;*
where others *vanished like drops of water and fell down like a storm of hail.*
Where still more sank down *into the transparent fiery globe of the New World.*
For Dee and Kelley: opprobrium, scandal, poverty.

After Dee's death, the mirror moves again,
through great men and titled houses, through centuries:
Cotton, Smyth-Pigott, and Walpole.
Petersborough. Londesborough. The Bishop of Woolwich.
Christie's. The British Museum.
Among other things, it will be known as *The Devil's Looking Glass.*

Diabolist. Alchemist. Astrologer.
But above all, the man who coined the phrase, who invoked the world to come:
Nowe (at length) ame I come to my chiefe purpose . . .
to stire vpp yo' . . . most noble hart, and to directe you' Godlie conscience,
to vndertake this Brytish discovery, and recovery Enterprise . . . of yo' Brytish Impire.
1576: the first time the two words appear together in print,
addressed to the Virgin Queen,
the Queen of Virginia.

Empire was not first seen in candlelight reflecting against the darkness of itztli.
But the mirror saw these places connected and connecting,
saw a new kind of story: a new world,
bound together in flame and sails and the streets near the river.[1]

2. Dawnland Telescopes

Making Colonial Knowledge in Algonquian London, 1580–1630

The way to the Ghost World lies over there. It is many days' journey.
Going to the Ghost World is walking many days, endless walking
through water. Their feet are walking on the top of the World Beneath
the Earth. Their bodies are walking through the Water World. Their
heads are walking in the sky. Their eyes are seeing nothing but water; it
stretches blue and shining all around them, to the very edge of the edge.
—Ruth Holmes Whitehead (Mi'kmaq), 1988

The ink looped and vined on the page, leaving whorls and lobes and the
occasional cursive thorn. Penned by a black-garbed polymath who tutored
gentlemen and pirates, measured rooms full of rain, and drew the moon, it
was one of the many secret codes of its day. It was the descendant of ciphers
created by Greek slaves, of the angelic languages of medieval mystics, and
of codes used by Tudor cardinals. Sibling and contemporary to the Enochian
scripts of John Dee and his scryers across the Thames in Mortlake, the script
was one of many guarded attempts to write down that which was occulted:
the order of the spheres, the creation of gold, the mechanics of conspiracy.
But these were not sigils of the zodiac or alchemical symbols; rather, they
were the first English attempt at an alphabet for a language that had never
needed one. These were the sounds of Roanoke and Croatoan, of "new"
and "old" worlds and lost colonies, of Virginia and Carolina: of a territory
called Ossomocomuck, "The Dwelling-Place Opposite." They were written
mostly in the hand of an Englishman named Thomas Harriot.[1]

Born in Oxford in 1560, Harriot had been a student at St. Mary's Hall
and Oriel College, hearing lectures on geography from mapmaker and imperial advocate Richard Hakluyt and following lessons alongside an ambitious

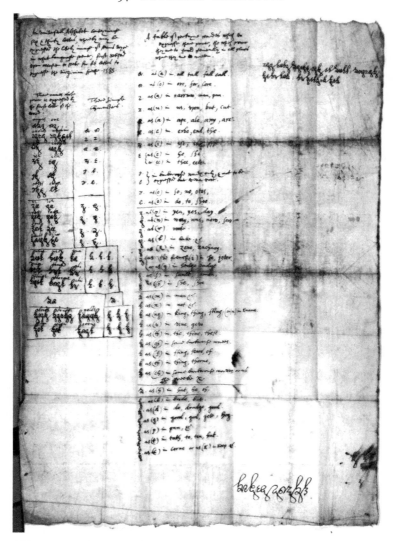

The Ossomocomuck orthography, created by Thomas Harriot, Manteo, and perhaps others. (Reproduced by kind permission of the Governing Body of Westminster School)

West Country nobleman by the name of Walter Raleigh. Sometime around 1582, Harriot joined Raleigh's household in London. Within just three years, Harriot would cross the ocean to Ossomocomuck, where he first encountered the language he would struggle to represent in written form. In his "brief and true report" of the voyage, he wrote of *wapeih*, a blue clay akin to that known as terra sigillata by physicians in Europe; he called a local black pigment "shoemake" just as in England. He noted *winauk*, "sassafras," whose bark was prized as a cure for many diseases, and *pagatowr* and *uppowoc*, which would transform England and the world under other Indigenous names: maize and tobacco. Harriot also provided training in the language to mariners and colonists—one ship's manifest includes the line "What is this. Kecow hit tamen" alongside inventories of powder and shot, copper, and hatchets. Meanwhile, Harriot's account would become forever linked with the watercolors of colonist John White and the engravings of Flemish artist Theodor de Bry, providing to Europe some of the first detailed—if fanciful—images of the people of "Virginia."[2]

But Harriot's linguistic work was never solely his own, and he was as much a pupil as an expert. Without the direct engagement of the citizens of Roanoke (People Who Polish Shell-Beads), Secotan (River Bend), and other towns, "Virginia" would have remained merely a projection of the English imagination. Instead, Harriot's work was the result of Indigenous knowledge and labor, and in particular, of Manteo and Wanchese, two Roanoke men from Croatoan, a community whose name probably meant something like "Talking Town." Together, Manteo and Wanchese made Harriot's accounts of Ossomocomuck possible. Although absent from the title page of *A brief and true report*, they and others were its co-authors.[3]

We might imagine Harriot laboring over his new alphabet in precious moments of quiet. Widening our gaze from the hunched shoulders and the scratching of quill on candlelit parchment, we can envision Wanchese and Manteo alongside Harriot, teaching the scholar simple acts of listening and speaking in a combination of English and their own language. If we pull back just a little farther, we would see that such exchanges took place not only in colonial encampments or an Ossomocomuck town. Much of Harriot's research and writing was done at Durham House, Raleigh's palace on the Strand. There, on the north bank of the Thames, Harriot, Manteo, and Wanchese constructed a new English future during the winter of 1584 and 1585. Meanwhile, young adventurers and scholars came to Durham for training, while artists, scientists, courtiers, and others came and went, carrying the knowledge of Wanchese and Manteo with them along urban networks of elite patronage, intellectual exchange, mercantile deal-making, and common gossip. Ossomocomuck had even begun to establish a material footprint in

London: the first whiffs of tobacco in parlors and taverns, for example, or the sassafras being used to treat syphilis at a shop just down the street from Durham House.[4] But perhaps the most telling evidence of Roanoke presence in London was a signature of sorts at the bottom of the Ossomocomuck orthography, in a different hand than the rest of the text: "King Manteo did this."[5]

London had to learn to be colonial. From the very first moments of sustained encounter in the late sixteenth century, places like Ossomocomuck and London were entangled through the creation of knowledge. Even before Harriot and others stepped ashore in "Virginia," they were propelled there by an unprecedented urban crisis that threatened the stability of London, and English, society. This urban context shaped how English explorers and colonists saw the territories and people they encountered and how they attempted—often unsuccessfully—to organize themselves and others in these unfamiliar places. Such incipient imperialism depended on the participation of Indigenous people, not just aboard English ships or in colonial outposts, but in London itself. Whether as captives or emissaries, Indigenous people in Tudor and Stuart London were concrete sources of empirical information and symbolic representations of an incipient empire, which in the late sixteenth and early seventeenth centuries was as much London's as it was England's. Meanwhile, the experiences of Indigenous travelers to London, and in particular those originating in the homelands of the eastern Algonquian peoples—from Ossomocomuck and the Powhatan chiefdom of Tsenacomoco in the south to the Wampanoag, Abenaki, and Mi'kmaq polities in the north— suggest that parallel Indigenous processes of exploration and meaning-making were taking place.[6] Like the script created at Durham House, this new world was neither urban nor Algonquian. It was both.

In the work of empire building, England, even by its own accounting, was a laggard. Although Bristolian fishermen and explorers like Giovanni Caboto had extended an ephemeral English presence along the coasts of the northwestern Atlantic around the turn of the sixteenth century, such efforts had little effect on either side of the ocean and often met with disdain and indifference in London, particularly among merchants, the satisfied masters of a lucrative trade with continental Europe who were less than impressed with accounts of America's resources. Meanwhile, Ireland served as a cautionary tale for the moral, economic, and human costs of colonialism, and tales of Spain's atrocities in Mexico and Peru highlighted the dangers of such projects, even as it inflamed calls for religious and economic competition. By the middle of the sixteenth century, neither profit nor gospel had compelled England to look beyond the Atlantic. Meanwhile, Londoners themselves were famously parochial. Thomas Platter, a visitor from Basel, noted, "for the most part the English do not much use to travel, but are content ever to learn of foreign matters at home." While historian Peter Mancall has shown that the English learned about the larger world from sailors, fishermen, and printed materials, the reality was that English colonialism was, as late as the 1570s, a contradiction in terms, at odds with the practices and proclivities of English life.[7]

In the late sixteenth century, though, a new rationale for colonialism came to the fore. Between 1500 and 1600, London exploded in population, from perhaps seventy-five thousand to almost a quarter million. The vast majority of this burgeoning originated not from natural growth—indeed, deaths far outpaced births in the plague-ridden city—but rather from immigration, as enclosure, famine, rural economic stagnation, and the discharge of soldiers from ventures in Ireland and Europe unmoored thousands upon thousands of men, women, and children. Most of these people headed for London, and the result was a growing elite discourse of urban anxiety. In 1587, John Howes decried the "caterpillars of the commonwealth . . . lustie roges and common beggers . . . cometh hither to seke reliefe." The city, he wrote pointedly, "can not releve England." Parliament and the Crown made unsuccessful attempts to curb the bewildering speed and chaotic form of the city's expansion. In 1580, for example, Queen Elizabeth made a decree intended to halt the uncontrolled construction at the edges of the city, but this had little or no effect; indeed, in the time of Elizabeth's successor, James I, one observer described the "great concourse of all sorts of people drawing near unto the City," often forced to live in sheds and crowded tenements. In places like Wapping, Limehouse, and Southwark, plague, pollution, and sheer population tested the ability of London's elites to manage their city.[8]

For at least some Londoners, one solution seemed clear: colonization. Sending the city's excess population across the ocean became one of the primary justifications for colonial ventures, often expressed with at least as much urgency as the drive for profit or the call to spread Christianity. Richard Hakluyt was among the first to explicitly make the case, writing that the "idle persons . . . having no way to be sett on worke be either mutinous and seeke alteration in the state, or at least very burdensome to the common wealthe and often fall to pilferage and thevinge and other lewdness." His gesture toward the threat of social unrest was tempered by a humanitarian impulse regarding his fellow citizens who, "for trifles may otherwise be devoured by the gallowes." In a sermon in 1622, clergyman and satirist John Donne made a similar point, arguing that colonization "shall redeeme many a wretch from the Jawes of death, from the hands of the Executioner." Others, like Thomas Churchyard, warned that the "lustie Bodies" invading the city might be "ready too spoyle and cut the throates of the welthy and ritch." In 1583, soldier and naval commander Christopher Carleill argued that colonization could provide hope to English men and women who "fall into sondrie disorders, and [are] ledd on, to one shamefull ende or other." By the early seventeenth century, colonization had become an accepted response to urban problems. In October of 1618, John Chamberlain recorded in a letter that "The City is now shipping thither an hundred young boys and girls that lay starving in the streets, which is one of the best deeds that could be done with so little charge, not rising to above £500." Edwin Sandys, a member of Parliament and one of the founders of the Virginia Company, announced in 1619 that one hundred children of whom "the Citie is especially desirous to be disburdened" had been identified for transportation to Virginia. Noting that many of the children were "ill disposed" to go, he hoped that "vnder severe Masters they may be brought to goodnes."[9]

The city, then, cast a particularly large shadow over the process of colonization; indeed, colonization *was* an urban process. This was also true of the ways in which the English saw the lands they planned to colonize. Instructions to Sir Humphrey Gilbert for a failed expedition in 1578 included admonishments to find "thinges without which no Citie may be made nor people in civill sorte be kept together," including stone, timber, tile, lime, and thatch. A generation later, the Virginia Company organized four "Cities or Burroughs": Jamestown, Charles City, Henrico, and "Kiccowtan," a name taken from one of the towns of Ossomocomuck. Martin Pring, head of a little-known voyage in 1603 to the coasts of what would come to be known as Massachusetts and Maine, wrote of Abenaki canoes being "in proportion like a Wherrie of the River of Thames . . . a thing almost incredible in regard of the largenesse and capacitie thereof." John Brereton described the tools carried by Wampanoag people, which included "a flat Emerie stone (wherewith Glasiers cut glasse, and Cutlers glase blades)" and "a piece of Touchwood (much like our Spunge in England)." This was not idle language for a culture of exploration with its roots in the merchant trades of London; despite their seeming strangeness, these new lands also could be understood through urban similes.[10]

The native peoples of the American continent were also seen by English observers, both in America and at home, through the lens of urbanity, reading their own urban past onto the peoples they encountered in Ossomocomuck and elsewhere. Strachey, for example, argued that "we might yet have lyved overgrowen satyrs, rude and untutred, wandering in the woodes, dwelling in caves, and hunting for our dynners" if the Romans had not built "castells and townes, and in every corner teaching us . . . to knowe the powerfull discourse of divine reason." As Nicholas Canny has noted, many, if not most, early English advocates of colonialism, whether in Ireland or Virginia, explicitly looked to Romanized models of civil structure and law as they imagined what settlements might look like. We can see this way of thinking in the illustrated versions of Thomas Harriot's own writings, in which Ossomocomuck communities like Secotan and Pomeiooc (Good Landing-Place) were labeled with the ancient word for Romano-British towns such as Londinium: "oppidum."[11]

The urban past was one thing; organizing an urban future in "Virginia" was another. As in so many other cases throughout European encounters with the world, in Roanoke, Virginia, New England, and elsewhere, the kinds of problems—many of them distinctly urban—that the English were seeking to escape followed them to the new lands. If we were to excise specific references to location, we would be hard pressed to determine whether a particular complaint arose from Jamestown or London. Directives aimed at controlling nascent urban English landscapes brought to mind similarly hopeless efforts in London. Governor Thomas Gates was given instructions that in Jamestown and other settlements, "in buildinge your towns you shall as easily keepe decorous and order as confusion . . . for every streete may answere

one another and all of them the markett place or storehowse in the middle"—
which was obviously an attempt to leave behind the higgledy-piggledy medieval welter of London streets. And when martial law was enforced at Jamestown in 1611, the laundering of clothes in the streets or even within forty
feet of Jamestown's palisades would bring whipping and court-martial, as
would the washing of dishes near a well or pump, or urination or defecation
anywhere within a quarter mile of the fort. Such prohibitions, both mundane
and draconian, make the most sense when understood in the context of the
streets of London, where suds, shit, and piss all flowed in the streets, causing
disease and disorder, which had helped make the case for colonial transport
in the first place.[12]

Like the alphabet that was neither of Ossomocumck nor of London
yet somehow of both places, urban anxieties drove colonialism and inflected
the experience of the colonies. London and Indigenous territories were enmeshed from the beginning. No term illustrates this better than one that
appears so often in the literature of the day: "adventurer." To the modern
mind, the word conjures images of manly explorers at the prows of ships.
But in the late sixteenth and early seventeenth centuries, an adventurer could
also be an overweight cloth merchant or an aging grocer, a priest or courtier
who had no intention of going anywhere at all but who might invest in a
colony in hopes of eventual profit. In fact, there were probably more of the
latter than the former. The word itself sutures together the two sides of the
Atlantic, blurring the boundaries between center and periphery, embodied
practice and abstract knowledge, and Indigenous and urban places. But in
addition to the Londoners who migrated among these spaces, there was one
other kind of migrant of a very different sort altogether: Indigenous people
themselves, whose knowledge of their homelands would animate England's
transatlantic aspirations.

How to capture a human being, early modern English style:

First, lure them to your ship by ringing a bell; when one rows alongside, quickly pull him up over the gunwale. Many do not wear much in the
way of clothing and some coat themselves with the grease of animals, so it
may be best to grab their long hair. Consider paying or threatening a neigh-

boring chief into betraying one to you under the guise of safe transport. You may be surprised at their strength and their desire for freedom; plan ahead and outnumber them solidly. If your crew fears one of their women may be a witch, remove her skin boots to check for cloven feet. If, after displaying ten very ordinary toes, she still seems powerful—or is just too ugly—leave her behind and look instead for a young woman with an infant. For the men, employ a Cornish trick, a wrestling move likely well known among your sailors. It may break his ribs or puncture a lung, but it will be worth it, as will the information gained from the autopsy. The children matter most of all. Try purchasing them. Certainly, separate them from their families and from their religious leaders, imprisoning and killing the latter if necessary. Taking one or more of their people can also help ameliorate the lack of hospitality you might face while conducting your work. Invite them aboard your ship; tie up your mastiffs to create a more welcoming environment. Sharing meals, both on ship and on shore, will also put them at ease. Should you capture both a woman and a man, put them together and watch to see if they might breed. A number of them will of course die. Prior to this sad outcome, make every effort to baptize. If all goes well, you may be lucky enough to receive permission and funding for a second voyage. Repeat.[13]

At its core, colonization depends on violence. In 1609, for example, Virginia Company instructions to Governor Thomas Gates included specific directives to remove Indigenous people—and in particular children—from their families in the towns of Tsenacomoco:

> You must procure from them some convenient nomber of their children to be brought up in your language and manners, and if you finde it convenient, we thinke it reasonable you first remove from them their Iniocasockes or Priestes by a surprise of them all and detaininge them prisoners.

James Rosier, returned from his wanderings along the coast of the Abenaki Dawnland (now Maine) in 1605, provided the most in-depth description of what capturing another human being might require. After encountering Wabanaki warriors in seafaring canoes, Rosier's captain George Weymouth and his crew "determined so soone as we could to take some of them." After several failed attempts, they finally captured two young men. Rosier described the moment:

> And it was as much as five or sixe of us could doe to get them into the light horseman. For they were strong and so naked as our best hold was by their long haire on their heads; and we would have been very loath to have done them any hurt . . . being a matter of great importance for the accomplement of our voyage.

In the end, Rosier reported that "we shipped five Salvages, two Canoas, with all their bowes and arrowes." This was not the worst of such cases; in 1614 Thomas Hunt, an associate of the famous John Smith, captured two dozen Wampanoag men and women to sell into slavery in Spain.[14]

In most cases, the circumstances by which Indigenous people ended up aboard English ships are unclear. What is clear, however, is that Indigenous communities were often well aware of foreigners' designs. During an encounter in Wampanoag territory in 1602, Gabriel Archer wrote that even after pantomimes of friendship and exchanges of gifts between the local sachem and expedition leader Bartholomew Gosnold, the Wampanoag were "all in love with us," but when invited aboard the English ships, "they refused and so departed." Similarly, Rosier had experienced significant resistance from Abenakis, who were clearly skeptical of his motivations, noting that one of their leaders would not allow his men to come aboard the English ship. Several years later, in 1617, Virginia planter John Rolfe wrote to Edwin Sandys that the people of Tsenacomoco were largely unwilling to allow their children to attend a settler school, while Rolfe's colleague George Yeardley wrote to Sandys in 1619 that "the Spirituall vine you speake of will not so sodaynly be planted as it may be desired, the Indians being very loath vpon any tearmes to part with theire children."[15]

Occasionally, however, Indigenous people openly sought to be taken aboard ships. One participant in an expedition to the Dawnland wrote that "one of the savages, called Aminquin . . . would also have come with them for England."[16] Perhaps Aminquin had been sent on a reconnaissance mission; perhaps he was hoping to increase his own or his family's stature through establishing a trade relationship with the English; perhaps he was an outcast seeking a new life. But in a handful of other cases, we do know why Indigenous people sought passage to England. A Powhatan delegation in 1616 that included Pocahontas, for example, was just that: a diplomatic mission tasked with learning more about the newcomers, their homeland, and the potential threats and benefits they represented. A few years later, in 1629, a Mi'kmaq sagamore named Segipt traveled to England with his wife and sons to establish an alliance against French colonists. They were received at Whitehall by King Charles but ultimately returned home without any formal agreements between the Crown and their people. Contrasting sharply with the accounts of deception, abduction, and outright enslavement, such journeys are more in keeping with the diplomatic journeys made by Indigenous people in later periods of London's history.[17]

Meanwhile, the presence of Indigenous people in England, and London in particular, served a set of very specific and urgent colonial purposes. Rosier, headed home with Weymouth's captives, laid it out clearly: "having some of the inhabitant nation . . . who (learning our language) may be able to give us further instruction . . . of their governours, and government, situation of townes, and what else shall be convenient, which by no meanes otherwise we could by any observation of our selves learne in a long time." The stakes were geopolitical: through the "conueying away of Saluages," England could gain an edge over other European nations who might have designs on the lands of North America. Sir Ferdinando Gorges, an adventurer who never saw America but who oversaw the funding and planting of a failed colony in the Dawnland, saw a similar urgency in the abduction of Indigenous people, believing firmly that "the Natives . . . must be acknowledged as the meanes under God of . . . giving life to all our Plantations." Without Indigenous knowledge, it would be impossible to transform the Dawnland, Tsenacomoco, or any other Indigenous homeland into a subject realm or even a new England. What Gorges could not foresee, however, were the ways in which Indigenous knowledge and presence in the cultural crucible of London would also transform his own society.[18]

Whether as captives or emissaries, Indigenous people found themselves in London. Like the movement of urban anxieties and urban residents back and forth between the city and places like Virginia, the physical presence of Indigenous people in the streets, courts, and guildhalls of London entangled center and periphery—or rather, multiple centers, some English and others Indigenous—and their knowledge mattered to the creation of the thing now known as English colonialism.

Almost all of the travelers were from the Algonquian homelands that stretched from what is now North Carolina northward to Nova Scotia. From Ossomocomuck (present-day North Carolina) in the 1580s came Manteo of Croatoan and Wanchese of Roanoke, along with a third man named Towaye, about whom the archives say almost nothing. Many men, women, and children came or were brought from Tsenacomoco (currently Virginia). These included the young boys Totakins and Namontack, the latter traded for an English boy by captain Christopher Newport; Matchumps, thought to have been a kinsman of Wahunsunacawh, the *mamanatowick* (high chief) more commonly known by his title of Powhatan; Nanawack, brought in 1610 or 1611 by Virginia governor Lord De La Warr; Eiakintomino and Matahan, who appeared on a Virginia Company lottery circular in 1615; the 1616 delegation that included Pocahontas; and a handful of poorly documented travelers from as late as the 1630s. A man named Jack Strawe is the sole recorded traveler from Pequot territory (present-day Connecticut), but four visitors to London—Epenow and Coneconam from Capawack (Martha's Vineyard), Sakaweston from Canopache (Nantucket), and Tisquantum, or Squanto, from the mainland we now call Massachusetts—were citizens of the Wampanoag Confederacy. A total of seven men from the Abenaki Dawnland found themselves in London during the early seventeenth century, and at least one family from the L'nu, or Mi'kmaq, of present-day Nova Scotia arrived in the late 1620s. These, along with a handful of others who remain unidentifiable in the records—in total, perhaps a little more than forty— made up Algonquian London in the Tudor-Stuart era.[19]

Despite their small numbers, Algonquian people and peoples were central to the cultural productions of the day and to notions of what it meant to be English. William Shakespeare is the most well known writer to have employed "Indian" symbolism in his plays. In *All's Well that Ends Well* (1601–5), for example, the young gentlewoman Helena explains,

> Indian-like,
> Religious in mine error, I adore
> The sun.

While never identified specifically as an American, Caliban has long been understood as a thinly veiled stand-in for Indigenous North Americans. Meanwhile, in *Henry VIII* (ca. 1613), a "strange Indian" draws a pressing crowd of curious Englishwomen with his "great tool." As Rebecca Ann Bach has argued, works like these were "signs of—and . . . agents of—the emerging new Atlantic world" at the same time that they were "home-making fantasies that envision England in terms of its colonial spaces and as a colonial space." For example, *The Memorable Mask,* created in 1613 by Inigo Jones and George Chapman, involved a massive production that included musicians "attir'd like Virginean Priests," and "chiefe Maskers, in Indian habits . . . like the Virginian Princes." The masque ended with a clear statement of the new relationship between England and Tsenacomoco. Its final scene called on the *weroances* (political and military leaders) of the Powhatans to renounce their "superstitious worship of these Sunnes," and turn instead

> To this our Britain Phoebus, whose bright skie
> (Enlightend with a Christian Piety)
> Is neuer subiect to black Errors night.

Subtle stuff.[20]

Plays, masques, and other urban rituals involving Indian imagery were influenced to no small degree by actual Indigenous people and practices. The sun worship ascribed to Helena and referenced in *The Memorable Mask,* for example, jibes with early accounts of Indigenous religious devotions in Tsenacomoco that were in wide circulation at the time. In *The Tempest,* Caliban indignantly declares at an important juncture that he will build "no more dams . . . for fish," resonating with Virginia colonists' accounts of Indigenous fish weirs, which had at first helped feed the newcomers, being destroyed by Powhatans in punishment for bad English behavior. The "strange Indian" in *Henry VIII,* meanwhile, has been identified by scholars Sidney Lee and Alden Vaughan as having likely been based on the Wampanoag captive Epenow, who was "shewed up and down London for money as a wonder." Similarly, in Ben Jonson's *Epicœne,* from 1609, the characters included an idiot knight who made "maps of persons," including one of Namontack, the Powhatan youth. Almost two decades later, Jonson's *The Staple of Newes* (1625), noted that

> The blessèd
> Pocahontas (as the historian calls her)

And great king's daughter of Virginia
Hath been in womb of a tavern,

revisiting Rebecca Rolfe's stay at the Bell Savage Inn in Cornhill, a former theater—a place of fiction becoming a place of history becoming a place of fiction again.[21]

Perhaps more than any individual Indigenous person, it was another sort of migrant from Ossomocomuck, Tsenacomoco, and elsewhere that became the center of debates about the relationship between London and Indigenous territories. For Indigenous peoples throughout much of the Americas, tobacco was a sacred being, central to ceremonial life and to the orderly working of the cosmos. Thomas Harriot appreciated its special gifts and described its use in London. "We used to suck in the smoke as they did, and now that we are back in England we still do so," Harriot wrote. "There is sufficient evidence in the fact that it is used by so many men and women of great calling, as well as by some learned physicians." The plant became so popular that many elite Londoners decried its effects on society. In one screed against tobacco smoking from 1602, called "Worke for Chimney Sweepers," the anonymous author spoke directly to the sacred being itself, writing, "Come not within our Fairy Coasts to feed . . . Go charm the priest and Indian cannibals." In 1613, the men of Gray's Inn performed *The Maske of Flowers*, a contest between Silenus, representing wine, and Kiwasha or Potan, representing tobacco. The connections to Tsenacomoco were clear: Kiwasha was the name of a manitou (spirit being) described by Harriot and others, and Potan was an ill-veiled reference to Powhatan. The actors, meanwhile, wore fake tobacco leaves and hats shaped like chimneys. Linking an Indigenous plant to the urban landscape, critics folded American heathenism and the filth of city life into each other. Even King James himself made the connection. "With the report of a great discouery for a Conquest," he wrote in 1604, "some two or three Sauage men, were brought in, together with this Sauage custome . . . but the pitie is, the poore wild barbarous men died, but the vile barbarous custome is yet aliue, yea in fresh vigor." In myriad places at the heart of London society—the Shakespearean stage, guild pageants, tobacco shops, and even the royal court—the presence of Indigenous people and the material evidence of their territories shaped urban discourses.[22]

Perhaps no place was as entangled in this manner as Sir Walter Raleigh's Durham House, where Harriot, Wanchese, and Manteo lived and worked side by side. Having once been home to such Tudor luminaries as Cardinal Wolsey, Simon de Montfort, Catherine of Aragon, Anne Boleyn, and Robert Dudley, it was here that Manteo and Wanchese also worked, no doubt encountering many of the scholars, courtiers, and sailors who came and went and thus finding themselves at the center of one of London's hubs of knowledge production. Its neighborhood was one of the fast-growing suburbs that the civic elite decried and tried to control through limits on building, to no effect, and its chaotic growth, combined with its connections through men like Raleigh to colonial ventures, led to its being given another name in the late sixteenth and early seventeenth centuries: the Bermudas. Ben Jonson, for example, complained to Edward Sackville, Earl of Dorset, about unscrupulous adventurer-merchants who "turne Pyrats here at Land" and "Ha' their Bermudas and their streights i'th'Strand." Similarly, Charing Cross, practically in front of Durham House, may have been a medieval monument to a beloved queen, but by the time Manteo and Wanchese moved in, it was also the name of an Arctic headland "discovered" by Martin Frobisher. Although Wanchese and Manteo did much of their work in private—no records exist of them having been paraded in the streets like Epenow or being received at court like Pocahontas—they lived in an urban landscape that was already dense with meanings derived from the colonial experience.[23]

There was a more private set of encounters, however, taking place in Algonquian London, in places that were quite distinct from the streets and stages of tobacco debates and pageant costumes. In private homes and in the meeting rooms of the charter companies, Indigenous women, children, and men lived and worked. These spaces were hardly a lord mayor's inauguration or a new play at the Globe, but they likely did more to facilitate the processes of colonization through everyday, face-to-face encounters. By simply tracking where and with whom Algonquian people lived during their sojourns in London, we can see how deeply embedded they were in networks of urban and colonial power.

For example, when the Abenaki sagamore Tahanedo arrived in London in 1605, he was placed in the home of jurist and speaker of the House of Commons Sir John Popham, a primary investor in several colonial ven-

tures. "It should be made known to your Majesty," he wrote shortly after
Tahanedo had returned home, "that among the Virginians and Moassons
[Abenaki] there is no one in the world more admired than King James. . . .
Tahanida, one of the natives who was in Britain, has here proclaimed to
them your praises and virtues." While serving Popham's own interests, such
a statement also likely reflects Tahanedo's own diplomatic maneuvering.
Amoret, one of Tahanedo's fellow Abenaki captives, was sent to live with
John Slaney, a merchant in Cornhill, and almost a decade later, Slaney, who
served as treasurer of the Newfoundland Company, hosted the Wampanoag
man Tisquantum. And when Epenow was not being "shewed up and down,"
he and his four fellow captives—his Wampanoag brethren Coneconam and
Sakaweston, and the Abenakis Manawet and Pennekimme—lived with Sir
Ferdinando Gorges, who credited them with inspiring him to seek, along
with Popham, charters for the London and Plymouth Companies. Indigenous presence in the homes of these Londoners was not so much an outcome
of colonial ventures as it was concurrent to them. Indeed, one of the most
important early accounts of the Abenaki homeland was, like much of Harriot's work, crafted not in America but in London, in Gorges's own home,
with his charges as uncredited as Manteo and Wanchese.[24]

Similarly, women, children, and young men from Tsenacomoco lived
with merchants and ministers throughout the city. In 1613, a young boy named
Totakins joined the Gracechurch Street household of Thomas Smythe, the
merchant-tailor treasurer of the Virginia Company. There, Totakins, young
and ultimately alone as he was, must have received a crash course in the
nature of power in London. Three years later, a female member of the delegation that included Pocahontas, christened Mary, went to live as a servant
in the home of a mercer in Cheapside. She did not stay there long; ill with
tuberculosis, she was taken in by one of London's most celebrated Puritan
preachers, William Gouge, whose sermons at St. Ann's Blackfriars electrified audiences and who raised a subscription for Mary's treatment and up-
keep, along with Virginia investors William Throckmorton and George
Thorpe. Thorpe, himself, meanwhile, hosted a young boy from Tsenacomoco. Baptized rather unimaginatively as Georgius Thorpe, the boy served
as an amanuensis for his namesake, copying patents and other important documents that were sent between London and the Virginia Colony.[25]

At Durham House and the rectory of St. Ann's Blackfriars, as captive diplomats or colonial clerks, Indigenous people like Manteo and Wanchese, Mary, Tahanedo, and Georgius Thorpe played key roles in a network of Londoners engaged in the business of empire. More than just passive subjects, they were active agents in the creation of knowledge about their homelands, even if the specific ways in which this took place left little trace in the archive. Certainly, in Harriot's reports on Ossomocomuck, Popham's missive to King James, and Thorpe's patents, we can see direct evidence of Indigenous labor. Beyond that, we might imagine more the ephemeral ways in which Indigenous presence facilitated London's encounter with America: the ripple of gossip up and down streets as Epenow passed by; the impassioned plea of a minister on behalf of an ailing young "maid of Virginia" (who, if not too ill, was likely to be seen in a nearby pew); or the young Totakins presented to an alderman's guests as evidence of investment potential. Such moments are not unimportant. Indeed, they are perhaps one of the most important ways London came to first know itself as a colonial center. But we have to imagine it, because it is ultimately beyond the archival record. All we are left with are textual fragments and our own historical imagination.[26]

"Ventriloquism"—the word if not the practice—was invented in the early modern period, and the archive of Algonquian London, spare as it is already, is filled with words put in others' mouths. One example involves Eiakintomino and Matahan. We know almost nothing about them, but their likenesses appear on a Virginia Company lottery circular from 1615, which would have been read out in public places such as Smithfield or St. Paul's Churchyard. It included a powerful message attributed to the two men from "Virginia":

> Once, in one State, as of one Stem
> Meere Strangers from IERVSALEM,
> As Wee, were Yee; till Others Pittie
> ought, and brought You to That Cittie.
> Deere Britaines, now, be You as Kinde;
> Bring Light, and Sight, to Vs yet blinde:
> Leade Vs, by Doctrine and Behauiour,
> Into one Sion, to one SAVIOVR.[27]

It is difficult to imagine two Powhatan representatives making such a statement; indeed, the circular's text is more akin to the scene in *The Tempest* in
which Prospero boasts of his own ventriloquism through Caliban:

> When thou didst not, savage,
> Know thine own meaning, but wouldst gabble like
> A thing most brutish, I endow'd thy purposes
> With words that made them known.

Aside from Pocahontas, Eiakintomino and Matahan are the only residents
of Algonquian London of whom contemporary images exist. There is even
a second portrait of Eiakintomino, a watercolor of him walking among a
menagerie of animals—a goose, a crane, a ram—in St. James's Park. He
wears the regalia of a man of wealth: a deerskin mantle, three necklaces and
an armband made of beads or pearls, and a beaded or painted purse. Clearly,
this was a man with a transatlantic agenda, but instead of his voice, we have
that of a Virginia Company publicist.[28]

Which brings us to the most difficult question: What did Eiakintomino,
Matahan, and all the others make of London? Is it possible to re-create their
subjective experiences, informed by Algonquian ways of knowing and conducted according to Wampanoag, Powhatan, or other agendas? Certainly,
modern Indigenous scholars have attempted to reclaim some of these earlier travelers using Indigenist approaches. The Laguna Pueblo scholar Paula
Gunn Allen retells the story of Pocahontas in the broader sweep of colonial
and world history. According to Allen, Pocahontas "would be involved in a
great world change . . . because it was the role of a Beloved Woman to do
these things, and, because it was a time of vast change, it was the responsi-
bility of a particularly able Beloved Woman to do so. That woman, as the
manito seem to have decreed, was Pocahontas." Allen reinterprets the voyage
of Pocahontas and her delegation to London as an extension of Tsenacomoco's political and spiritual power. Following Allen's lead and drawing upon
both archival and ethnographic materials, it is possible to re-create something of the larger Indigenous worlds of which London was becoming part,
which is to say, it is possible to imagine London as something other than the
center of the world.[29]

We can begin, for example, with the geographies of Algonquian home-

A Declaration for the certaine time of dravving the great standing Lottery.

Eiakintomino · **1125 li.** · li. **500** · li. **500** · *Matahan*

Once, in one *State*, as of one *Stem*, Meete *Strangers* from IERVSALEM, As *Wee*, were *You*; till O:hers *Pitie* Sought, and brought You to *That Citie*.

Deere *Britaines* now, be *You* as kinde; Bring *Light* and *Sight*, to *Vs* yet blinde: Leade *Vs*, by *Doctrine* and *Behauiour*, Into one *Stem*, to one SAVIOVR.

IT is apparent to the world, by how many former Publications we manifested our intents to haue drawne out the great standing Lotterie long before this day: which not falling out as our selues desired, and others expected, whose moneys are already aduentured therein, we thought good therefore for auoiding al vniust and sinister constructions to resolue the doubts of al indifferent minded, in thee speciall points for their better satisfaction.

The first is, for as much as the aduentures came in so slackly with such poore and barren receits of moneys at the Lottery house for this twelue moneth past, that without too much preiudice to our selues and the aduenturers in lessening the blankes & prizes. we found no meanes nor ability to proceed in any competent proportion, but of necessity are driuen to the Honourable Lords by petition, who out of their Noble care and disposition to further that publike plantation of Virginia, haue recommended their letters to the Counties, Cities and good Townes in England, which we hope by sending in their voluntarie Aduentures, will sufficiently make that supply of helpe, which otherwise we should not in any reasonable time haue effected.

The second poynt for satisfaction to all honest and wel affected minds, is, that notwithstanding this our meanes of Lottery answered not our hopes, yet haue we not failed in that Christian care of the Colony in Virginia, to whom wee haue lately made two sundry supplies of men and prouisions, whom wee doubt not but they are all in health and in so good a way with corne and cattell to subsist of themselues, that were they now but a while supplied with more hands and materials, we should the sooner resolue vpon a diminution of the Country by lot, and so lessen the generall charge, by leauing each seuerall tribe or family to husband and manure his owne.

The third and last is our constant resolution, that seeing our credits are now so farre engaged to the Honourable Lords, & to the whole State for the drawing and accomplishment of this great standing Lotterie. which we intend shall be our last of all standing Lotteries for this plantation, that our time fixed and determined for accomplishing thereof, shall be if God permit. without longer delay, the 26. of June next being in Trinity teame, desiring all such as haue vndertaken with bookes to solicite their friends, and all such as intend the prosperity of that worthie plantation, that they will not withhold their monies till the last weeke or moneth be expired, lest the be vnwillingly forced to proportion a lesse value and number of our blankes and prizes which hereafter follow.

And whosoeuer vnder one name or posie shall ad-

VVelcomes.

To him that first shall bee drawne out with a Blanke	100.	Crownes.
To the second	50.	Crownes.
To the third	25.	Crownes.
To him that euery day during the drawing of this Lottery shall be first drawne out with a Blanke	10.	Crownes.

Prizes.

1. Great Prize of	4500	Crownes.
2. Great Prizes, each of	2000.	Crownes.
4. Great Prizes, each of	1000.	Crownes.
6. Great Prizes, each of	500.	Crownes.
10. Prizes, each of	200.	Crownes.
10. Prizes, each of	200.	Crownes.
100. Prizes, each of	100.	Crownes.
200. Prizes, each of	50.	Crownes.
400. Prizes, each of	20.	Crownes.
1000. Prizes, each of	10.	Crownes.
1000. Prizes, each of	8.	Crownes.
1000. Prizes, each of	6.	Crownes.
4000. Prizes, each of	4.	Crownes.
1000. Prizes, each of	3.	Crownes.
1000. Prizes, each of	2.	Crownes.

Rewards.

To him that shall bee last drawne out with a Blanke	25.	Crownes.
To him that putteth in the greatest number of Lots vnder one name or Posie	400.	Crownes.
To him that putteth in the second greatest number	300.	Crownes.
To him that putteth in the third greatest number	200.	Crownes.
To him that putteth in the fourth greatest number	100.	Crownes.

If diuers bee of equall number, then these Rewards are to be diuided proportionally.

Addition of new Rewards.

The Blanke that shall bee drawne out next before the Greatest Prize, shal haue	25.	Crownes.
The Blanke that shall bee drawne out next after the said Great Prize, shall haue	25.	Crownes.
The Blankes that shall be drawne out immediately before the 2. next Greatest Prizes, shall haue each of them	10.	Crownes.
The seuerall Blankes next after them shall haue also each of them	10.	Crownes.
The seuerall blankes next before the foure Great Prizes, shall haue each of them	15.	Crownes.
The seuerall Blankes next after them shall haue also each of them	15.	Crownes.
The seuerall Blankes next before the six Great Prizes, shall haue each of them	10.	Crownes.
The seuerall Blankes next after them shall haue also each of them	10.	Crownes.

uenture twelue pounds ten shillings or vpward. if he please to leaue & remit his Prizes and Rewards, hee they more or lesse the Lottery being drawne out, hee shall haue a bill of Aduenture to Virginia, for the like sum he aduentured, & shall be free of that Company, & haue his part in Lands, & all other profits hereafter arising thence. according to his aduenture of twelue pounds ten shillings or vpwards.

Whosoeuer is behinde with the payment of any sum of money, promised heretofore to be aduentured to Virginia, if hee aduenture in this Lotterie the double of that sum, & make payment therof in ready money to Sir Thomas Smith Knight, Treasurer for Virginia, he shall be discharged of the forelaid summe so promised to haue been aduentured to Virginia, and of all actions and damages therefrom arising, and haue also the benefit of all Prizes and Rewards whatsoeuer in this Lottery, due by reason of the like sum which he shall bring in. and yet notwithstanding, if after the Lottery drawne, he list to remit at his said Prizes and Rewards, he shall haue a bill of aduenture to Virginia for the said entire summe according to the last preceding Article.

And if vpon too much delay of the Aduenturers to furnish this Lottery. We bee driuen to draw the same before it be full. the we purpose to shorten both blanks and Prizes in an equall proportion, according to that wherein wee shall come short. bee it more or lesse. that neither the Aduenturers may be defrauded, nor our selues, as in the former, any way wronged.

The Prizes. Welcomes, & Rewards shall be paid in ready Money, Plate, or other goods reasonably rated. If any dislike of the said Plate or other goods, he shall haue ready money for the same. abating onely a tenth part: except in small Prizes of tenne Crownes or vnder, wherein nothing shall be abated then.

The money for Aduentures is to be paid to Sir Thomas Smith Knight. Treasurer for Virginia, at his house in Philpot lane: or to such officers as shall be appointed to attend for that purpose at the Lottery house: or to such other as shall elsewhere, for the ease of the Countrey be authorized, vnder the Seale of the Company, for receipt thereof.

The Prizes, Welcomes & Rewards being drawne, they shall be paid by the Treasurer for Virginia, without delay. whensoeuer they shall be demanded.

And for the better expedition to make our sum compleat, as wel to hasten the drawing of our Lottery. as chiefly to inable us the sooner to make good supplies to the Colonie in Virginia: Whosoeuer vnder one name or posie shall bring in ready money three pounds, either to the Lottery house, or to any Colledge, the same party receiuing their money. for euery three pounds so receiued shall render them presently a siluer spoone of 6. shillings 8. pece price, or 6. shillings 8. pece in money.

Imprinted at London by *Felix Kyngston*, for *William Welby*, the 22. of Februarie. 1615.

Eiakintomino and Matahan, both from the Powhatan people, on a Virginia Company lottery circular, 1615. (Broadside 151, Society of Antiquaries of London) lands such as Tsenacomoco. The Powhatan territory dwarfed the tiny English settlements that clung to riverbanks and tidewater shorelines, and Tsenacomoco stretched far inland along a network of rivers, roads, and trails, with trade networks that reached to the Appalachian Mountains, the Great Lakes, and the Mississippi Valley, and the people had rituals for incorporating powerful objects from these places, whether copper from the Haudenosaunee Confederacy to the northwest, or muskets from the small English communities on their eastern edge. The Powhatan world consisted of concentric circles: facing east, one began at Tsenacomoco in the center, then rippled out through the ocean, to England, and then ultimately to another, world-encircling ocean. In this Indigenous mapping, London was not the center of anything.[30]

Parallels to Powhatan territoriality existed to the north among the Mi'kmaqs and the Abenakis of the Dawnland, although in these cases, the homelands also included the ocean. For the Mi'kmaqs, the ocean is but one of six worlds, and their oral traditions are full of stories set far out at sea, in which ancestors traveled great distances to fight enemies, enticed whales to beach themselves and feed the people, or received the sacred gift of spiritual power. Similar stories exist in the Dawnland tradition, and Abenaki historian Frederick Wiseman has written that the "shaman-helmsmen" of his people were "supremely adept at reading the ocean spirit and its signposts . . . fearlessly striking out for new territory beyond the horizon to see and to fish," noting the prevalence in ancestral village sites of bones from open-ocean species such as swordfish. Even James Rosier noted in 1605 that the Wabanaki used "a multitude of their boats" in search of great whales.[31]

It was from these deeply inhabited homelands (and home-seas) that Indigenous peoples engaged newcomers such as the English. From Mi'kmaki to Ossomocomuck, the religious leaders and visionaries of the nations had prophecies about changes that might one day come from the east. Indeed, among the Abenakis and Mi'kmaqs, one of the most important figures in their history, Kluskap, had come from the east, from across the ocean, to bring change to their world. Among the peoples of the Wampanoag Confederacy, traditions included stories of a great eagle that carries people away over the water, accompanied by thunder and lightning, which were likely grafted on to abductions like those involving Epenow and Tisquantum. And in Tsenacomoco, Powhatan priests warned their leader Wahunsunacawh of a new nation that would arise out of the eastern sea and challenge his primacy. These geographies no doubt inflected Algonquian travelers' experiences of London.[32]

But what did Algonquian travelers from these various homelands make of England's metropolis? Certainly the sheer scale and bewildering sensory texture of London were like nothing in Ossomocomuck or the Dawnland. One observer in 1606, for example, described the sound of London as "a thundering as if the world ran upon wheels."[33] Combine that with the pressing crowds of the densely packed city, and we can understand why one commentator described Pocahontas as tiring quickly of the throngs clamoring outside the Bell Savage Inn. Inside was not much better; colonist John Smith wrote of taking "divers courtiers and others my acquaintances to see her" and that she was visited by "divers persons of great rank and quality." That she was under intense scrutiny is without question; of her portrait made by Simon van de Passe, one courtier snipped, "here is a fine picture of no fair lady and yet with her tricking up and her high style you might think her and her worshipful husband to be somebody." Her itinerary beyond this was enervating in its own right; in addition to being entertained at Lambeth Palace by Bishop King with, according to Samuel Purchas, "festival state and pomp, beyond what I have seen in his great hospitality to other ladies," she also visited the Tower, meeting with Raleigh and Henry Percy, the "Wizard Earl" of Northumberland, whose brother she had known in Virginia. One gets the sense that when she finally retreated to Northumberland's estate west of London, Syon Park, Pocahontas must have been exhausted, and according to at least some accounts, she was already ailing.[34]

There was one moment, however, that allows us to engage in more exact imagining about how an elite Powhatan woman might have understood her time in London. It took place on January 18, 1617, when Pocahontas attended a Twelfth Night celebration at the court of King James. She was, according to one courtier, "well placed," seated on the royal dais at the invitation of Queen Anne. From there, she witnessed the debut of a new masque called *The Vision of Delight*, a didactic spectacle penned by Ben Jonson and designed by Inigo Jones, which included characters such as Delight, Love, and Peace and emphasized the sun and stars. It ended with a paean to James,

Simon van de Passe's 1617 engraving of Rebecca Rolfe, or Matoaka, better known as Pocahontas. (© The Trustees of the British Museum, all rights reserved)

"whose presence maketh this perpetuall *Spring*, the glories of which . . . are the marks and beauties of his power" and who was "lord of the foure Seas [and] King of the lesse and greater Iles."[35]

What might Pocahontas have made of *The Vision of Delight*, which so crudely made the case for King James's Christian dominion over her people? Certainly the peoples of Tsenacomoco had their own sophisticated traditions of performance; John Smith would alternately refer to one such event as a "maske" and an "anticke" in various versions of his memoir. Meanwhile, Powhatan religion included a creator being, Ahone, who was associated with the sun and the stars and responsible for the abundance and wealth of the natural world. These things would have made Jonson and Jones's lavish production legible to an Algonquian noblewoman. But what did she think of it? Was she impressed and entertained? Could she see similarities between her people's traditions and beliefs and those of the English, or did she see straight through the ham-handed attempt to establish English authority over her father's chiefdom? Was she bored, tired, or struggling with the early symptoms of the illness that would soon kill her? That we have no record of her reaction is no doubt an artifact of an imperfect archive, but it may also be a result of her own circumspection: trained as an elite woman and political emissary, and under such close observation, it may simply not have been in her interest to express a strong reaction one way or the other.[36] The Twelfth Night performance, including Pocahontas's performance as an audience member, marked an important turning point in public attitudes about the possible benefits of the colonial experience. Pocahontas's presence at court, like her time in London more generally, was a public-relations coup. But whether it was a turning point in Pocahontas's mind, we cannot know. And two months later, she was dead, likely of dysentery, struck down as her ship descended the Thames on its way back to Tsenacomoco, and buried at Gravesend.[37]

Pocahontas had not been alone on that dais with James and Anne and their favorites. Her kinsman Uttamattomakin, statesman and shaman, had been there with her, and although they come to us through something like ventriloquism, his opinions on London stand out sharply. During his time in London, Uttamattomakin held a series of conversations with John Smith and the chronicler Samuel Purchas. In their accounts, we see an Indigenous leader who was decidedly unimpressed. He had been disappointed in the English religion, seeing little evidence of the Christian God in London and coming to despise the missionary impulse among many of the people he met. Uttamattomakin told Purchas he preferred his own religion to Christianity, even if their respective creators might in fact be equal, a statement that led the minister to call him a blasphemer. Uttamattomakin was also particularly disappointed by King James, who had so little charisma that he could be missed in a crowd. Perhaps the most telling comment of all was the diplomat's comment to Purchas that he would not be able to enter the temples of Tsenacomoco until called by manitou, likely because his time in London had polluted him spiritually. Uttamattomakin's actions after returning home also speak to his conclusions regarding London and the English. With several members of his retinue left behind in the city, and having watched his young relative Pocahontas die, Uttamattomakin arrived back in Tsenacomoco in the summer of 1617 and began to foment an uprising against the Virginians, speaking out against the English both to Wahunsunacawh and Governor Thomas Dale. Although Uttamattomakin was ultimately ignored and marginalized, his anger presaged the eventual collapse of Anglo-Powhatan relations that led to all-out war in 1622.[38]

If we want to understand the Algonquian experience of London, then we should look to what happened after Indigenous people left the city. The outcomes of their individual stories, where visible, suggest that while there was no single experience of London, their time spent there—which in most cases constituted their primary or only sustained experience of the English—shaped the course of the rest of their lives. For example, although Ferdinando Gorges had claimed that Epenow had learned enough English to shout "Welcome! Welcome!" as he was paraded in the streets, the Wampanoag man's actions suggest he might have harbored altogether different feelings. He convinced Gorges that his home island of Capawack was a sure prospect for mining gold, and in 1614, three years after he was captured, he led an expedition back home. During a meeting with a group of kinsmen, Epenow escaped, and five years later, he would laugh as he told this story to another English captain, Thomas Dermer. When Dermer returned in 1620, Epenow took things a step further: he and his men killed most of Dermer's crew and mortally wounded Dermer himself. He would then go on to become an important figure in conflicts with the English settlers who arrived on the *Mayflower* soon after.[39]

Some Algonquian people chose other paths. When Epenow and his warriors attacked Dermer's ship in 1620, they made sure that at least one person on board survived: a fellow Wampanoag man, Tisquantum, who had finally returned home six years after his capture. Tisquantum had escaped slavery in Spain, lived in London, ventured to the colony in Newfoundland,

and then returned to London. Captured by Epenow and taken to the leaders of the Wampanoag, Tisquantum would shock the *Mayflower* colonists by greeting them in English and would come to play a critical role in relations between the settlers and the Wampanoags, which eventually descended into violence in which Epenow appears to have played an important part. While ending their days on opposite sides of a war, Epenow and Tisquantum were part of a single story.[40]

Other Algonquian people also made it home. Of the five Abenaki men captured by Rosier in 1605—Tahanedo, Amoret, Maneddo, Skicowares, and Sassacomoit—at least three made it home as part of expeditions to the Dawnland funded by John Popham. Tahanedo, on one ship, was likely accompanied by his kinsman Amoret. A second ship, carrying Sassacomoit and Maneddo, was intercepted by Spanish pirates; Maneddo appears to have died in Spain, and it is unclear what ultimately happened to Sassacomoit; Skicowares made it back to the Dawnland later. Ultimately, there was little time for any of the survivors to decide how to engage with Popham's Sagadahoc Colony, which failed after only two years. But stories would be told among the Abenaki about the hero Kluskap, who traveled in a stone canoe with buffalo-skin sails and a crew of birds all the way to London, where the people marveled at him. A Pequot named Jack Strawe, meanwhile, who lived in London with the Puritan adventurer Sir Walter Erle in the 1620s, quickly "went native" upon his return to his Connecticut River territory, serving as a translator for his people in their relations with English colonists. (As historian Alden Vaughan suggests, "Jack Strawe" was a common epithet for a worthless person; one wonders if the Pequot man discovered its meaning and thus Londoners' true attitudes toward him.)[41]

Last, like Pocahontas, many Indigenous travelers to London never made it home. The young Namontack of Ben Jonson fame was murdered, for instance, by another Powhatan man, Matchumps, for reasons that are unclear. Matchumps's own trail goes cold in Bermuda, where two of Pocahontas's retinue, Elizabeth and the unwell Mary, ended up as English settlers' wives. One source suggests that Sakaweston, a Wampanoag captured along with Epenow in 1611, became a soldier in Europe. Many more, however, simply died. In 1610, Edwin Sandys complained that Nanawack, a young Powhatan boy, had been "living here a yeare or two in houses where hee heard not much of

Religion, but saw and heard many times examples of drinking, swearing, and like evils, remained as he was a meere Pagan." Sandys saw that Nanawack was "removed into a godly family," where his moral condition quickly improved, even as his physical condition deteriorated. Nanawack "gave such testimonies of his love to the truth," wrote Sandys, "that hee was thought fit to be baptised: but being prevented by death, left behinde such testimonies of his desire of Gods favour, that it mooved such godly Christians as knew him, to conceive well of his condition." A similar fate probably befell Totakins, the young boy sent to live with Thomas Smythe in 1613; indeed, at least two Powhatan children seem to have died in Smythe's custody. Virginia governor Thomas Dale hinted at this in a letter to Smythe: "I sent one Totakins to your self . . . but . . . as yet I never herd what becam of him." And Georgius Thorpe, the member of the Powhatan delegation who stayed on to live with his namesake, died soon after his baptism in 1619, the phrase "Homo Virginiae" written in the parish register of deaths.[42]

More often, though, Indigenous Londoners simply vanish from the historical record, which in most cases likely means that they died in the city. Even Eiakintomino, pictured in the lottery circular and the painting of St. James's Park, disappeared, as did his compatriot Matahan. And herein lies the great irony of Algonquian London: even the most highly visible Indigenous people—the ones who inspired plays or pageants—could be lost among the dangers and silences of early encounter. In September of 1603, for example, several "Virginians"—a term that at that point could refer to someone from almost anywhere in North America—thrilled audiences with their canoe skills on the Thames and stayed as guests in the home of Robert Cecil on the Strand. Their canoe might be the one that ended up in the private curiosity collection of Cecil's friend Sir Walter Cope, but of the canoeists' fate we know nothing. We do know, however, that a plague was raging in London at the time, forcing the newly crowned King James and many other elites to escape the city. Like so many other Algonquian people in Tudor and Stuart London, they simply vanish from the English archive. They are the mirror of Roanoke's lost colony, disappeared without a trace.[43]

Manteo and Wanchese both made it home. After a few months at Durham House in London, the two men, along with Harriot, departed for Ossomocomuck under the leadership of Sir Richard Grenville. At stops in the Caribbean, Manteo and Wanchese observed Spanish traders, who in turn observed the "two tall Indians, whom [the English] treated well, and who spoke English." Once home, their paths diverged radically. Manteo played the role for which he had been trained in London: he translated between his people and the English, guided expeditions into the lands beyond the shore, and at one point even saved an expedition from an attack by enemy warriors. Despite outbreaks of violence between the colonists and the Roanokes, Manteo remained loyal to the English. When Sir Francis Drake fortuitously appeared and offered to take most of the colonists back to England, Manteo, apparently with another Indigenous man named Towaye, returned with them. After nine more months in London, Manteo and Towaye made yet another voyage over the Atlantic to Ossomocomuck along with more than a hundred colonists who were on their way to found "the Citie of Raleigh."

Almost from their first step on the shores of Ossomocomuck, this new group of colonists found themselves at odds with a hostile faction of the Roanokes, led by Wanchese. Soon after returning in 1586, Wanchese had realized that the English intended to settle nearer to his Roanoke community than to Manteo's hometown of Croatoan, and having seen London, he almost certainly could envision the filth, chaos, and violence that would soon follow, so he began to work against those who had sought to create in him an ally. Wanchese was likely among those who burned the English outpost and killed the three Englishmen left behind in 1586. By 1587, Roanoke reticence and hostility toward the colonists had spread despite Manteo's efforts at diplomacy. In return, the English baptized Manteo and named him "Lord" of Dasemunkepeuc, a town the English had just attacked. He still held that title when the colony's leaders departed for England, leaving behind more than one hundred colonists at the mercy of Wanchese and others. The rest is history—or rather, the opposite of it: silence.[44]

After the loss of the colony at Roanoke, Harriot continued his work. He must have thought often of Manteo, Wanchese, and Towaye; he might have been reminded, for example, by the "Princes of America," archery targets set up in Finsbury Fields past the ragged north edge of the city and likely named after the men from Ossomocomuck. Caught up in the intrigues surrounding Sir Walter Raleigh's disastrous romantic and colonial over-reaching, Harriot eventually left Durham House and the Strand for Syon Park, the estate of the Wizard Earl Henry Percy. There, where he spent much of his later years developing new optic technology. On July 26, 1609, he made the first known drawing of the moon using a telescope, and the telescope was a fitting metaphor for his life. His observations of the world around him—whether of the towns of Ossomocomuck or the angles of the stars over Westminster, the waterworks at Syon or the moons of Jupiter—informed the early tasks of empire. In his writings and his lectures, Harriot projected London, and England more generally, into Indigenous territories, just as Indigenous people and places projected themselves, through Harriot, back into the city around him. From the earliest moments, we might say, Indigenous and urban histories were telescoped into each other, neither of London nor Algonquian, but both.[45]

We might imagine other telescopes that allowed the people of Tsenacomoco and the Dawnland and other Indigenous homelands to look out into the larger world that included London. Certainly, Algonquian peoples had their own astronomies. Observing his five Abenaki captives as they crossed the Atlantic to England in 1605, James Rosier noted that "they have names for many starres, which they will shew in the firmament." And Puritan settler Roger Williams wrote a poem later in the century about his Wampanoag neighbors' knowledge of the night sky:

> The very Indian Boyes can give,
> To many Starres their name,
> And know their Course, and therein doe
> Excell the English tame.

Among the seafaring Mi'kmaqs, astronomy was both science and religion: their traditions speak of celestial bears, robins, chickadees, ospreys, rattlesnakes, and old men, all offering spiritual strength to navigators. But there were more metaphorical telescopes that allowed Algonquian people to make sense of encounters with newcomers, just as the work of people like Harriot, Raleigh, Smith, and others did for the English. John Smith described a visit to a sacred Tsenacomoco precinct called Uttamusak, where he observed—or more likely, was incorporated into—a ceremony in which singing priests surrounded a great fire with a ring of cornmeal, then laid down two more concentric circles of whole corn kernels with sticks laid between the circles. As uneducated as he was, he understood what he was looking at: a map. Smith came to understand that the fire and the cornmeal represented the civilized, known world of Tsenacomoco, the first ring of raw corn the Atlantic, the sticks England, and the outermost ring of corn the ocean beyond all land. This was a ceremony of world-creation, bringing London and other newly discovered places into the Powhatan universe—in other words, a telescope of sorts.[46]

These were Dawnland telescopes: they allowed people to peer into each other's worlds at the opening of a new era. When Thomas Harriot was first in America in 1585, he had been fascinated by the appearance of a comet in the sky, and he and other observers, Roanoke, Croatoan, and English alike, found it difficult not to connect the apparition to the epidemics raging through the towns of Ossomocomuck. And many years later, in 1618, just after Harriot's former patron Sir Walter Raleigh had been executed for his failed attempt to project England into the larger world, another comet appeared in the sky over London, for many an omen of the injustice of Raleigh's death. Surely, the people of the Algonquian world also looked up—and wondered what would come next.

A Debtor's Petition, 1676

Come listen to me and I will declare
a story as true as you ever did hear
I merry will be while my money doth last
and only will shew that the worst is past.

King's Bench. Queen's Bench. Wood Street. Poultry.
Fleet. Ludgate. Tothill Fields. Coldbath Fields.
Southwark. Bridewell. Newgate. Marshalsea.
Names of fear, of privation, and of penury,
names of begging through an iron grate,
names of the impoverished punished,
names of desperation.
Justice.

To the Kings most Excellent Majestie.
The humble Peticon of John Wampas alias White.

John Wampas is a Nipmuc man, imprisoned for fifty shillings,
two pounds ten; two hundred pounds in today's money.
Wampas is a trading man, buying and selling
on the Massachusetts land market,
buying and selling and profiting
from his people's wide,
forested home.
Capital.

Oh this is a silver age,
Oh this is a spending age.

That your Petitioner being a poore Indian
having a certaine parcell of Land in Massÿ Chussit Bay
the which he hath held for many yeares

175
49

To the Kings most Excellent Ma:tie

The humble Peticon of John Wampas als White.

Sheweth

That yor Petr being a poore Indian having a certaine Parcell of
Land in Masijchusset Bay the wch he hath held for many yeares he having
received the Oaths of Allegiance and Supremacy and being now reduced
to great distresse was cast into Prison about six months since for a debt of
fifty shillings where he hath remained ever since to his utter Ruine.

Wherefore yor Petr most humbly prayes that yor Matie will be
graciously pleased to grant yor Petr yor Mats Royall Letter
to Sr John Leverett Knight Governr of Masij Chusset Bay
whereby he may be restored to his said Lands or else that
he may free liberty to make Sale thereof for his present
releife and towards paying of his debts.

HER MAJESTY'S STATE PAPER OFFICE

And yor Petr shall ever pray &c

174

Nipmuc debtor John Wampas's petition to King Charles II. (With permission of the National
Archives of the United Kingdom)

Natick. Manexit. Chaubunagungamaug.
Place of Hills. Where We Gather. Boundary Fishing Place.
Wabaquasset. Makunkoag. Pakachoag.
Place of White Stones. Place That Is a Gift. At the Turning Place.

Kupshagkinausu, he is in prison;
noh kobshagkinuk, one who is imprisoned.
Roots:
Kuppogki, it is closed;
sh, a forced or violent action.

When Pheobus and Luna no longer shall shine
and the clouds they drop down great showers of wine,
when Seamen shall fear e'ry pittiful blast,
then you may know that worst is past.

The sober praying towns of New England,
the new villages of evangelism.
Even with the Bible, the dead
are buried with red ochre,
not facing Jerusalem
but curled into
themselves.
Cornfields.

he having received the oaths
of Allegiance and Supremacy
and being now reduced to great distresse
was cast into Prison
about six months since . . .
where he hath remained ever since
to his utter Ruine.

His is not the only petition; others cry from other prisons,
pen stories of penurious life inside the compters:
corporal punishment, a grief and torture of the mind
deep wounds of our afflictions . . . noisome smells
infected like a ship in a Storm.
Starvation.

Oh this is a silver age,
This is a mercifull age.

> *Wherefore your Petitioner most humbly prayes*
> *that your Majestie will be graciously pleased*
> *to grant your Petitioner your Majestie's Royall Letter*
> *to S^r. John Leveritt Knight Governor of Massy Chussitt Bay.*

Across the Atlantic, war has been lit, in fire and musket-ball.
The first peoples rise up against the new peoples;
Puritans *feele the hethens shot* as towns burn.
King Philip's War they will call it—
King Philip, a skull on a stake.
Thanksgiving.

When Souldiers no more to the Warrs they shall go
nor Watermen on the River shall row
when Debtors no more into prison are cast
then you may be sure that the worst is past.

In the middle of war: Deer Island. The dead and dying,
young and old driven from the ruins of towns
for their own promised safety, left to spend
winter in the Boston Harbor,
hundreds to die.
Exposure.

> *whereby he may be restored to his said lands*
> *or else that he may free liberty to make Sale thereof*
> *for his present releife and towards paying of his debts.*

Remnants of warriors in the hills, hiding and gathering.
At Deer Island: survivors carrying prayers and Bibles
are herded onto English ships and sent outward
into southern seas, to Bermuda and Jamaica,
purified in a new baptism of surf
and misery and invisibility.
Enslavement.

Oh this is a silver age.
This is a friendly age.

Machaug, The Place of Departure. Now Sutton.
Nashoba, The Place Between. Now Littleton.
Okommakamesitt, Plowed Field. Now Marlborough.
Washacum, Surface of the Sea. Now Sterling.
Quabaug, The Bloody Pond. Now Brookfield.

And when all these things you do perfectly see
I hope you will not be forgetful of me
but then will conclude I spoke truth at the last
and so may conclude that the worst is past.

A second petition, in 1678, goes deeper than the first, invoking
Nipmuc names on the land: Aspatuck and Susquanaugh.
Invoking names of family and kin: wife Anne, her father
the sachem Romanock. And invoking names
of his tormentors: Nathan Gold, the
entire town of Fairfield.
Conspiracy.

Now for as much s Yo' Pet' & other
native Indians there inhabiting are miserably compterized
within the Laws made by the English
calculated only for their particular advantage . . .
Yo' Pet' humbly prays Yo' Ma^{ty}
to take the premises into Yo' Royal consideration
& appoint indifferent persons there inhabiting
to hear the matters in difference.

Petitions granted by Charles, John Wampas returns
to a countryside utterly transformed by war.
He warns the settlers of new Indian attacks:
you shall feel them. Nipmuc survivors meet,
call to have his land sales annulled.
He is arrested twice in Boston,
drinks, beats his wife.

Dead in his forties.
Commonwealth.

And your Petitioner shall ever pray &c

Commonwealth. Conspiracy. Enslavement. Exposure.
Thanksgiving. Starvation. Cornfields. Capital. Justice.

Oh this is a silver age,
Oh this is a mending age.[1]

3. Alive from America

Indigenous Diplomacies and Urban Disorder, 1710–1765

Gaudy things enough to tempt ye, showy outsides, insides empty;
Bubbles, trades, mechanic arts, coaches, wheelbarrows, and carts.
Warrants, bailiffs, bills unpaid, lords of laundresses afraid;
Rogues that nightly rob and shoot men, hangmen, aldermen, and
　　footmen . . .
Many a beau without a shilling, many a widow not unwilling;
Many a bargain, if you strike it: this is London! How d'ye like it?
—John Bancks, 1738

How it all becomes fantastical here.
All elephants and castles, chalk farms and canaries. All mile ends and
　　mudchutes. All circus.
—James Thomas Stevens (Mohawk), 2006

Had he come all this way, just for this? To lie down on a garden path, blood-ied, drunk, and surrounded by a mob?

All night, thousands of people had pressed in around Utsidihi and his two countrymen among the promenades, pavilions, and supper-boxes of the pleasure gardens at Vauxhall. Shouting. Pointing. Jeering. Grabbing. Even before they'd come ashore at Plymouth, dockside crowds had clamored to catch sight of them, and the situation only worsened after their arrival in the capital. After years of war between their Cherokee people and the English— towns burned, hostages slaughtered, trade relations collapsed—they had crossed the ocean only to find themselves the center of spectacle. For weeks, nobles and commoners alike had gawped at them, even forcing their way into the lodgings in Suffolk Street.

On this muggy July night at Vauxhall, though, Utsidihi reached his limit. The throng had amassed almost immediately after he and his compatriots entered the gardens' gates. Englishwomen accosted them there; one, a singer of dubious reputation, took Utsidihi forcibly by the arm, promenading him before the crowd that separated them. The night wore on; the alcohol flowed; the crowds grew, and grew threatening. Finally, he and his friends retreated into the orchestra pit of one of the music buildings. Someone brought more muscat. They tried to entertain the throng by fumbling with the violins and the organ and by mimicking the ensuing applause. By two in the morning, with the sea of people crashing against the pavilion's walls, it was clearly time to leave, and quickly. In the rush and crush outside, Utsidihi's cloak suddenly snagged on the hilt of a stranger's sword. The man drew his weapon, and the crowd surged open around them. For Utsidihi, this was the final indignity. Grabbing the blade, he wrenched it from the stranger's grasp and snapped it in two. Palms bleeding, he lay down on the ground. He refused to move. He was done. What a disaster.[1]

Chaotic scenes like the one at Vauxhall, one of the premier recreating grounds of eighteenth-century London, would have been familiar to any Londoner, and indeed are quite familiar to us, largely thanks to William Hogarth, whose art captured the hubbubs, huzzahs, and horrors of the Hanoverian metropolis. It was the city he knew all too well; son of a failed writer who had spent time in Fleet Prison, Hogarth understood firsthand the inequalities of the volatile city, even as he found success. His works portrayed the everyday London of fairs, parlors, and bedchambers and infused them with an unalloyed outrage at violence, inanity, and corruption. Ruffians sodomized dogs with arrows and threw cats from windows; apprentices and country maids went to their fates at Tyburn and Bedlam; and the victims of collapsed financial schemes whirled about on great wheels of fortune. Bad gin, cruelty, and venality were all too common in Hogarth's city, and his oeuvre is a window into the vernacular world of one of the most transformative eras in London's history. Hogarth was also at Vauxhall the night that Utsidihi lay down in the dirt. The artist had been responsible for turning around the fortunes of the gardens in the 1730s; under his guidance, they had become a showplace for contemporary English artists, a venue for composers such as Handel, and one of the most influential see-and-be-seen settings of the eighteenth century. Perhaps he was among the crowd on the night Utsidihi snapped; if he wasn't, his fingerprints were all over the place.[2]

Empire was also there that night. In the supper-boxes, Hogarth's stable of artists had created scenes meant to amuse and divert: happy drunks returned home to their wives; sophisticates played a game of quadrille; children skated on ice or played on a seesaw; fairies danced under the moon. But in the pavilions, one could view images of Britain's great warships in action, while in the Pillared Saloon, a vast mural depicted Lord Amherst's benevolence toward the citizens of a defeated Montreal only two years before; in one corner of the painting, a stone was inscribed, "POWER EXERTED, CONQUEST OBTAINED, MERCY SHEWN! MDCCLX." Such images made direct connections between pleasure and power, between gardens of amusement and delight at the heart of the empire, and between the fields of victory and defeat at its margins. One wonders if Utsidihi made those connections himself.[3]

Empire, after all, was why Utsidihi was there. Also known as Ustanakwa or Ostenaco (Big Head), he preferred to go by Utsidihi (Mankiller), a name he had earned as a young man. An important *asgayagusta,* or "military leader," from the Cherokee town of Tomotley, he had been accompanied to London by two other Cherokee leaders, Atawayi (Wood Pigeon) and Kunagadoga (Standing Turkey). Born into the same generation as Hogarth, the three Cherokee men had lived through violence that outstripped anything the artist had experienced in London. Devastating epidemics, mercurial economies, and near-constant violence had shaped their lives in profound ways. Only a year before their arrival in London, their nation had agreed to peace with the British, ending a particularly brutal war that had brought destruction to most of the Cherokee towns in the valleys and mountains west of the colonies of Virginia, North Carolina, and Georgia. Accompanied by Henry Timberlake, who had lived among the Cherokees for a time and been closely involved in the diplomatic rituals that created peace, the three men sailed for England in May of 1762.

The oceanic journey of Utsidihi, Atawayi, and Kunagadoga was part of a broader pattern that took shape in the early eighteenth century. Unlike in the sixteenth and seventeenth centuries, Indigenous North Americans were now more likely to come as emissaries seeking to cement political, military, and economic relations with the Crown within a deepening transatlantic system of trade, political alliance, and warfare. In 1710, four men—three of them Mohawk, the fourth from the allied Mahicans—captivated the city, becoming known as the Four Kings. In 1734, a group of Yamacraw elites came from the new colony of Georgia to establish themselves as brokers between their Mvskoki (Creek) relations and the British. The 1762 visit of Utsidihi, Atawayi, and Kunagadoga, meanwhile, came some three decades after another Cherokee delegation achieved celebrity status in 1730.[4] Day-by-day accounts of their doings appeared in the burgeoning print and popular culture of the era in everything from elite poetry and street doggerel to formal painted portraits and shopkeepers' signs. In these forums, the visitations became a way for Londoners to make sense of their own urban world, focusing in particular on three increasingly alarming aspects of city life: violence, the consumption of alcohol, and the changing roles of women. Meanwhile, as English and other immigrant populations began to grow in Mohawk, Mahican, Cherokee, and Yamacraw territories, the very same issues—violence, alcohol, and gender relations—were at the core of Indigenous-settler encounters there as well. These connections between diplomacy and disorder would also have echoes that lasted long after the travelers had returned home.

As for Utsidihi, that night at Vauxhall, he eventually got up. Timberlake quickly bundled him and the others into a carriage, escaping the drunken crowds and returning to the relative peace of Suffolk Street. Over the next several days, the debacle at Vauxhall became fodder for the newspapers, which declaimed "savage" appetites for alcohol and disorder among both the English and Cherokee participants in the night's events, while the government decreed that they should not be allowed in places of public entertainment because of the rioting and mischief they said such events caused. In response, Timberlake claimed that Utsidihi had never even gone to the pleasure gardens, that it was either Atawayi or Kunagadoga who had caused such a deplorable scene. But the damage was done: after weeks of public appearances, the three Cherokee men would not be allowed to appear in public again.

Soon after, Hogarth unveiled a new engraving called *The Times*. In it, the city is on fire, and competing groups of politicians, some pumping bellows and others aiming water cannons or carrying buckets of water, add to the frenzied scene. In the darkened foreground, impoverished Londoners

Designed & Engraved by W Hogarth   Published as the Act Directs
The Times   Sep.t 7 1762
Plate I

Plate 1 of William Hogarth's series of engravings entitled *The Times*, printed in 1762. (© The Trustees of the British Museum, all rights reserved)

wail and waste away as flames threaten to destroy a globe perched above the prime minister's door. For Hogarth, chaos on the streets—flames leaping between too-close buildings, the wretched lying in the road—reflected, and was reflected in, chaos at a much broader, nearly hemispheric scale: that globe on fire was an unsubtle metaphor indeed for the trauma of what would become known as the Seven Years' War and the possibility of new conflagrations yet to come. Hogarth's city was the world; the world was also the city.

And there, at the left edge of the engraving, a sign hangs from the side of a building. On it, a shirtless, long-haired man in a makeshift loincloth-cum-kilt holds aloft what appear to be wineskins and stands before two wine barrels. Beneath him, the words "Alive From America" appear. Earlier in the year, Hogarth had mounted a gallery exhibition of shop signs, aping and mocking the pretensions of high art; here, a shop sign became a satirical, if not exactly comical, commentary on world affairs. It was also, no doubt, a sly reference to the spectacle of the Cherokee delegation and perhaps even to the events that night at Vauxhall. The seemingly random presence of an "Indian" amid Hogarth's urban scene was part of an archive of disorder that reflected the tumult of eighteenth-century London and North America. The laying down of this archive had started decades before, with four men, very much alive indeed.[5]

In the early seventeenth century, when Epenow, Pocahontas, and other Algonquian people came to London, the city's print world had centered on St. Paul's Cathedral. Handbills and lottery circulars had changed hands in the churchyard and great aisle, and from there returned to the streets, almost as though the church inhaled information into its precincts and then exhaled it back into the city in the form of paper and its sibling, gossip. In the eighteenth century, this all changed. While the noise of printers' presses, the smell of ink, and the cries of news-hawkers still filled the spaces near the great church, printshops had begun to appear all across the city. In the early decades of the century, they could be found everywhere from Little Britain and Smithfields in the City proper to Fleet Street in the west. Wealthy printers plied their trade in main thoroughfares like Cornhill and Aldersgate, while marginal, dissenting, and underground presses printed materials in places like Moorfields, Grub Street, and Dark Lane. Indeed, two of these places—Fleet Street and Grub Street—have remained metonyms for highbrow and lowbrow presses respectively.[6]

In the spring of 1710, these arteries of print could have been mapped by following a single, remarkable document. If we are to believe its provenance, it is the first largely unvarnished Indigenous voice in London's history:

The Four *INDIAN* KINGS SPEECH To Her MAJESTY.
LONDON, April 20. 1710.
Yesterday the Four Princes of the Continent of America, *between* New-England *and* Canada, *had their Publick Audience of Her Majesty with great Solemnity, and by their Interpreter made the following Speech to Her Majesty.*

Great Queen!

We have undertaken a long and tedious Voyage, which none of our
Predecessors could ever be prevail'd upon to undertake. The Motive
that induc'd us was, that we might see our GREAT QUEEN, and relate
to Her those things we thought absolutely necessary for the God of
HER and us Her Allies, on the other side of the Great Water.

We doubt not but our *Great Queen,* has been acquainted with our
long and tedious War, in Conjunction with Her Children (meaning
Subjects) against Her Enemies the French; and that we have been as
a strong Wall for their Security, even to the loss of our best Men. . . .

The memorial went on to describe how the Mohawks and their allies had
agreed to the queen's instructions on the understanding that she would send
a fleet to support them against the French in Canada, who had been encroaching on their territories. When that fleet failed to materialize, the communities
began to fear French reprisals. Presenting a belt of wampum—white and
purple quahog shells woven into an authoritative record of legal and other
agreements—along with their statement, the four men made a veiled threat
that the Mohawk might "stand Neuter" on the question of the French versus
the British. Their appeal ended with an invitation to Protestant missionaries,
entreating the queen to "send over some Persons to instruct us, they shall
find a most hearty Welcome."[7]

The "Four Kings," as they quickly became known, instantly captured
the city's attention, having arrived from a place that anyone who kept abreast
of world affairs would have heard of: Canada. They were members of the
Iroquois Confederacy, or the Haudenosaunee as its citizens called it, made
up at that time of five related peoples—the Mohawks, the Oneidas, the On-
ondagas, the Cayugas, and the Senecas—who dominated the vast, abundant
territory between the English colonies and New France. They managed diplomacy with European newcomers and other Indigenous nations through
the Covenant Chain, a religious metaphor and set of diplomatic rituals that
linked the Haudenosaunee to other peoples in keeping with the Gayanasha-
gowa, the Great Law of Peace. At the beginning of the eighteenth century,
the Haudenosaunee was the most important geopolitical force in the north-
eastern quarter of North America. In the summer of 1702, for example, the
Haudenosaunee leader Oucheranorum told a gathering at Albany "our Cov-

Tejonihokarawa, one of the "Four Kings" of 1710, with wampum and a representation of his Wolf Clan status in a painting by Jan Verelst. (Courtesy of the Library and Archives Canada, acc. no. 1977-35-4, acquired with a special grant from the Canadian government in 1977)

enant Chain is so strong that the Thunder and Lightning cannot break it." He was correct, and the chain's rattles could be heard in London too.[8]

The four men embodied the kinds of changes that were taking place in Haudenosaunee territories during the late seventeenth and early eighteenth centuries. Three of the Four Kings, Sagayenkwaraton, Onioheriago, and Tejonihokarawa, were from the Mohawks; the fourth, Etowaucum, was a leader of the Mahicans, an Algonquian people from the Hudson Valley who had allied themselves with their Haudenosaunee "uncles" in 1675. All four were Christian converts but, unlike most Haudenosaunee Christians, were Protestant rather than Catholic, having been influenced by both Dutch and English colonists. Most important, they were go-betweens, key human links in the Covenant Chain; in fact, they may have been chosen by Haudenosaunee clan mothers and other leaders to go to England. Although their place in Haudenosaunee politics was likely somewhat tenuous, their geographical, religious, and social status seems to have given them advantage in both Haudenosaunee and British eyes.[9]

Soon after their arrival, the four men were ushered into the presence of Queen Anne at St. James's Palace. After that, things got busy very quickly. The press of the day offers details of a social calendar that must have been exhausting. For example, during a single three-day stretch at the end of April, they waited for hours outside a special meeting of the Society for the Propagation of the Gospel, which was considering their request for missionaries and the construction of a chapel; they took a meal with William Penn at the Devil Tavern in Fleet Street; and they heard a sermon by the bishop of London before spending the evening socializing at the extravagant Bloomsbury home of the Duke of Montague. Over the course of the spring of 1710, the Four Kings found themselves at the centers of British power. They dined with the illustrious military leader James Butler, Duke of Ormonde; were entertained by the archbishop of Canterbury; and met with the trade commissioners who oversaw British interests from New York to Virginia, Jamaica, and beyond. They toured the Guildhall, seat of London's powerful mercantile community; Gresham College, where the city's leading minds taught law, geometry, and divinity; and the Royal Exchange, venue for the deals that drove Britain's growing empire. They experienced rituals of British sovereignty in the Banqueting House at Whitehall, on the queen's private yacht, and at the parading of the Life Guards in Hyde Park. They saw firsthand British maritime power and its human consequences, visiting both the dockyards at Woolwich and the naval hospital at Greenwich. They were also the first Indigenous people known to have surveyed the entirety of the city from the top of St. Paul's Cathedral.[10]

The Four Kings did not, however, interact only with London's elite. Their lodgings were at a Covent Garden inn called The Crown and Two

Cushions, situated among the noisy theaters and crowded closes. They met the city's poor and middling classes in places like Leadenhall Market, where Londoners of all sorts sold and bought meat; the bearbaiting venues at Hockley-in-the-Hole in Clerkenwell; and even Bedlam Hospital. It was an itinerary that would deplete any visitor, and yet they appear to have taken it in stride: "they are generally affable to all that come to see them," wrote one observer. If the foreigners, with their dark skins, tattoos, and limited English, were exotic and strange to many observers, they were clearly intensely popular; the editor of *The Spectator* wrote that "when the four Indian Kings were in this Country . . . I often mix'd with the Rabble and followed them a whole Day together."[11]

That we know so much about the Four Kings' day-by-day activities is thanks to a new print culture that ranged from broadsides of monsters and human freaks to elevated discussions of politics, shared not just by printers and publishers but by shopkeepers and stevedores.[12] The Four Kings' speech was part of this transatlantic urban echo chamber. Soon after its first printing, the speech proliferated throughout London, typically appearing in its entirety. One J. Baker of the Black Boy in Paternoster Square reprinted and sold it under the title *The Four Kings of Canada*, along with commentary lauding the four men who, "tho' unpolish'd by Art and Letters, have a large Share of good Sense and natural Reason." A similar reprint, *History & Progress of the Four Indian Kings*, noted that the makers of the speech were "very kind and affable to the *English*." Meanwhile, poets and others began to create a small flood of material related to the Four Kings, most of which acknowledged the broader transoceanic geo- and Christo-politics of their presence. Playwright Elkanah Settle, for example, opined in his *Pindaric Poem* from 1711 that

> You'll find the Phosphor of the advancing Day
> In our Plantations gratefully arise
> And Jesus dawning thro the *Indian* Skyes.
> See there their *Indian* Majesties on Knees
> Waiting for Heav'ns, & Royal *Anne*'s Decrees.[13]

Other parts of this growing archive of Mohawk and Mahican London were elaborate fictions, perhaps inspired to some extent by real events. One lengthy account drew on a visit the Four Kings made to St. James's Park.

After a few stanzas about the diplomatic mission of the visitors, the author described one of the Four Kings being "love seiz'd" among the "troops of handsome ladies . . . rich and gaudily attir'd," with one particular woman "in the christian land and city . . . far exceed[ing] them all." Even though he knew she would never deign to be his, the visitor asked for her hand. The ballad included her answer: "Nor will I ever wed a heathen, / For the richest Indian store." While at one level a commonplace sentimental romance, at another level, this popular account both drew attention to the cruel snobbishness of elite, park-frequenting women and highlighted the Indigenous visitors' difference and supposed inferiority. Whether it really happened or not is almost irrelevant.[14]

In fact, the more popular the source, the more critical it tended to be, both of the Four Kings and of elements within London society—including, most notably, women. One tract described sexual relations between European traders and Indigenous women in Canada by noting that "this Correspondence makes 'em learn the *Indian* tongue with more facility." Having thus gestured toward the alleged bawdiness of Indigenous women, the piece went on to describe them as being "full shore of the Impudence of our own *English* Whores in many Respect," although, to their credit, it was "impossible to find a Scold" among Indigenous Americans, compared to English women who made such good use of "that unruly member the Tongue." As in the decades to come, the presence of Indigenous emissaries—almost all of them men—combined with widespread racism and sexism would be an opportunity for male Londoners to engage in easy misogyny against their countrywomen while also denigrating Indigenous women.[15]

Other references to Etowaucum and his three colleagues took the forms of ballads and bits of rhyming verse. For a mere penny, one could learn "A Ballad on the Progress of the four Indian Kings, that have come so many thousand Leagues to see her present Majesty," which went like this:

> FOUR Kings, each God's viceregent, with Right divine inherent,
> Have lately cross'd the Main, Sir, and Audience to gain, Sir,
> Of *Britain's* Empress *Anne*.
> Which she has kindly granted, to know what Aids they wanted,
> By giving each an Answer, when they had kiss'd her hand, Sir,
> As pleas'd 'em ev'ry Man.

Another piece, "render'd into Pleasant and Familiar Verse," simultaneously emphasized the nobility of the visitors, but also their supposed poverty:

> Four Monarchs of Worth, from their Kingdoms set forth,
>   Without Hose or Shoes to their Feet;
> In order to know, how Affairs did here go,
>   And of Things of Importance to Treat.

Meanwhile, images of the Four Kings moved through the city. The most well known example consisted of four very large painted portraits by the Dutch painter Jan Verelst, for which the men were dressed to look something like Turks. At shops in the Poultry and the Strand, meanwhile one could purchase John Faber's print of the four visitors "Done from ye Life"—likely a spurious claim—while a mezzotint called "The true Effigies" was based on Verelst's portraits. Meanwhile, one storekeeper near the visitors' lodgings in Covent Garden changed his sign during their sojourn from the Jackanapes on Horseback to the Four Indian Kings.[16]

Some sources claim to offer evidence of Mohawk or Mahican opinions of the city, but in truth, most are primarily swipes at competing factions within London society. One account in *The Spectator,* for example, printed Sagayenkwaraton's alleged perspective on what he saw at St. Paul's—Londoners bowing to each other rather than to God, and sleeping in the church—but then went on to describe the Mohawk's disdain toward Whigs and Tories, idle men being carried in "little covered Rooms," strangling clothes and monstrous hair, and fat urbanites who sat in dark rooms when they should be out hunting. "Amidst these wild Remarks," the editor added, "there now and then appears something very reasonable." Only once does their perspective come through relatively clearly: the visitors had hoped to "tire down [a] Deer, and catch him without Gun, Spear, Launce, or any other Weapon" in one of London's parks, but the request was never granted. So perhaps the editor of *The Spectator,* with his account of fat Londoners who couldn't hunt, spoke some truth after all.[17]

Even if we cannot know their specific responses to the city, we can be sure of one thing: the Four Kings asserted their Indigeneity in London. When the Society for the Propagation of the Gospel conceded to send missionaries to their people, the Mahican and Mohawk representatives signed a letter agreeing to the arrangement with symbols representing Haudeno-saunee clans: two wolves, a bear, and a turtle. In Verelst's paintings, mean-while, these ancestral beings come to life. Behind both Onioheriago and Te-jonihokarawa, a wolf snarls and prances; Sagayenkwaraton's red cloak hides a bear in its shadow; and a turtle ambles at Etowaucum's right. These are not accidental. The animals' presence can only be explained by the Four Kings' own system of ancestral clan kinship: the portraits are not just of four indi-viduals; they are portraits of entire communities stretching back to at least the formation of the Haudenosaunee in the centuries before contact. But per-haps the most important element of Verelst's work from the spring of 1710 is there, hanging on Tejonihokarawa's arm: wampum. It is almost certainly a representation of the exact wampum the four men presented to Queen Anne; if so, it is yet another version of the speech and another link in the Covenant Chain that now stretched from the Sacred Tree at the heart of the Haudeno-saunee homelands to St. James's Palace.[18]

Whatever their opinions of the city, the Four Kings at times found themselves in situations where the lines between elite and popular cultures blurred with potentially violent results. One such moment took place on the evening of April 24, when the four men were taken to the Queen's Theatre to see a performance of the opera *Macbeth*. The rowdy audience, referred to in the surviving accounts as a "Mob," made it clear that they had come not to see an opera but to see the Four Kings, warning "we have paid our money, the Kings we will have . . . otherwise there shall be no play." Faced with this threat, the stage manager conceded, placing chairs on the stage so the audience could watch the foreigners watching *Macbeth*. It is impossible to know what the four men thought of this display of the sheer force of a London crowd (or of the backstabbing violence of Shakespeare's story, so at odds with the Great Law of Peace). But by all accounts, after the fiasco at the Queen's Theatre, the four men were kept out of such situations.[19]

The Four Kings were implicated in a second violent episode not long after. In November 1709, a dissenting preacher named Henry Sacherevell had delivered a sermon that scandalized London's elites and mobilized its radicals, lambasting Britain's engagement in the years-long war with France. The sermon inspired a storm of protest that turned into violence soon after. A mob of thousands poured through the city, lighting huge bonfires, looting houses, and even going so far as to tear down a meetinghouse belonging to a member of the opposition. One of the mob's leaders, a queen's waterman named Daniel Demaree, was arrested. On the same day that the Four Kings had their audience with the queen, Demaree was sentenced to death, but the queen pardoned him "at ye Intercession of 4 Indian Kings," according to one writer. Most historians of the Four Kings' visit doubt that they even knew about the trial, but the fact that they were linked to it illustrates the ways in which "Americans" could be used to talk about urban problems.[20]

The third and last episode of violence linked to the visit of the Four Kings took place nearly two years after Tejonihokarawa and his colleagues had returned home. In March of 1712, the pamphleteer and essayist Jonathan Swift wrote in his diary, "Here is nothing talked about but men that goes in partys about the street and cuts people with swords or knives, and they call themselves by som hard name that I can nethere speak nor spell." That name was "Mohocks." Swift continued over the next few days to describe numerous assaults in the streets around Covent Garden and the Inns of Court. On March 14, he wrote that the Mohocks "put an old woman into a hogshead, and rolled her down a hill, they cut some nosis, others hands, and several barbarass tricks." Identifying them as young men of the upper classes, Swift noted that the "Grubstreet Papers about them fly like Lightning," and he was right: the *Spectator* in particular covered the violence and broadsides titled *The Town-Rakes* and *An Argument Proving from History, Reason, and Scripture, That the Present Mohocks and Hawkubites are the Gog and Magog mention'd in the Revelations, etc.* Meanwhile, the dramatist John Gay penned a play entitled *The Mohocks* in which a character asked, "Who has not trembled at the *Mohock's* Name?" and in which the gang's members sang a refrain of unfettered urban violence:

> Then a Mohock, a Mohock I'll be,
> No Laws shall restrain, our Libertine reign,
> We'll riot, drink, and be free.

But only a couple of weeks later, Swift seemed confused. On March 22, he wrote, "Our Mohocks are all vanisht," but four days later fretted, "Our Mohawks go on still." Like the queen's pardon of Daniel Demaree, later observers have questioned whether the Mohocks even existed, or if they were a literary device to critique certain elements of London society or a titillating urban legend to thrill Gay's and Swift's audiences.[21]

And that is exactly the point: as real as the Mohawk and Mahican visitors had been, the "Four Kings" offered an opportunity for eighteenth-century Londoners, with their new culture of print, to tell stories about themselves and their city. Although "Indian" violence might be attributed to urban criminals, imagined or otherwise, the real thing—violence between settlers and actual Indigenous people—could leave its mark on the city: two years after the Four Kings' visit, a statue of Queen Anne was erected in the square in front of St. Paul's Cathedral; on one side of the pedestal, a feathered Indian representing America sat, her foot resting on a very European and very severed head. Meanwhile, the Atlantic world descended into a series of wars that linked violence in Britain and Europe to violence in Indigenous homelands. As the century progressed, Londoners and Indigenous travelers alike tried to make sense of their increasingly entangled worlds.

On the high bluff above the wide, slow river, the people came dancing. They had shared *asi'*, the White Drink from the Beloved Tree, with each other and now came dancing in welcome to the strangers who had arrived in their territory. They came singing out of the council ground of their young town; they came shaking rods covered with bells. They came with muskets, some of the men shooting into the air in memory of past military victories. They carried fans made from the tails and wings of Eagle, the ruler of the Upper World, who offers a peace that flies across the expanse of the earth. They stroked the bodies of the newcomers with their fans, they shook their hands, and they sat down to talk with them. More ceremonies would happen in the days and weeks to come, filled with dancing and the language of hospitality and obligation. They called themselves the Yamacraws; the river was the Savannah; and the strangers included British parliamentarian James Oglethorpe. For Oglethorpe and those who came after him, the first day of February 1733 would be remembered as the moment in which the colony of Georgia was born. For the Yamacraws, it was the beginning of an extension of their already complex world into the Atlantic and of a challenge to the peace expressed in Eagle's feathers.[22]

A year later, the presence of Eagle would be required again, but this time the ceremony linking the Upper World to the lives of human beings took place near the banks of another, very different river: the Thames. Tomochichi, the same Yamacraw *mico* (chief) who had shaken hands with James Oglethorpe, now stood in the throne room of St. James's Palace alongside his wife, Senauki, his teenaged grandnephew Toonahawi, and several of his kinsmen and attendants. There, they presented themselves to George II and Queen Caroline, expressing through an interpreter their desire for trade and their curiosity about Christ. To cement this new relationship, they presented eagle feathers to the royals. Eagles also appeared in paintings of the visitors: in a scene portraying a meeting between the Yamacraw visitors and investors of the Georgia Company, two members of the delegation hold feather fans and a live eagle sits in the lower corner of the painting, while in another portrait, Toonahawi holds an eagle in his lap, the bird no doubt representing for British audiences American "wilderness" but also serving as evidence of Yamacraw religious beliefs and political practices.[23]

Four years earlier, other Indigenous eagles had come to London. In 1730, a delegation of Cherokees also presented themselves at court, offering five eagle tails, four human scalps, and a ceremonial headdress made of a dyed opossum skin. As they laid the feathers on a table before the king, the Cherokee said through their interpreter that "this is our Way of Talking . . . we deliver these Feathers, in Confirmation of all that we have said." This association of Indigenous visitors with eagles and with birds and feathers in general was commonplace; back in 1713, for example, Alexander Pope, inspired by the visit of the Four Kings, had written in "Windsor-Forest" of the "Feather'd People" of America, and in 1762, most portraits of Utsidihi and his colleagues included feather headdresses. Like the appearances of wampum and clan symbols in Verelst's portraits of the Four Kings, feathers were both symbols of exoticism in English minds and assertions of ancestry and authority by Indigenous visitors.[24]

Beyond their use of feathers, the three delegations that arrived in the decades after the Four Kings' departure shared other similarities. All three came in the context of profound upheavals in their own societies resulting from encounters with Europeans. The Yamacraw who greeted Oglethorpe in 1733 at what would become Savannah, for example, were themselves a people of war and diaspora. In 1715 and 1716, a war between the Yamasee

Isaac Basire's 1730 engraving of the seven Cherokee emissaries with Adgalgala, listed here as "Oonacanoa," on the far right. (Courtesy of the Museum of Early Southern Decorative Arts [MESDA] at Old Salem)

people of the Carolina Low Country and the young colony of Carolina had proved particularly devastating for both sides. Many Yamasee survivors moved south along the Atlantic coast, where they joined with a group of Mvskoki people, led by Tomochichi, who had split from the main polity of the Mvskoki for reasons that are unclear and who had traveled to a place on the lower Savannah River where his ancestors were buried. There, with the eventual approval of the Mvskokis, the Yamacraws created a new *talwa*, or town, whose members welcomed the Georgia colonists.[25]

Cherokee journeys to London similarly came at a time of growing tension and trauma. Though sundered by epidemics and increasingly drawn into the Atlantic economy through the deerskin trade, Cherokee towns and their Beloved Men (their chief political leaders) continued to hold sway over

George Verelst's painting of the Yamacraw delegation of 1734, including Tomochichi and Senauki, meeting with trustees of the Georgia Company. (Courtesy of the Winterthur Museum, Painting by William Verelst, Gift of Henry Francis du Pont, 1956.567)

a vast region. Wars between the Cherokees and other Indigenous nations, many of them refugees from earlier wars, led the Cherokees into alliance with the British, and in 1730, a delegation left for England to deepen the relationship. The decision to travel was not taken lightly by the Cherokee delegates. A quarter century after his journey, a young Cherokee man named Adgalgala told Governor James Glen of South Carolina that not one of the Cherokee would consent to the 1730 trip; it was only after much cajoling and detailed descriptions of the nature of a transatlantic voyage that the young man and his colleagues agreed to go. They included Oukah Ulah, who was being groomed to become a Beloved Man; three warriors named Scallelocke, Kerragustah, and Collannah; and two additional men named Clogoittah and

Okanackah. Their "handler" was a ne'er-do-well by the name of Alexander Cuming, who had lived in Cherokee territory for some time.[26]

Thirty-two years later, at the end of another war, Utsidihi, Atawayi, Kunagadoga, and Henry Timberlake prepared to make the same journey to find a solution to the continued pressures of European settlement in their traditional territories (and Utsidihi wanted to know if Adgalgala had been lying about what he had seen in England). Kunagadoga had been named as Beloved Man of the Cherokee only two years earlier, and thus he likely had higher standing than Utsidihi, even if he would appear less prominently in the London press. In fact, it was he who had signed the peace treaty with the British in 1761.[27]

The ways in which the Yamacraw delegation of 1734 and the Cherokee delegations of 1730 and 1762 moved through London was not unlike those of the Four Kings. Their itineraries were equally grueling, and the pressures of being observed were intense. For Oukah Ulah, Adgalgala, and their companions, the schedule in 1730 included Windsor Palace in the west and the Royal Hospital at Greenwich in the east, the fair at Croydon in the south and Sadler's Wells in the north, with the Tottenham Court fair, Bedlam, and numerous inns and theaters in between. Throughout, persons "of all Ranks and Distinctions" were allowed to observe them in their lodging, and they sat for several portraits. The Yamacraws appear to have had something of a more relaxed schedule in 1734, but they were certainly under as much scrutiny as their Cherokee predecessors. During a meeting with the archbishop of Canterbury, for example, they were questioned about the nature of their religious beliefs and practices, but they refused to answer; one of their group had just died, and Tomochichi and the others believed his death to be the result of sharing too much during an earlier religious interrogation. Meanwhile, they were spied on by a Spanish friar, disguised as a Dutch diplomat, who had managed to infiltrate the court in order to gain insight into British-Yamacraw alliances on Spain's northern colonial frontier in Florida. The 1762 Cherokee emissaries, for their part, made appearances at Mansion House and the Temple, toured the Woolwich Arsenal and Greenwich, and took in entertainments at Bagnigge Wells and Haymarket Theatre. Timberlake noted that his Cherokee charges felt "the highest disgust [at] being stared at while dressing or eating [and] they grew extremely shy of being seen." So perhaps it was not Utsidihi's sword-grabbing outburst, but rather his and his colleagues' fatigue and frustration, that led to their disappearance from public view after the fracas at Vauxhall. Such experiences had broader ramifications; Utsidihi said after his return that "the numbers of warriors and people being all of one color which we saw in England far exceeded what we thought possible," suggesting that London's spectacle could shape international diplomacies. (Tomochichi, meanwhile, commented upon returning that he "Saw nothing was done without money" in England, but that he doubted the English were happier than his own Yamacraw people and their Mvskoki kin.)[28]

Even though none of these delegations ever saw or heard an English monarch make a specific political commitment to them, and even though most of their negotiations took place in private with colonial trustees or other figures, their presence inspired Londoners to tell stories about urban life, as discussion of the Yamacraw and Cherokee visitors easily slipped into commentary on the state of the city and its residents. In particular, Indigenous presence in the public spaces of city, and the chaos that so often resulted, inspired complaints about the irrational and potentially dangerous nature of London's lower classes. The editor of *The Gazette and London Daily Advertiser,* for example, fretted over "people running in such shoals to all public places, at the hazard of health, life, or disappointment, to see the savage chiefs that are come among us," and noted that "to read in the papers, how these poor wild hunters were surround by as wild gazers on them at Vauxhall . . . I should like to read a letter (if they could write one) . . . in order to learn what they think of the mad savages of Great Britain." A similar story stated that the three Cherokee men would observe an execution at Tyburn "to see the mob throw dogs and cats at each other . . . and afterwards the battle of the mob who shall have the body, in order to form an idea of European Savages." This emphasis on "the mob" and on London's lower classes was an intrinsic part of accounts of Indigenous visitors.[29]

As in the case of the Four Kings, later Indigenous visitors also inspired London's men to comment on their female neighbors. In 1730, for example, the Cherokee emissary Scallelocke had two rings stolen by a prostitute named Jenny Tite, prompting their host Cuming to refer to lower-class women as little more than animals, and another woman allegedly stole one of the delegation's sword-belts and was later caught trying to pawn it. Tomochichi's wife, Senauki, meanwhile—the only female member of these eighteenth-century delegations—compared favorably with English women. When she and the others were taken on a tour of the Tower, they were shown, among other things, Henry VIII's codpiece. When their guide flipped it up to show what was behind, according to one account "many women crowded in and liked the sight, but the Queen [Senauki] turned her head away."[30]

These portrayals took place in a context of swift changes and intense anxieties over the status not just of women but of the changing mores of English society as a whole. In the eighteenth century, women increasingly demanded a place in the public realm. They called for access to education, they conspicuously consumed new goods, they became involved in humanitarian projects, and they began to craft voices for themselves in both the press and literary circles. These were largely upper-class initiatives, but among more middling populations, women became more likely to keep shops, inns, and other small businesses than ever before. Others even went on to become part of the Grub Street printers' world. In response, a discourse of male virtue developed that began to assert the separate spheres that would become so central to English life in the nineteenth century. This virtue was closely—and perilously—linked to colonial goings-on outside of Britain, where trade and warfare could create both anxiety and confidence among elite male Britons. The expansion of the colonies into Indigenous territories, especially during what eventually became known as the Seven Years' War, reshaped notions of both male and female identities, brought new kinds of trade goods and tall tales into circulation within the city, and transformed the ways in which Londoners, male and female alike, talked about "Indians" and other foreign peoples.[31]

Perhaps the raunchiest example of the narrative connections between the status of English women and the presence of Indigenous travelers came in the form of a "New Humorous Song" published as a broadside in 1762 by one H. Howard. After a description of the hordes that turned out to see Cherokee and other Indigenous visitors, and a reference to the notorious events at Vauxhall, the song suggested a particularly sexual answer to the problems of colonial conflict:

An engraving entitled "The Three Cherokees, came over the head of the River Savanna to London, 1762," with Utsidihi/Ustanakwa at the center and translator William Shorey at far left. (© The Trustees of the British Museum, all rights reserved)

Ye Females of *Britain,* so wanton and witty,
Who love even Monkies, and swear they are pretty;
The *Cherokee Indians,* and stranger *Shimpanʒeys,*
By Turns, pretty Creatures, have tickl'd your Fancies;
Which proves, that the Ladies so fond are of Billing,
They'd kiss even M———rs [Moors], were M———rs as willing.
No more then these Chiefs, with their scalping Knives dread, Sir,
Shall strip down the Skin from the *Englishman's* Head, Sir;
Let the Case be revers'd, and the Ladies prevail, Sir,
And instead of the Head, skin the *Cherokee* T———l [Tail], Sir.
Ye bold Female Scalpers, courageous and hearty,
Collect all your Force for a *grand Scalping Party.*
For Weapons, ye Fair, you've no need to petition,

No Weapons you'll want for this odd Expedition;
A soft female Hand, the best Weapon I wean is,
To strip down the bark of a *Cherokee P——s* [Penis].
Courageous advance then, each fair *English* Tartar,
Scalp the *Chiefs* of the *Scalpers,* and give them no Quarter.

At first glance a bit of tawdry, puerile frippery, the song also captured the complicated ways in which Indigeneity and gender could be linked in the transatlantic world.[32]

If the London mob and English women were often central to depictions of Indigenous visits, there was a third concern that brought even more furrows to the brows of observers, and that was alcohol. In the eighteenth century, London was the epicenter of a plague of spirits known as the "gin craze." William Hogarth's famous *Gin Lane* (1751), with its swinging suicides, cadaverous dissolutes, and crumbling buildings captured the anxiety among urban elites about the effects of widespread alcohol, especially on the city's poor. "Dead drunk" could be literal: the 1740s were one of the deadliest postplague decades in London's history, thanks in no small part to the eight thousand spirit-houses that had sprung up in places like the Rookeries in St. Giles, the inspiration for Hogarth's engraving. For lawmakers and other elite observers, fears of a generation of sickly children twisted by "mother's ruin" and of a shortage of controllable labor dominated discussions of gin shops and chandlers where liquor was sold for pittances. While a law passed in 1751 finally had the effect of controlling distillery trade, the middle of the eighteenth century would be remembered as a time when London's social fabric had almost frayed entirely.[33]

While hand-wringing over the gin craze focused largely on London's destitute, similar fretting about alcohol could also be inspired by Indigenous visitors. A drunk Indian in London was worthy of comment; Utsidihi had discovered that to his great chagrin. But it was not Indigenous drinking, in these cases, that was the primary problem; rather, it was alcohol abuse on the part of English interpreters that most worried observers. Lord Egremont, for example, complained at some length about John Musgrove, the drunkard who served as interpreter for the Yamacraw delegation: in his cups, Musgrove "so confounded the Indians that they did not understand our proposals. . . . Hereupon we desired to see what he could settle with the Indians to-morrow when Musgrove should be sober." The Yamacraws likewise complained about Musgrove, and no wonder. The stakes in such meetings were exceedingly high: war, trade, and land were all on the table. In 1762, the situation was even worse. William Shorey, a notorious inebriate, had been assigned to interpret for that year's Cherokee delegation, but just before sailing, he was thrown, drunk, into a cold creek by his Cherokee wife and died of either pneumonia or tuberculosis en route. As a result, the audience of Atawayi, Kunagadoga, and Utsidihi was almost derailed entirely. Coming at the end of a protracted war between the two nations, the audience was something of a debacle, likely explaining much of the satire that developed around the emissaries, from Hogarth's *The Times* to the "New Humorous Song." Such were the dangers of Indigenous-British diplomacy in London.[34]

Prostitutes and gallows, Riot Acts and gin shops, thieves and thrown cats: all were part of London's landscape of unrest in the eighteenth century. Georgian England, Roy Porter has written, "was pockmarked with disorder," and Indigenous delegations were unwittingly enlisted in Londoners' fractious conflicts. In fact, stories of Tomochichi and the other travelers tell us as much about the English as about the Yamacraws or any other Indigenous visitors. Take, for example, the two-part essay printed in *The Universal Spectator, and Weekly Journal* in 1742, which cast one of the Four Kings as a "Voice of Nature and Reason" in order to critique many things about London society, in particular affectation. A similar letter appeared twenty years later during the second Cherokee visitation; this time, the letter claimed to be from the Four Kings to Utsidihi and his colleagues, decrying the English as a people of folly, London as a den of immoral materialism, and St. Paul's as little more than a big rock. It is easy to see such artifacts as little more than colonial self-referentiality. But behind such projections, there was something real going on, and it is in Indigenous experience, not in London, but in the homelands, that we can see the real consequences of colonial encounter. And the same three issues that dominated urban discourses about Indigenous visitors—class conflict, the status of women, and alcohol—were central to events in Mohawk, Mahican, Cherokee, and Yamacraw territories.[35]

While elite colonial officials had regular contact with elite Indigenous officials, it was everyday encounters between European and Indigenous commoners that could most shape relations between peoples. In the case of all four peoples who sent representatives to London, migrants from the city were central to Indigenous experiences of colonialism. In the case of the Mohawks and the Mahicans, they became hosts to some of London's most outcast residents, when a group of Palatine German refugees living on the outskirts of the city were sent to the colony of New York to produce turpentine for the Royal Navy. Described by some Londoners as a "parcel of vagabonds" and "strange we know-not-whats," the Palatines had experienced violent attacks on their encampments on Blackheath and in Camberwell. Soon after their arrival near Schoharie outside of Albany, the Palatines quickly became a vassal people to the Mohawks, who, in the words of one German settler, "sukled them at their breast." Meanwhile, in both Yamacraw and Cherokee territories, Indigenous people complained about the caliber of Englishmen and women who were coming into their territories. Georgian colonial leaders, for example, found themselves in the tricky position of trying to satisfy new, lower-class migrants while also maintaining the alliance, articulated through Tomochichi, with the Mvskoki nation of the interior. In Cherokee country, the nation's leaders complained in the 1740s that "the white People every Day come nearer and nearer and settling up near us," and one colonial official noted in the 1760s that the Cherokees were "proud, despising the lower classes of Europeans." Many of the wars of the eighteenth century, meanwhile, would be started not just by tensions between settlers and Indigenous people but by differences between lower-class settlers and colonial officials, mirroring conflicts in London.[36]

If urban migration, class conflict, and land encroachment built up the tinder in colonial North America, it was often alcohol that lit the spark. Rum and other spirits had a devastating influence on Indigenous-settler relations throughout the colonies, and time and again Indigenous leaders raised their concerns about it. Almost immediately after the Four Kings' return, Mohawk leaders asked colonial leaders "to prohibit the selling or giving of any rum, strong drink, wine or beer upon very severe penaltys, because many mischiefs doth ensue." A decade later, Aupaumut, a Mahican chief, told the governor of New York that "we desire our father to order the tap . . . to be shut," and a few years after that, another local Indigenous leader told officials at Albany that "you may find graves upon graves . . . all which misfortunes are occasioned by Selling Rum to Our Brethren." Similar stories came from Cherokee territories, where both colonial and Cherokee leaders struggled to regulate the liquor that drove Cherokee people into "jug Debts" and into violence and despair, although these laws were flouted just as openly as London's gin laws were. In both places, alcohol threatened to throw the entire world into disorder.[37]

It was often women who bore the burden of all of these changes; while London men fretted about the changing status of their female counterparts, in Indigenous territories, women were becoming increasingly vulnerable over the course of the eighteenth century. Mohawk women would continue to control much of the political landscape of the Haudenosaunee for generations to come, but for Yamacraw and Cherokee women, the story was altogether a different one. While it is quite likely that Senauki, as the Yamacraw matriarch, was in fact the most powerful member of the 1734 London mission, upon her return, she saw her status decline dramatically. From playing a role in local diplomacy—literally offering milk and honey to the Georgians as symbols of hospitality and goodwill—she found herself forced to negotiate, unsuccessfully, for the land reserved for the Yamacraws living north of the Savannah River. And when the War of Jenkins' Ear broke out between the Spanish and the English in 1739, the rape of Yamacraw and other Indigenous women became central to the prosecution of the conflict and negotiations over compensation. Meanwhile, the sexual exploitation of Cherokee women by English settlers and traders became commonplace as midcentury approached, facilitated by a free trade in rum and other spirits. As women refused to go into the fields for fear of rape or capture, food shortages became endemic throughout the Cherokee towns, and as male warriorship became increasingly central to Cherokee politics, women's matriarchal roles became increasingly marginal. Like class conflict and the disorder created by liquor, the ways in which women's lives were shaped on both sides of the Atlantic give the lie to simplistic and moralistic narratives about scolds and queens. The truth was that to be a woman in either place was a dangerous affair.[38]

It would be wrong to think about these seemingly disparate moments— the chaos at Vauxhall, a rape on the outskirts of Charles Town, a petty thief transported to New York, an Indigenous petition presented to a monarch—

as directly causal, one leading exactly to another. Instead, they are entangled, indeterminate, constellated. In his work on circum-Atlantic performance, Joseph Roach has referred to the network of cities around the ocean's edges as "a vast behavioral vortex." In this way of thinking, the thuggery of the Mohocks can resonate with the Seven Years' War; the gin craze has its echo in rapacious rum traders on the Georgia frontier; stories about fussy ladies flirting with "Indians" run up against Cherokee matrons terrified to tend their sacred crops. The archive of unrest, then, is a disorderly thing in its own right, rhizomatic and imbricated, multivalent and omnidirectional. In his first encounter with the English, on the bluff overlooking the river of his home, Tomochichi is said to have exclaimed that the newcomers were "swift as the bird," that they "flew from the utmost parts of the earth," and that "nothing could withstand them." That may or may not have been true, but certainly the effects of such encounters flew back and forth across the Atlantic, often with very little of the peace that Eagle had once promised.[39]

In 1764, a visitor to London would have been able to see waxwork copies of "Indians," in the form of replicas of Utsidihi and his colleagues, at Mrs. Salmon's Waxworks in Fleet Street. Or they could have gone to see the real thing. Between ten in the morning and six in the evening, customers could pay one shilling to view two young Mohawk men, Sychnecta and Trosorogha, in "their Country Dress, with Belts of Wampum; likewise Tomahawks, Scalping-Knives, Bows, Arrows, and other Things too tedious to be mentioned." The fact that Sychnecta and Trosorogha carried wampum suggests that they may have seen themselves as being on a diplomatic mission. The press and the House of Lords, however, found the situation deplorable, and in March of 1765, the Lords declared a moratorium of sorts on such displays "to prevent any free Indian, under his Majesty's Protection, from being carried by Sea . . . without a proper License for that Purpose." King George III even stepped in, ensuring that Trosorogha and Sychnecta were compensated for their labor and then transported home, where their fellow Mohawks were "much offended" by the public display of their people.[40]

    One of the first applications of the new law was, interestingly, against Henry Timberlake himself. When a group of Cherokee leaders petitioned the governor of Virginia in 1764 to allow them to visit the king in England, their request was denied. Flouting the ruling, Timberlake set sail with three of them not long after, but their trip was a failure: Crown officials refused to meet with an unauthorized diplomatic mission. Ultimately, the law did little to stop travelers from coming. When a delegation of five Cherokee and Mvskoki leaders arrived in 1790 under the sponsorship of their adopted kinsman and British loyalist William Augustus Bowles, they had very little success politically, and the travelers left disappointed.[41]

In fact, the journey to London, for all its possible benefits, rarely conferred long-term prestige and influence upon those who risked the Atlantic crossing. For the Four Kings, certainly, the outcomes were mixed. In 1722 Tejonihokarawa was in Boston at a negotiation with Indigenous representatives from French-allied nations, even though he had been removed from his leadership position in 1716. Of Sagayenkwaraton, Onioheriago, and Etowaucum, less is known, although their families continued to be prominent among Mohawk and Mahican Christians, and a descendant of Sagayenkwaraton, Thayendanagea (Joseph Brant), would eventually visit London twice, in 1776 and 1785, a story we shall take up in a later chapter.[42]

For Tomochichi and the Yamacraws, at first the gains of the visit were clear. Their status as intermediaries between Georgia and the Mvskoki towns was stronger after the journey, which had conferred firsthand knowledge of London as well as spiritual power drawn from its wondrous nature. Fairly soon, however, Tomochichi seems to have overreached, with Mvskoki leaders claiming he exaggerated stories of London to "keep them in Awe." Tomochichi's final years saw him struggling to prevent settlers, both free and enslaved, from encroaching on Yamacraw holdings, at the same time that he and his community were caught up in small-scale wars between the English and Spanish. After Tomochichi's death in 1739 and the dissolution of the Yamacraw reserve on Pipemaker's Creek in 1746, the Yamacraws lost their status as a talwa, and by the nineteenth century, they had ceased to exist as a distinct people, their descendants either gone to live with Mvskoki relations or married into African- or European-descent communities.[43]

Adgalgala of the Cherokee, meanwhile, made good use of his 1730 sojourn in England after his return. Recounting the voyage a quarter century later, he told one colonial governor, "I am the only Cherokee now alive that went to England," and in fact, he had achieved such clout from the voyage that leaders of the following generation seem to have seen a trip to London as an important facet of political leadership, even if only a handful were able to make the journey, like Utsidihi and his colleagues were in 1762. As for Utsidihi, he would remain one of the most important military leaders of the Cherokee people well into the 1770s, taking up arms against the American rebels alongside Adgalgala's son Tsiyu Gansini (Dragging Canoe). Utsidihi's fellow 1762 traveler Kunagadoga, meanwhile, courted the Spanish as allies against the Americans into the 1780s. What happened to Atawayi is unclear.[44]

Tejonihokarawa, Tomochichi, Adgalgala, and all the others left echoes in the city. For one particularly influential and prolix Londoner, politician and antiquarian Horace Walpole, references to Indigenous people became part of his urban lexicon, appearing throughout his voluminous correspondences with various English and foreign elites across several decades. He called the French "the most Iroquois of nations," but in another letter, after tut-tutting over salacious rumors about the French queen, he exclaimed, "What Iroquois we must seem to the rest of the world!" and he castigated the notoriously callous General Edward Braddock as being "very Iroquois in disposition." Walpole's scorn was especially sharp when directed at disorder within Britain. In 1780, Walpole excoriated London rioters, declaiming, "the savages of Canada are the only fit allies of Lord George Gordon and his crew." Four years later, he wrote in shock that dissenters at Dover had "roasted a poor *fox* alive by the most diabolic allegory! a savage meanness that an Iroquois would not have committed. . . . I detest a country inhabited by such barbarians!" When Jacobites threatened to sweep south toward the capital in 1745, Walpole let Toonahawi stand in for Charles Stuart: "everybody seems as much unconcerned, as if it was only . . . Tooanohowy, the young prince, [who] has vowed he will not change his linen till he lies at St. James's." Walpole's contempt toward actual Indigenous people, meanwhile, was all too clear: during Utsidihi's 1762 visit, he reported dismissively to Lord Montague that "the Cherokee majesty dined here yesterday at Lord Macclesfield's . . . don't imagine I was there."[45]

The Indigenous visitors of the eighteenth century could also leave traces in more public venues. In 1794, composer Stephen Storace's new opera *The Cherokee*, set in London and North America, debuted to great acclaim. One passage in the libretto involved a run of Indigenous names that was clearly meant as a kind of savage glossolalia, but which also chronicled eighteenth-century British engagements with Indigenous nations: "There were Chicksaws and Cherokees and Mohawks and Miamis Schenectaws and Catabaws Algonquins & Iroquois." More tellingly, the main Cherokee character, portrayed by legendary bass Charles Bannister, sang an aria that recalled real Indigenous experiences:

> "Then if to England I shou'd go on weighty affairs of my nation
> There shall I be the first rate show and for nine days lead the fashion
> Bond Street flaunting and Caps enchanting *a la mode de l'Iroquois.*
> With tomahawks & rings and hatchets hung to strings
> Ev'ry belle will seem a squaw, ev'ry belle will seem a squaw . . .
> Oppress'd yet pleas'd, oppress'd yet pleas'd with their approbation
> My grateful heart beats in my breast, my grateful heart beats in my
>   breast
> Success to the British nation, success to the British nation."

The genealogy of this scene is obvious: it descends not only from the theatergoing of actual Cherokee people but from other Indigenous appearances in the city as well as fictionalized accounts, such as the alleged romance between one of the Four Kings and an English lady in St. James's Park in 1710. Like Walpole's epithets, Storace's opera is proof of Indigenous passing. Meanwhile, the score offered a new texture to London's soundscape. Along with sounds of thunder and bloodcurdling war whoops, for the first time in English music, an iconic musical trope appeared. Whenever a group of Cherokee characters came on stage, they did so to music that has resonated ever since. It is the stereotypical sound of Native America: DUH-*dum-dum-dum*, DUH-*dum-dum-dum*.[46]

The other piece of music that was left behind, if indirectly, by Indigenous visitors, became part of the soundtrack of the British Empire. When the Mohawk and Mahican emissaries stayed at the upholsterer's house in Covent Garden in 1710, the crowds thronging around the place must have been an enormous burden on the householder's wife, who was nursing a small infant. Many years later, that baby, educated at Eton and grown into one of Britain's most well known composers, created stridently rousing music to accompany some of the most assertive lyrics in the English language. There are no Mohawk or Yamacraw or Cherokee characters in the song. Instead, it is flush with other symbols: shouting angels crowding a commanding heaven, native oaks and foreign tyrants, generous flames and shining cities of commerce. First heard in 1745 in London, the song's influence expanded along with Britain's, as part of what Winston Churchill would famously refer to as the "first world war." The composer Thomas Arne had no doubt grown up with family stories of Tejonihokarawa and his compatriots, and perhaps even had faint memories of his own to fuel his transatlantic imagination. He had also no doubt read newspaper accounts of other delegations or had even seen men like Adgalgala, Tomochichi, and Kunagadoga in the city's public places. Surely, he had a few "Indians" in mind when he set these words to music:

> Rule, Britannia! Britannia rule the waves:
> Britons never will be slaves.[47]

Atlantes, 1761

Atlantes (n. pl.): The plural form of atlas; stone carvings of male figures, used as columns to support the entablature of a Greek or Greek-style structure.

What a cannonball does to a human body:
blossoms it in pink and white and red and grey and yellow,
leaves it blackened and open among its fellows on the field.
Such was the fate of Roger Townshend, who flowered open in 1759,
twenty-five on the field of Tekanteró:ken, the River Junction, Ticonderoga.

It is a war of names—the French and Indian War,
la Guerre de la Conquête, the Seven Years' War,
bleeding into wars before and after, a continent in ash.
In America and Britain, a sea of memorials.

Major General George Townshend, elder brother of the blossomed Roger,
when he is not leading troops against the French and the "Indians,"
fancies himself an artist, makes caricatures of his enemies:
"Outewas" with beetling brows and skinny legs, loping along in half-drawn landscapes,
women and tobacco-smoking children in tow.
An Indian who has wounded his enemy & pursues with his tomahawk to scalp him.
War chief completely equipped with a scalp in his hand.
Writes to his wife, calls the people *savages & American butchers.*
At the end of Ticonderoga's victory,
he carries an Odawa child, spoil of war and spectacle,
back to London.

> *The first rejoicing night he was terribly frighted,*
> *and thought the bonfire was made for him,*
> *& that they were going to torture and devour him.*

Robert Adams's study of the atlantes for Roger Townshend's memorial in Westminster Abbey. (Courtesy of the Trustees of Sir John Soane's Museum; photograph, Ardon Bar-Hama)

A child can be a gift.
A child before a fire can be a prize.
Townshend brings the boy to Craven Street. Craven Street,
a few doors down from Benjamin Franklin,
a short walk from Whitehall and power.
There, the boy lives as a stranger in a strange home.

> *He is mighty fond of venison blood-raw;*
> *& once they caught him flourishing*
> *his knife over a dog that lay asleep by the fire,*
> *because (he said) it was* bon manger.

The only memory of the boy—with no name—lies
in the letters of Thomas Gray,
Thomas Gray of the famed *Elegy:* of ploughmen and beetles, elms and applause.
Without this poet of country churchyards and senates,
no Odawa boy would live in the archive.

> *He has brought home an Indian boy with him*
> *who goes about in his own dress*
> *& is brought into the room to divert the company.*
> *the Gen.ᴸ after dinner one evening had been showing them*
> *a box of scalps*
> *& some Indian arms & utensils.*

A scalp is a thing of commerce and certainty;
a gift to crowns and proof of countrysides emptied.
Knives and muskets, hair and skin, boxes of people.

> *When they were gone, the boy got to the box*
> *& found a scalp wᶜʰ he knew by the hair*
> *belong'd to one of his people of his own nation.*

Red ochre along the parting of hair, perhaps.
Maybe the head shaved before the ears.

Townshend calls it polishing: the civilizing mission
to bring the Odawa and others under the Crown;
here, it happens under a Robert Adam ceiling,
a Scots filigree of plaster acanthus and rococo.

Adam is entertained, is inspired. Creates a monument
and aims it toward the cannonballed Roger Townshend,
but also to the boy, whose fate is to be polished.

> *He grew into a sudden fury (tho' but eleven years old)*
> *& catching up one of the scalping-knives made at his master*
> *with the intention of murthering him,*
> *who in his surprise hardly knew how to avoid him,*
> *& by laying open his breast, making signs, & with a few words of French Jargon,*
> *that the boy understood, at last with much difficulty pacified him.*

What does eleven-year-old rage look like?

In another room, a mother mourns,
pens an epitaph for her Roger, her loyal and loved English son:
His Life was glorious, enrolling Him with the Names
of those Immortal Statesmen and Commanders, whose Wisdom and Intrepidity,
In the course of the comprehensive and Sucessfull war,
have extended the Commerce, enlarged the Dominion,
and upheld the Majesty of these Kingdoms, beyond the Idea of any former Age.

Sir John Soane, years later architect of the Bank of England,
collects the sketch of the monument,
the one image of the boy, become an atlas.

> What London does to an eleven-year-old Odawa body:
> captures its curves in graphite and parchment-yellow and white
> doubles it in marble and burdens it with a relief honouring an exploded soldier.
> The unnamed boy twinned in the Abbey's south aisle,
> made into two men,
> polished atlantes bearing a war,
> literally,
> on their shoulders.[1]

4. "Such Confusion As I Never Dreamt"

Indigenous Reasonings in an Unreasonable City, 1766–1785

> On several occasions people have brought savages to Paris, London, and other cities. They have been quick to lay out our luxuries, our riches, and all our most useful and most interesting arts. All that has never excited from them anything other than a stupid admiration.
> —Jean-Jacques Rousseau, 1754

> There is never an unrecognizable place.
> —Simon Qirniq (Inuit), 2004

It was the century of the city and of the savage and of the imagined spaces in between.

The view from the top of St. Paul's Cathedral in the latter years of the eighteenth century was breathtaking. The city had grown faster than ever before in the hundred and some years since the Great Fire of 1666, and St. Paul's was the best place to take it all in. In 1782, German tourist Karl Moritz described the vista:

> Below me, lay steeples, houses, and palaces in countless numbers; the squares with their grass plots in their middle that lay agreeably dispersed and inter-mixed, with all the huge clusters of buildings, forming, meanwhile, a pleasing contrast, and a relief to the jaded eye.
>
> At one end rose the Tower, itself a city, with a wood of masts, behind it; and at the other Westminster Abbey with its steeples. There I beheld, clad in smiles, those beautiful green hills, that skirt the environs of Paddington and Islington; here on the opposite bank of the Thames, lay Southwark; the City itself seems to be impossible for any eye to take in entirely, for, with all my pains, I found it

impossible to ascertain, either where it ended, or where the circum-adjacent villages began; far as the eye could reach, it seemed to be all one continued chain of buildings.

At the limits of understanding, yet somehow pleasing to the eye and mind of the observer, this was the grandeur of Georgian London.[1]

It was, ideally at least, a city of reason. In the precincts that had grown the fastest over the course of the eighteenth century, the north and west, the urban landscape was designed in keeping with the dominant ideas of the day. Row upon sightly row of three- and four-story townhouses stretched in straight lines and graceful arcs through new neighborhoods like Mayfair and Bloomsbury, their neoclassical details harkening to the intellectual and aesthetic traditions of the ancients. Doric orangeries, temples to classical deities, and Palladian porches all expressed the virtues of polite, learned sociability. Above all, taste and wealth were, in the words of architectural historian John Summerson, "foundation stones" of this new urban form. The proliferating squares, patches of orderly green within the burgeoning new districts, were places where the best of London society could "gather occasionally without confusion" and were copied throughout the British realm in places as far afield as Bristol and Philadelphia. Elsewhere in the city, register and excise offices, botanical and pleasure gardens, and architectural pattern books served to edify and organize a new kind of civil society dedicated to reason, respectability, and replicability. London was quite literally enlightened, with gas lighting spreading throughout the wealthier parts of the city and changing that most profound of relationships: the one between night and day. Even the city's language was becoming ordered, with the standardization of spelling and the great lexicographic projects of men like Samuel Johnson.[2]

Birmingham native William Hutton had first visited London in 1749, and when he returned in 1784, he wrote that "the stranger will be astonished at improvements which have been introduced in the last thirty-five years." "Improvements" was an apt choice of words; it was not so much a description of change as an articulation of an ideology. Improvements of the self, of society, of the nation, and of the land itself were paramount concerns of the day, and this was especially true of the urban environment. In 1771,

James Stuart described the ways in which attention to improvement might remake society to manifest its own better nature: "people accustomed to behold order, decency, and elegance in public" in the form of canals, new lighting, and other improvements, he wrote, "soon acquire that urbanity in private, which forms at once the excellence and bond of society." Every aspect of urban life was an opportunity to refashion not just the city but human nature itself, and the eighteenth century was the moment in which projects as diverse as dictionaries and pavements came together under a single ideology of improvement.[3]

Each of these changes was a manifestation of power. "Publick magnificence may be considered as a political and moral advantage to every nation," wrote John Gwynn, author of the 1766 tract *London and Westminster Improved,* and such power extended beyond Europe as notions of improvement and urban primacy informed virtually all aspects of Britain's efforts toward dominance around the world. Gwynn continued:

> The English are now what the Romans were of old, distinguished like them by power and opulence, and excelling all other nations in commerce and navigation. Our wisdom is respected, our laws are envied, and our dominions are spread over a large part of the globe. Let us, therefore, no longer neglect to enjoy our superiority; let us employ our riches in the encouragement of ingenious labour, by promoting the advancement of grandeur and elegance.

This was a vision of dominance in which other societies, lacking in such imposing grandeur, were fit to be ruled first and foremost—to be improved. The city was the avatar of all this.[4]

There was, however another London. In the lanes off the bright new thoroughfares and in the older parts of the city, Londoners lived in abject poverty in warrens of tiny streets and ramshackle houses. The squares were not only spaces of the attempted pastoral within the fabric of the city; they were the sites of assignation and of robbery. For all the pavements, filth and overwhelming amounts of chaotic traffic still flowed in the streets, and the Thames remained the city's primary sewer. The threat of riot was constant. Disorder, unrestricted growth, and profound inequalities of wealth meant that the purported city of reason was, in every sense of the word, unreasonable. Poet William Cowper captured this tension in 1785, writing that "London is, by taste and wealth proclaim'd / The fairest capital of all the world, by riot and incontinence the worst."[5]

What these two Londons, the city of reason and the unreasonable city, shared, though, was spectacle. Together, they were sublime, the apotheosis of human ambition written on the landscape for better or for worse. They also shared a relationship with their opposite: the savage. Over the course of the eighteenth century, the increasing complexity and influence of the press, protracted wars in North America, and growing numbers of firsthand accounts from the colonies and by explorers meant that descriptions of Indigenous peoples became more specific at the same time that they became more contradictory, sometimes trafficking in noble savagery and sometimes offering lurid accounts of Indigenous rapacity. For some, like biographer and journalist James Boswell, the noble savage was a salve to urban life. Writing to Lord Monboddo in February 1767, Boswell commiserated, "You are tempted to join Rousseau in preferring the savage state. I am so at times. When jaded with business, or tormented with the passions of civilized life, I could fly to the woods." Similar to accounts of Indigenous diplomatic expeditions in earlier decades, the noble savage served many purposes in the latter part of the century. As historian Robert Berkhofer Jr. noted in the 1970s, "the noble American Indian scored specific points against religious beliefs and institutions, the nature of education, the organization of government and codes of laws, the prevalence of commerce and the organization of the company, the general social system and social inequality, and the very complexity of life and corruption of civilized and sophisticated customs in general."[6]

Accounts of Indigenous bloodthirstiness and cruelty, though, kept apace with those of Indigenous nobility, and for many, the very notion that a savage might be able to teach anything to an Englishman was absurd. For example, Boswell's great subject, Samuel Johnson, warned Boswell, "Don't cant in defense of savages! . . . What can savages tell, but what they themselves have seen? Of the past, or the invisible, they can tell nothing." Similarly, the philosopher William Robertson derided the possibility of Indigenous intelligence: "A naked savage, cowering over the fire in his miserable cabin, or stretched under a few branches which afford him a temporary shelter, has as little inclination as capacity for useless speculation . . . [;] his mind is totally inactive." For all their differences, these two kinds of savages, the noble and ignoble, had something in common. As literary scholar Kate Full-agar has described, eighteenth-century British notions of savagery, whether admiring or derisive, tended to focus on what supposed savages lacked. These included the things so central to London life: architecture, history, taste. In the words of Anthony Ashley-Cooper, Fifth Earl of Shaftesbury, a trustee of the colony of Georgia and one of the leading intellectual patrons of the day, the difference between the city and the savage was between the "polished" and the "monstrous," and his writings invoked the Great Chain of Being that placed Indigenous peoples at one end of a spectrum of human possibility, and places like London at the other.[7]

But when the city and the perceived savage met in person and Indige-nous visitors were "exposed to the laboratory of polite society," to borrow historian Roy Porter's phrasing, a different set of stories emerges.[8] While Indigenous visitors did often find the Georgian city overwhelming, their di-verse reactions tell us something not just about the "savage mind" but also about the city itself. Far from stupid, as Rousseau had claimed, the Mohegan minister Samson Occom, an Inuit shaman named Atajuq and his family, and a Mohawk military leader named Thayendanagea, or Joseph Brant, were the intellectual contemporaries of Boswell, Johnson, Gwynn, and Shaftesbury, and in a London that was both unreasonable and recognizable, they reasoned themselves and the city into a broader transatlantic world.

"It Looks to me Some like a Dareing Presumption, that I Shou'd Stand be-fore you this Day as a Teacher," the Reverend Samson Occom began. "What Can I Say to You, you that are highly Priviledg'd of the Lord of Hosts . . . and you that are refin'd with Literature and kinds of Sciences?" He spoke these words from the pulpit of a tabernacle in Moorfields, a part of the city that was hardly "refin'd": nearby, noxious foundries smoked amid the hovels of the poor, and raucous fairs appeared and disappeared around the wheel of the year with chaotic regularity. On this February Sunday in 1766, though, Occom sought to create a space for the implacable, liberating logic of Chris-tian salvation. Describing himself as a "Babe in Religion" whom Providence had taken "from the Dung Hill, and from Heathenish Darkness and Gross

Idolatry,—to this Sacred Desk," Occom knew that the pews were filled with people who had come there to see him as much as to hear his words. "If it may be for Gods Glory and Honor," he continued, "I think I am ready to Stand before you all, if it is only as a Spectical and a Gazing Stock." He knew what he represented and what his audience wanted. Occom then began his sermon proper, on the "inexhaustible Text" of Matthew 22:42. "*'What do you think of the Messiah? Whose son is he?' They said to him, 'The son of David.'* "It was, he told his audience, the most important question in Christianity, and he went on to warn against the restless mind that forgets God and Christ, that is "Continually runing after other objects."[9]

Samson Occom was an Atlantic man whose life and work connected that "Sacred Desk" to the homeland of his people. Born among the Mohegan in 1723, he came of age in a time of great change. In the seventeenth century, the Mohegan had allied themselves with the English against their relatives the Pequot, but by the eighteenth century, the English-Mohegan alliance had largely been broken, as settlers from the colony of Connecticut sought to expropriate Mohegan lands and sow discord by helping to create factions within the community. In 1742 Occom became an adviser to Ben Uncas II, leader of the colonists' favored faction, and a year later he attended hearings on a case brought to protect Mohegan lands from further encroachment. Establishing a pattern that would persist throughout his life, Occom devoted himself to bettering the condition and protecting the rights of his and other Indigenous New England communities through engagement with settler political institutions.[10]

Concomitant with this political awakening was a spiritual one. At age seventeen, Occom heard an itinerant preacher in nearby Norwich. That preacher, John Davenport, was part of a radical Christian revitalization movement that would come to be known as the Great Awakening. A whole host of minor sects—Methodists, Baptists, and others—became influential around the shores of the Atlantic, while others, like the Congregationalists and Presbyterians, were transformed by the ferment of the day. Especially in the American colonies, women and men of all sorts, including both the free and the enslaved, found themselves drawn to new ways of manifesting their relationship with a higher power. Democratic, radical, and mobile, and led by preachers known as New Lights, the Great Awakening linked places

The Mohegan minister Samson Occom in a 1768 mezzotint by Jonathan
Spilsbury. (© The Trustees of the British Museum, all rights reserved)

as far-ranging as Connecticut and the Cotswolds. Two years after hearing
Davenport at Norwich, Occom met the man who would come to play the
most important role in his spiritual education and career as a minister. Eleazar Wheelock, a Congregationalist minister, had founded Moor's Charity
School for Indigenous boys at Lebanon, some ten miles from the main Mohegan settlements. Occom joined the student body there in 1743, and it was
through Wheelock's influence and tutelage that Occom developed ambitions
to be a minister and educator in his own right.[11]

Occom's Christian calling did not lessen his commitment to and connections with his Mohegan community; if anything, it deepened them. His
training with Wheelock, combined with the itinerant practices of the Great

Awakening, the New Light emphasis on social justice, and his preexisting networks of kinship and alliance, allowed Occom to maintain and even extend his relationships with other Indigenous communities throughout southern New England and beyond, a region Abenaki literary scholar Lisa Brooks has described as a "common pot" for Algonquian peoples such as the Mohegan. He established Christian worship groups in nearby communities, and after his studies were complete he set up a school for Montaukett children on Long Island, where he also studied traditional herbal medicine and met his Montaukett wife, Mary. He also undertook missions to the Haudenosaunee (in particular the Oneida), from whom he received wampum in a Christian echo of the Covenant Chain. Meanwhile, Occom continued advocating for the rights of his Mohegan people to territory and sovereignty—so much so that his church superiors disciplined him in 1765 and forced him to promise he would desist—and by the 1760s Occom had become a fluent preacher, comfortable sermonizing to both English and Indigenous audiences.[12] Through his connections to the broader networks of the Great Awakening, and in particular to Reverend George Whitefield, Occom and some of his colleagues launched an ambitious project: a journey to Britain to raise funds for the charity school. In 1765, Occom sailed for England.[13]

During his travels prior to 1766, Occom had seen Boston, New York, and Philadelphia, the colonies' largest cities. But little in his experience had prepared him for London. His journals betray Occom's primary initial reaction: dismay. Two weeks before his sermon in Moorfields, George Whitefield and others were advising Occom against traveling in the city openly. "We rode with Mr Whitfield in his Chaise to a good Friends and din'd there," he noted, "but We Were Private about it." No doubt this was because they knew Occom would be an immediate spectacle should he appear in public. It was not just the gawping crowds, however, but the very nature of urban life that merited caution. When Occom finally did venture out on foot, one week before preaching at Whitefield's tabernacle, the resulting journal entry captures his shock:

> Saw Such Confusion as I never Dreamt of—there was Some at Churches, Singing & Preaching, in the Streets some Cursing Swaring & Damning one another, others was hollowing, Whestling,

talking gigling, & Laughing, & Coaches and footmen passing and repassing, Crossing and Cross-Crossing, and the poor Begars Praying, Crying, and Beging upon their knees.

Nothing in his life thus far could have softened the blow of the sublime disarray of London.[14]

Occom was born in a small Indigenous community at the edges of a far-flung colony, so it is not surprising if he found London's bewildering street-scapes daunting, with their numbing cacophony and riotous motion. But we would be wrong in thinking that his response had anything in particular to do with his being Indigenous. Other visitors to the city also quailed before its spectacle. When rake and adventurer Giacomo Casanova arrived in London in 1763, he called it "a town which is sometimes described as a chaos, especially for a stranger." The same could be true not just for continentals but for Britons themselves. In his 1771 novel *The Expedition of Humphry Clinker,* Scottish reformer Tobias Smollett offered scenes that were almost verbatim to Occom's. "All is tumult and hurry," he wrote; "one would imagine they were impelled by some disorder of the brain, that will not suffer them to be at rest. . . . In a word, the whole nation seems to be running out of their wits." Even when the tumult was a source of pleasure, it was still a tumult; Boswell, writing of his arrival in 1762, offered that "the noise, the crowd, the glare of shops and signs agreeably confused me." Confusion, pleasurable or dismaying, was built into the very fabric of the city.[15] And Occom took much of it in. Three days before the sermon at Moorfields, Whitefield "Caried us to the Parlament House—there we Saw many Curiosities, from thence went over Westminster Bridge a Cross the River Thames made all of Stone—thence went to Greenwich, and had a glance of Hospital there." Three days later, Occom and Whitefield "went to Westminster Abey, and had a fuler Vew of the Moniments—saw Bedlem." He also viewed the menagerie at the Tower and watched displays of soldiers on horseback, all part of what had become a tradition for Indigenous and other visitors.[16]

There was a new geography to Occom's time in London, however, different from that of previous Indigenous visitors, whose social calendars primarily included the sights of the city and places of leisure. Instead, the Mohegan minister's itinerary is a map of London's new religious landscape.

It included the High Pavement Chapel of minister John Conder; St. Anne's Blackfriars, where William Romaine, an evangelical Anglican dissenter, preached to large, energetic audiences; Samuel Chandler's Presbyterian church at Old Jewry; and Haberdasher's Hall, where the Congregationalist Thomas Gibbons presided. Occom also interacted with London's abolitionist scene, visiting Bartholomew Close to buy a collection of hymns for enslaved people from printer John Oliver and meeting with John Newton, who would go on to write "Amazing Grace" seven years later. He also circulated within the city's commercial establishment, having an audience with William Legge, Second Earl of Dartmouth and president of the Board of Trade, and with merchants in Spitalfields and the Minories. And always, Reverend Whitefield and his benefactors were at the center of this whirlwind of activity.[17]

The most dramatic encounter of Occom's time in London, though, involved being taken to see George III, an encounter that inspired him to think on an altogether different kind of king:

> [We] saw the King, had ye Pleasure of Seeing him put on his Royal Robes and Crown.—He is quite a Comly man—his Crown is Richly adorn'd with Diamonds, How grand and Dazling is it to our Eye,—if an Earthly Crown is So grand—How great and glorious must the Crown of the glorious Redeemer be.

Rather than simply being overawed by the splendor of the royal personage, Occom quickly turned to what he understood to be the true monarch of his life and world.[18]

Another encounter with the royal family only heightened Occom's disdain for the gulf between those blessed with frivolous largesse and the downtrodden and outcast:

> This is the Queen Charlottes Birth-Day, was Conducted to St. James's where the Royal Family and the Nobility were to be together to keep a Joyful Day . . . [;] we Saw some of the Nobility in their Shining Robes and a throng of People all around,—the Sight of the Nobility put me in mind of . . . the Rich Gluton, and the poor reminded me of Lazarus—What great Difference there is Between the Rich and the Poor—and What Diference there is and will be, Between God's poor and the Devil's Rich, &c—O Lord God Almighty let not my Eyes be Dazled with the glitering Toys of this World.

Occom, who also used the term "confusion" to describe profound spiritual dis-ease and political strife, was clearly aghast at what he saw. Just one example of a common and particularly sharp critique of the city among Indigenous visitors, from Pocahontas's kinsman Uttamattomakin and Tomochichi to others who were yet to come, Occom drew attention to the failings of a supposedly civilized city and nation.[19]

In all, Occom would spend a total of nearly two years in Britain and Ireland, giving sermons and meeting with New Light luminaries across the two countries. By the tour's end, Occom and his companions had raised significant amounts of money. His diaries offer detailed accounts of his travels, but it is his descriptions of London that are the most incisive and critical; they stand out among all the other entries. Although it was unstated, Occom clearly had another city in mind as he measured the faults of urban life in the greatest city he would ever encounter. He must have been thinking always of the New Jerusalem.

In all his journeys, though, he never lost sight of commitment to his own Mohegan people, even as his superiors continued to pressure him to avoid speaking out on the tribe's claims against Connecticut. In early March of 1768, as his ship sailed from London and down the Thames, Occom made a shocking decision during a brief stop at Gravesend: he jumped ship. What happened next is not entirely clear; his diary falls silent at this point. But we know he returned to London. This was his last chance to make a case at the heart of the empire on behalf of his community, and he seems to have taken it. William Johnson, the barrister representing Connecticut in the case, complained to a colleague, "I fear he [Occom] has been induced to enter with an unbecoming spirit into this affair, and, in despite of the agreement he entered into before he left America, is to be made use of, by telling a doleful tale of imagined injuries and abuses, to excite as much compassion for the Indians, and make as much clamour against the Colony, as he can." Johnson might have characterized the minister as little more than a pawn in the hands of the Mohegan's few but powerful allies in Connecticut, but in late April, he let slip that Occom might in fact have more power than the barrister let on, noting that "Mr Occam is, I am told, returned home. . . . I do not find that he has made any very deep or dangerous impressions." Here, Johnson nonetheless hinted that the minister, if allowed to report on the situation of his people, might be a threat to Connecticut's position. Either way, by the end of April, Occom was gone, having become one of the most well traveled people in his social world. Whether his last-minute dash would make any difference to his people's situation, though, only time would tell.[20]

Four years after Samson Occom's departure from London, a party of six boarded a Thames wherry at Westminster and traveled downriver toward the heart of the city. One of them was home, more or less. An Englishman from an aristocratic Nottinghamshire family who had turned his life to exploration and entrepreneurship, his name was George Cartwright, and he was the mastermind of this small voyage. The other five members of the party were foreigners, newcomers to the city and to Britain. They were Inuit, from a place the English called Labrador, and included the shaman Atajuq, his youngest wife Ikkanguaq, and their toddler daughter Ikiunaq, along with Atajuq's youngest brother Tuglavingaaq and Tuglavingaaq's wife Qavvik. Cartwright was showing them the city's sights, much like he might show any group of visitors before or since, Indigenous or otherwise. But this particular tour was much more complicated for everyone involved. "I was exceedingly disappointed," Cartwright later complained in his journal, "to see them pass through London Bridge without taking much notice of it. I soon discovered that they took it for a natural rock which extended across the river. They laughed at me when I told them it was the work of men; nor could I make them believe it." Alighting at Blackfriars, Cartwright had more luck with the bridge there, using his fairly passable Inuktitut to encourage the five visitors "to examine with more attention [and] shewing them the joints, and pointing out the marks of the chizzels upon the stones. They no sooner comprehended by what means such a structure could be erected, than they expressed their wonder with astonishing significancy of countenance."[21]

The group then traveled by carriage into Blackfriars Street, up Ludgate Hill, and on to Sir Christopher Wren's iconic church. Cartwright noted that the group "had often passed St. Paul's without betraying any great astonishment," something that mystified him, until he learned that they had taken it for a natural feature of the landscape, comparing it to a mountainous headland and important landmark in their home territory. To correct this error, he took them to the top of the cathedral and there "convinced them that it was built by the hands of men," with the result that they were "quite lost in amazement. The people, they compared to mice; and insisted, that it must at least be as high as Cape Charles, which is a mountain of considerable altitude." If Cartwright's journal is to be believed, the five Inuit were taken aback by the experience. "Upon my asking them how they should describe it to their countrymen on their return," he wrote, "they replied, with a look of the utmost expression, they should neither mention it, nor many other things which they had seen, lest they should be called liars, from the seeming impossibility of such astonishing facts." Here again, the supposed savage was rendered nearly mute by the capacious, imposing order of the metropolis. What was really going on, however, was something altogether different. Over the course of their time in London, the Inuit would develop what appeared to be cogent critiques of the city's built environment and its environmental and social challenges. Like Occom, these critiques would parallel those of other urban observers.[22]

In the centuries between 1502, when those first Indigenous (and probably Inuit) visitors appeared at Westminster Palace, and 1772, when Ikiunaq and her family arrived, other Inuit people had come to Britain. In 1576, the explorer Martin Frobisher entered the territory of the Inuit with instructions to "bring hither above the number of iii or iiii or eight or ten at the most of the people of that country." The first such captive—taken in 1576 and unnamed in the historical record—had been lured near Frobisher's ship with a small bell. English crew members wrenched this "new pray," as sailor George Best described him, over the gunwale, where the Inuk, realizing he was a captive, "bit his tong in twayne within his mouth." In London later that year, the man served as a "sufficiente witnesse" of Frobisher's accomplishments before dying and being buried at St. Olave Hart Street. The next year, the Inuit infant "Nutaaq" would join him there (we will turn to the baby's story later). In the decades and centuries after the deaths of Frobisher's captives, English presence continued to be felt throughout the southeastern coasts of Inuit territories in the form of whaling crews and fishing boats. By the middle of the eighteenth century, trade relations between the Inuit and Qallunaat [non-Inuit] had become a mix of intimacy and violence, including in the territory that Atajuq and his family called home. In 1767, Inuit warriors killed three European crewmen; in the retaliatory assault, twenty Inuit men were killed and three women and six children captured. Of the latter, one woman, Mikkuq, her son Tutuak, and another young boy named Karpik would be taken to England, after Mikkuq had been forced to teach her captors her language. Of the three, only Mikkuq would return home alive.[23]

It was into this emergent Inuit-British world that the former military officer George Cartwright arrived. Primarily concerned with establishing sealing stations and salmon fisheries on the coast, Cartwright understood that relations with the local population would be key to his success. Over time, he became deeply involved in the everyday workings of at least some Inuit families, employing a number in his household, and according to at least one account, fathering a son by a local woman. Cartwright later wrote, "they are a most amiable, ingenious, tractable and well-disposed race of mortals, and would greatly and rapidly improve by proper management and cultivation." To facilitate this improvement, on October 29, 1772, Cartwright chose five individuals who would accompany him back to England.[24]

From the moment they arrived, the Inuit family was both subjected to the spectacle of Georgian London and cast as one of that spectacle's attractions. "On landing at Westminster Bridge," wrote Cartwright, "we were immediately surrounded by a great concourse of people; attracted . . . by the uncommon appearance of the Indians who were in their seal-skin dresses." Bundling them into coaches, Cartwright had the Inuit driven to their lodgings in Leicester Street. Soon, however, crowds angling to see the strangers "made my lodgings very inconvenient to my landlord as well as to myself," forcing Cartwright to find more private accommodations in Little Castle Street near Oxford Market. Again, the clamor made it almost impossible for him to sleep or conduct business. Finally, he set Tuesdays and Fridays aside for public viewings: "on those days, not only my house was filled . . . but the street was so much crowded with carriages and people, that my residence was a great nuisance to the neighbourhood."[25]

Like Timberlake and the others who had brought Indigenous visitors to London in decades past, Cartwright made sure to take his guests to the theater, in this case to a performance of Shakespeare's *Cymbeline* at the Covent Garden Theatre. They were seated in the royal box, with Cartwright noting, "their pride was mostly highly gratified, at being received with a thundering applause by the audience." The young Ikiunaq, in particular, paid "unremitting attention to the whole representation," and let out "a most feeling scream" at the first sword fight. On another occasion, Cartwright escorted Tuglavingaaq and Atajuq into Piccadilly Circus—no doubt to countless gaping stares—and took them into a menagerie where, among the parrots and snakes, they were horrified to see what appeared to be a tiny Inuk. Cartwright, agreeing that there did seem to be "considerable resemblance," explained the monkey's true nature to them, at which they were both "greatly diverted" and "not well pleased." Then, while dining at the home of the surgeon John Hunter, Atajuq stepped into the next room, only to return with "evident marks of terror." Cartwright wrote, "He hastily led me to . . . a glass case containing many human bones. 'Look there,' says he, . . . 'are those the bones of Esquimaux whom Mr. Hunter has killed and eaten? Are we to be killed? Will he eat us, and put our bones there?'" When Cartwright explained the situation, the company of diners exploded into laughter, and Cartwright spent the rest of the evening assuring the Inuit that the bones were those of a criminal and would help in healing the living. While the others seemed to relax, Atajuq only felt safe once back in Little Castle Street.[26]

In his account of these and other encounters, Cartwright described the Inuit in terms that echoed Johnson, Robertson, and Rousseau. "The uninformed mind of the savage, who never had the least hint given him, that certain things are in existence; consequently, they break upon him as unexpectedly, and forcibly, as the sun would do upon a man who was born deaf and blind, in case he should suddenly be brought to sight on a clear day." Cartwright also wrote of using the city itself as a tool of submission:

> I omitted nothing . . . to make their stay in England agreeable, or to impress them with ideas of our riches and strength. The latter I thought highly necessary, as they had often . . . spoken of our numbers with great contempt, and told me they were so numerous, that they could cut off all the English with great ease, if they thought proper to collect themselves together. . . . But they had not been long in London before they confessed to me, that the Esquimaux were but as one, compared to that of the English.

This hospitable domination permeates Cartwright's account.[27]

What, then, might Qavvik and her family have thought of all they saw? Reading between the lines of Cartwright's journal suggests that a central Inuit concept, *isuma*—a form of logic expressed in emotional restraint, cool circumspection, and an observant detachment—might explain some of their reactions (or lack thereof). The seemingly mute unresponsiveness to London spectacles such as St. Paul's was almost certainly isuma. Even if London did not make sense to the Inuit, Inuit understanding of the journey to London made sense and can be reinterpreted through isuma and other Inuit ways of knowing and being. As for the monkey in the Piccadilly menagerie, for example, the Inuit had throughout their history encountered miniature and very dangerous humanlike beings called *inugarulligaarjuit*, and had developed strategies for protecting themselves in such situations. Their reaction on seeing one so far "out of place" spoke not so much of Inuit confusion but of Inuit order: of an Inuit worldview transposed into the heart of the metropolis.[28] Thinking about isuma and other aspects of Indigenous ontology—in other words, thinking about Indigenous thinking—allows us to reframe Inuit experience of the journey to London. It dislodges racist notions of docility and primitiveness and replaces them with a specifically Inuit rationality or, as literary scholar Keavy Martin argues, a form of sovereignty.[29]

More important, perhaps, is how the Inuit reactions to the city paralleled those of other visitors. Certainly, they resonate with Samson Occom's account of the confusion that he had never dreamed. But more pointedly, they are remarkably similar to the reactions of other, non-Indigenous visitors. Arriving ten years after the Inuit, for example, German schoolmaster Karl Moritz was particularly impressed, even awed, by the activity of London's river. "On the Thames itself are countless swarms of little boats passing and repassing," he wrote, ". . . [and] there is hardly less stir and bustle on this river, than there is in some of its . . . crowded streets." In this, he echoed closely the responses of not only Samson Occom but Cartwright's female guests Qavvik and Ikkanguaq, who "were greatly astonished at the number of shipping which they saw in the river; for they did not suppose that there were so many in the whole world." Similarly, on seeing Ranelagh Gardens, a place the five Inuit visited and found quite overwhelming, Moritz wrote, "I felt pretty near the same sensations, that I remember to have felt, when . . . I first read the Fairy Tales." Tobias Smollett, ever the harsh observer, was more strident in his description of the irrationality of the pleasure grounds: "What are the amusements at Ranelagh? One of the company are following one another's tails, in an eternal circle; like so many blind asses in an olive-mill, where they can neither discourse, distinguish, nor be distinguished." In these accounts, Indigenous, European, and British alike, the alleged city of reason looks altogether different: sublime, uncanny, disordered, ridiculous.[30]

It was also a city that barely held itself together ecologically, and Tug-lavingaaq and the others had serious questions about the nature of the city. For example, Cartwright noted that they found it difficult to understand how many people actually lived in London and how those people were fed. Cart-wright chalked this up to their limited intelligence and a counting system that he claimed only went to twenty-one, but he also let slip that "nothing surprized them more, than to meet with a man who assured them he could not shoot, had never killed an animal, nor seen the sea in his life." In fact, the Inuit were on to something: in the era of land clearances and other forms of subsistence dispossession, failed agricultural experiments, and burgeoning urban slums where food provision was a constant worry, a small group of hunter-gatherers seemed aware of one of Britain's most pressing problems and the strange lack of self-sufficiency of the English. The food that only barely sated London's hunger came from throughout Britain: salmon from Scotland, beef from Wales and Yorkshire, fish from the Fens, vegetables from across the whole of England. Concerns over the relationship between London's appetite and the needs of the rest of the nation were forefront in many other critiques of the city. Smollett, ever the indicter, warned that "the capital is become an overgrown monster; which, like a dropsical head, will in time leave the body and extremities without nourishment or support," while architect and urban planner John Gwynn called the city "a Wen, or Excres-cence, in the Body Politic" that drained the body of the nation "to skin and bone." What seemed like an offhand remark by stranger newcomers was in fact an insight into one of the most pressing issues of the day.[31]

That expansion itself had always provoked criticism. In 1722, Dan-iel Defoe had complained of London's "most straggling, confus'd Manner, out of all Shape, uncompact, and unequal; neither long or broad, round or square." His concern was echoed by many of the city's observers in the de-cades to come. An anonymous Irish clergyman, for example, first visited the city in 1761, and when he returned eleven years later, the same year that

Tuglavingaaq, Qavvik, Atajuq, Ikkanguaq, and Ikiunaq, rendered in pencil by an unknown artist. (Courtesy of the Hunterian Museum, Royal College of Surgeons of England)

Atajuq and his family arrived, he wrote this of the construction in the city's West End: "Such Huge Piles such elegant Improvem^ts w^d most undoubtedly Amaze you. They are joyn.g Field to Field & House to House in so unbounded & precipitate a Manner y^t Hamstead will ere long reckond ye suburbs of this City." Confused, unbounded, precipitate: this was the very nature of the city throughout the eighteenth century (and really, throughout most of its history). Even an Inuit stranger could see this. After a long day on the Thames, at Westminster, and at Hyde Park Corner, Atajuq returned home exhausted and despairing, according to Cartwright. "Oh! I am tired; here are too many houses; too much smoke; too many people. . . . I wish I was back again." While a clear statement of homesickness, it was also a reaction to critical issues facing the city: too many houses, too many people, too much smoke. He knew what he was seeing.[32]

These were the kinds of intersections that could take place between Indigenous ways of knowing and the realities of London's urban landscape. Other, deeper intersections also existed between the Inuit and the city's own self-representations. At several points during their visit, members of the group sat for portraits, as had so many Indigenous visitors before. In one, reproduced here, all five can be seen, Ikiunaq mostly hidden in the hood of her mother's parka. But it is another pair of portraits that best capture the connections between the urban and the Indigenous. They are highly lifelike treatments of Atajuq and Qavvik, both standing. Atajuq holds a harpoon;

Qavvik stands with her hands clasped, a smile on her face. The man who drew them was named Nathaniel Dance, and it is his history that connects the Inuit to the very landscape of the city and to the broader networks of empire. Dance had been raised by his grandfather George Dance the Elder, surveyor of London and architect of, among other icons of the London landscape, the Lord Mayor's Mansion House. Nathaniel's uncle, George Dance the Younger, succeeded the Elder and was renowned for his architectural renderings. Nathaniel himself made the practice of architectural drawing a centerpiece of his Grand Tour of the continent, and it was this skill that would so realistically capture Atajuq and Qavvik. Dance's architectural heritage was, in turn, linked to his imperial connections: he had made the image for Joseph Banks, founder of the Royal Academy of Science and the naturalist aboard Cook's voyages around the world, and would go on to serve Britain in his own right as a celebrated naval commander in the seas around Asia. A single portrait of two Inuit visitors, then, reveals the intimate if subtle connections between empire, the urban built environment, and encounters between Indigenous people and the city at the heart of that empire. When Qavvik and her kin stepped out of that wherry at Blackfriars, they were stepping into deep connections between power and place and into the muscular extensions of British might, both into the far reaches of the earth and into the London skyline. In the end, the consequences of those connections would be devastating.[33]

They met at a Haberdasher's Ball in early 1776. Among the pantomime characters and costumes from exotic lands, one partygoer had stood out to James Boswell. He was a man like no other in the place: tall, dark-skinned, dressed in a combination of English and foreign clothing, and wearing an unusual metal gorget and brandishing a threatening-looking tomahawk. This was Thayendanagea, also known as Joseph Brant, a military leader who had come to London on a mission from his people, the Mohawk. From the moment he saw him, Boswell was utterly fascinated.

Not long after the ball, in mid-April, the two sat down for an interview at the Swan with Two Necks, a busy mail-coach inn near Cheapside. Boswell noted that Thayendanagea spoke English fluently, and that he "had not the ferocious dignity of a savage leader; nor does he discover any extraordinary

JOSEPH THAYENDANEKEN

COMMONLY CALLED BRANT,

A MOHAWK CHIEF.

The illustration that accompanied Boswell's 1776 *London Magazine* account of Thayendanagea (Joseph Brant). (Courtesy of the Toronto Public Library, accession no. JRR 1673)

force either of mind or body . . . [;] when he wore the ordinary European habit, there did not seem to be anything about him that marked preeminence." Although perhaps a little disappointed, Boswell understood this to be the result of the improvements of civilization: "His manners are gentle and quiet," he would write after Thayendanagea had returned to North America; "and to those who study human nature, he affords a very convincing proof of the tameness which education can produce upon the wildest race." Only Thayendanagea's tomahawk, carved with both his Mohawk and Christian names, hinted at what Boswell no doubt imagined as noble savagery. Inquiring into Thayendanagea's personal history, he discovered that the Mohawk man was related through marriage to one of the Four Kings of 1710, whose portrait was still hanging at the British Museum sixty-six years later, and he saw a clear trajectory in the course of history between the two visits. In 1710, he noted, the Mohawks had been "a very rude and uncivilized nation" and that "the very name of Mohock was terrible in London." More than half a century of exchange with the British, however, had resulted in "a very great change upon the Mohock nation" who were now "well trained in civil life." In Boswell's mind, they had been improved to the extent that Thayendanagea had been able to appreciate the sights he had seen in London—in particular, apparently, "the ladies and the horses."[34]

The interview between Boswell and Thayendanagea, published in the July 1776 issue of *The London Magazine* opposite an engraved portrait of the Mohawk leader, hinted at the ways in which Thayendanagea interacted with the city in the two visits he would ultimately make to London. In 1776 and again in 1785, Thayendanagea did not play the part of the benighted, uninformed savage. Nowhere in the accounts of him is there record of reactions such as Occom's dismay or Atajuq's astonishment. Nor is there evidence of strident critiques of the city's profound inequalities or its disorderly, unreasonable nature. Instead, Thayendanagea seems to have been an active, engaged participant in the spaces of the city's modern landscape, moving with ease between its entertainments and enlightenments alongside some of its most elite residents. Thayendanagea, in short, was a cosmopolitan.

This cosmopolitanism began long before Thayendanagea journeyed across the Atlantic, in the complex relationships between diverse Mohawk communities and their neighbors. Born in 1743 to Christian parents, he was a member of the Wolf Clan, and his mother would, over time, become one of the most important matriarchs of that clan at the major Mohawk town of Canajoharie. There, she married her second husband, a grandson of Tejonihokarawa. All of them were Christians. As a young boy, Thayendanagea must have heard stories about the 1710 delegation's trip to London: the incident at the theater, the pressing crowds, the sheer scale of the city. Certainly, Christian Mohawks still used the Bible and the religious paraphernalia that Queen Anne had sent to them in 1712. But Thayendanagea was connected to another Indigenous traveler as well: Samson Occom. As a teenager, he attended Eleazar Wheelock's school at Lebanon. The similarities in his and Occom's life ended there, however; by the time he reached adulthood, Thayendanagea had already participated in military engagements against the French and the Indigenous Lenape and had been awarded a medal by British colonial authorities for what they understood to be loyalty. By the 1770s, he was a well-known military leader among both his own people and the British.

The Mohawk people were in an increasingly tenuous position, though, caught like the rest of the Haudenosaunee between French and especially British expansion in and around their territory. Perhaps overstating his authority and influence to British officials, Thayendanagea used his connections with Sir William Johnson, the late superintendent of Indian Affairs, to secure passage to Britain. Bringing with them a second Mohawk man named Oteronyente, or John Hill, about whom scant evidence appears in the historical record, Thayendanagea, Sir William's son Guy Johnson, and others set sail in the *Adamant*, with the rebel Ethan Allen held prisoner in the hold. They arrived in London at the end of February.[35]

Soon after his arrival, Thayendanagea secured an interview with the new colonial secretary, Lord George Germaine. There, he presented the claims and grievances of his people in a speech he had prepared with the help of Guy Johnson:

> Brother. The Mohocks our particular Nation, have on all occasions shewn their zeal and loyalty to the Great King; yet they have been very badly treated by his people in that country, the City of Albany laying an unjust claim to the lands on which our Lower Castle is built, as one Klock and others do to those of Conijoharrie our Upper Village. We have been often assured by our late great Sr William Johnson who never deceived us, and we know he was told so that the King and wise men here would do us justice; but this notwithstanding all our applications has never been done, and it makes us very uneasie.[36]

Echoing the call of the Four Kings sixty-six years earlier, and using similar language of kinship—which the English invariably interpreted as a sign of submission—he also asked for missionaries to be sent among the Mohawks.

But his paramount concern, the issue that dominated all others, was the land. "Indeed it is very hard when we have let the Kings subjects have so much of our lands for so little value, they should want to cheat us in this manner of the small spots we have left for our women and children to live on," he told Germaine. "We are tired out in making complaints and getting no redress." (In the press, meanwhile, the issue of land was often lost, with the emphasis placed instead on the Mohawks' "fidelity on all occasions" as perceived subjects of the Crown.) At least on military matters, Germaine was somewhat sympathetic to the Mohawk's position. Unlike his predecessor, Eleazar Wheelock's friend Lord Dartmouth, he was keen to involve Indigenous nations in efforts to control uprisings among discontented colonists. In a letter to a General John Burgoyne, Germaine would write, "The Dread the People of New England &c have of a War with the Savages, proves the Expediency of our holding that Scourge over them." He was also secure in his belief that "Of the good will and Affection of the Indians, there seems to be little doubt, if they are managed with Attention, and proper Persons employed to negociate with them." On the question of Mohawk territorial sovereignty, Germaine said in the course of several meetings that he would deal with that matter once the rebels had been subdued. Whether he would make good on that promise remained to be seen.[37]

In the meantime, using the Swan with Two Necks as a base, Thayendanagea and Oteronyente set about taking in the sights of Hanoverian London. According to one newspaper account, they attended a review of troops on Wimbledon Common, accompanied by "by several ladies and gentlemen, the whole consisting of nine carriages and upwards of twenty attendants on horseback." At the review, which consisted of soldiers marching in formation and firing round after round, the two Mohawk men found themselves among an elite crowd. "There was the greatest number of persons of distinction present ever remembered," claimed the *Gazetteer and New Daily Advertiser,* "among whom were the Duke and Duchess of Wirtemberg [*sic*], the foreign ambassadors, Ministers of State, and a vast concourse of people of inferior rank." The Prince of Wales, a teenager who would come to play a large role later in Thayendanagea's life, also appeared on horseback in his regimental regalia. As for the soldiers, they would soon be sent to the colonies.[38]

Over the next few weeks, Thayendanagea found himself in the midst of high society. According to observer Daniel Claus, who would develop a close relationship with Thayendanagea, "Several Gentlemen of Distinction and Fortune took notice of him and used him very kindly," even though some of them were in sympathy with the American rebels. With these men, Claus claimed, Thayendanagea "listened to the Arguments with Calmness and answered with Discretion." At one masked ball—perhaps the one where Thayendanagea met Boswell—a pro-rebel aristocrat asked him directly whether he would take up arms against the colonists. When he carefully said no, the man "with a seeming degree of Satisfaction Kissed his Tomahawk." Thayendanagea's presence at a masked ball, among aristocrats, suggested the level of attention he was receiving while in the city. Another example came when the Earl of Warwick, George Greville, paid to have a portrait of Thayendanagea made by George Romney, a leading artist of the day who had made his career painting the luminaries of the era.[39]

The Crown was also closely involved in the nature of Thayendanagea and Oteronyente's visit to the city. Around the time of their first meeting with Germaine, they had been presented to George III at St. James's Palace, and while there is no further detail about this meeting beyond its brief mention in *The London Chronicle*, it is clear that the king saw something in Thayendanagea: two months later, on April 26, the Mohawk warrior was inducted into the Freemasons by George himself, at a ceremony at the Falcon Lodge near Leicester Square, one of dozens of masonic lodges throughout the city. In becoming a Freemason, Thayendanagea became part of one of the key social institutions of the Enlightenment, where the leading ideas of the day were replicated, discussed, and disseminated. Like those behind urban development—the squares, the lexicographies, the lit thoroughfares—Freemasons were particularly concerned with improvement. Moreover, their rituals and symbolism were replete with metaphors that recalled the urban landscape of men like Wren and Dance, in which a divine architect had created the harmonious geometry of a Newtonian universe. And as a transatlantic organization, Freemasons could also draw on the imagery of encounter; Erasmus Darwin, for example, told one philosophical society's members in 1784 that "their body would be, like the freemasons, a 'band of Wampum,' or 'chain of concord' collecting together the 'scattered facts' of philosophy . . . to exhibit the distinct and beautiful images of science." This was the intellectual and ritual world into which Thayendanagea entered when he received the Masonic apron from a reigning monarch.[40]

Soon after receiving his apron, and after receiving continued noncommittal answers from Germaine, Thayendanagea, presumably accompanied by Oteronyente, sailed for home. He would not return for nearly a decade.

In the intervening years, he was widowed and then married again, this time to an immensely influential Turtle Clan matriarch, whose powerful presence in his life no doubt enhanced his status within Mohawk society. Meanwhile, he took up a critical role as a military leader in the violent war between the British and the American rebels, a conflict that challenged all notions of Enlightenment rationalism and civilized improvement. He was particularly influential in battles throughout the northern theaters of the war, at the same time as he attempted to cement alliances between his people and the English—an initiative that won him enemies among some Mohawks, who saw him as collaborating with a polity that ultimately threatened their sovereignty. Meanwhile, the Mohawks' position became more tenuous as the war continued, and afterward, as British loyalists and others encroached into Haudenosaunee territory.[41]

In 1785, he returned to London, determined once again to secure rights to territory for his people, this time appealing to Thomas Townshend, Lord Sydney. In the three months that he would ultimately wait for an answer, Thayendanagea once again partook in the life of the city. His hosts on this trip, Daniel Claus and his son William, took him to freak shows and other entertainments, as well as to masked balls like the ones he had attended in 1776. At one of these, Thayendanagea put on yet another strategic performance of "savagery" for his elite audience. The Turkish ambassador mistook Thayendanagea's dark skin and face paint for a mask, and tried to remove it. The response from the otherwise famously mild-mannered Mohawk was to raise his tomahawk and let loose a war cry that stunned those gathered into frightened silence. He then laughed, and the party resumed. He also had another audience with George III, sat for more portraits, and circulated among the social networks of loyalists who had returned from the colonies at the end of the war. In his spare time—of which he no doubt had very little—he continued working on a project he had started some time before: the translation of a prayer book into the Mohawk language.[42]

He also became a favorite of that royal teenager who had also taken in the review of soldiers in Wimbledon Common nine years before: George, the Prince of Wales. Now in his twenties, the prince was notorious. He was a high-stakes gambler: the Duke of Cumberland kept a faro bank for the prince at his house on the Strand. The prince was a lush and a foul-mouth:

Horace Walpole noted wryly that the prince "drank royally" and wrote that "Nothing was coarser than his conversation and phrases . . . [;] in the place of piety and pride his Royal Highness had learnt nothing but the dialect of footmen and grooms." And he was a letch: in addition to his scandalous and illegal marriage in 1785 to a Catholic woman, he shared mistresses with his best friend, Charles James Fox, the dissolute foreign secretary whose father had amassed a fortune as paymaster general during the Seven Years' War. At Carlton House in Pall Mall, George would throw lavish and outrageously expensive parties that shocked much of London society. The extent to which Thayendanagea participated in any of this debauchery is unclear; a generation older and married with children, it is unlikely that the Mohawk man partook in the worst of the excesses, although one account did in fact describe Thayendanagea as being taken "places very queer for a prince to go."[43]

If the wild life of the Prince of Wales seems to have taken up much of Thayendanagea's time, the Mohawk leader did find time to engage in more sober pursuits. Most notably, he participated in a popular pastime among European intellectuals: archaeology. Fascinated by huge earthworks he had seen in the territories to the south of the Haudenosaunee homelands, Thayendanagea used at least part of his 1785 trip to pursue research into the matter. He had a theory that the tumuli had been built by an ancient race that had been extirpated centuries earlier by an alliance of peoples, including perhaps the Mohawks' own ancestors. While his research seems to have been largely fruitless, by engaging in it Thayendanagea became part of a key Enlightenment practice. The study of antiquities, from Stonehenge to the Temple of Solomon to the Roman ruins seen on every young aristocrat's Grand Tour, was a requirement of any proper education. This intellectual fashion was represented in the fabric of the city itself, from the Palladian porches of the West End and Dance's Mansion House to the rituals of the Freemasons and the Royal Society. Like the Londoners who engaged in these practices, Thayendanagea sought to find a deep, civilized genealogy for the peoples of North America, and he saw the resources of the European Enlightenment as a way to get there. In the three months that he awaited Lord Sydney's reply, and in his two visits to London more generally, Thayendanagea had participated in some of city's most important social institutions, appearing in all accounts not as a confused newcomer but as a participant in the rational city.

As one later chronicler would note, Thayendanagea had "the inquiring mind of a true man of the century." Whether Lord Sydney would recognize this and support Thayendanagea's appeals was another matter.[44]

Perhaps the greatest confusion of colonialism has been the notion that Indigenous people are lacking in reason, sophistication, or the capacity for understanding the technological and other achievements of European society. Like other ideas born out of the Enlightenment—notions of gender, race, or Indigeneity itself—this one has been remarkable in its persistence. Into the twenty-first century, colonial and settler societies around the world have continued to perceive Indigenous peoples as savage (either noble or ignoble), as inherently lacking, or in need of "improvement." Making sense of the ideological genealogies that undergird very material forms of oppression, from the dispossession of land to the cultural genocide of programs of "civilization," has been one of the primary tasks of Indigenous scholars and activists and their allies. For Samson Occom, the Inuit travelers of 1772, and Thayendanagea the outcomes of their voyages highlight the ways in which, for all their insights into the nature of the city and of urban life, their journeys to London could not inoculate, in some cases literally, against some of the worst effects of settler colonialism.

It might have turned out otherwise, especially for Samson Occom. His return to North America was celebrated among the Algonquian communities of New England, who were so keen to hear of his journey that he had to beg them to allow him to stay home with his family for a time, not having seen them for nearly two years. But the success of the journey ended there. Eleazar Wheelock and his superiors decided to redirect the funds raised across the Atlantic to a school not for Indigenous youth but for young English men. It would be named after one of its chief benefactors; it would be called Dartmouth. Occom was outraged. "I was quite Willing to become a Gazing Stock, Yea Even a Laughing Stock, in Strange Countries to Promote your Cause," he wrote Wheelock, noting also that "we shall be Deem'd as Liars and Deceivers in Europe, unless you gather Indians quickly to your College." In a very sharp turn of phrase, he criticized Wheelock by saying that "instead of your Semenary becoming alma Mater, she will be too alba mater." He shared his disgust with others; he wrote to a John Bailey that "if I was to be in England again, I should not dare look any gentleman in the face, I should seem to them, as if I had been telling Lies to them."[45]

Occom's disappointments after his return also seem to have inflected his descriptions of his time in Britain, amplifying the critiques he had leveled while in London. He wrote:

> Now I am in my own country, I may freely inform you of what I honestly and soberly think of the Bishops, Lord Bishops, and Archbishops of England. In my view, they don't look like Gospel Bishops or ministers of Christ. I can't find them in the Bible . . . and I am apt to think they don't want the Indians to go to Heaven with them.

Later, infused with revolutionary rhetoric, he would report to the Oneida that English nobility "are very Proud and they keep the rest of their Brethren under their Feet, they make Slaves of them." And after the American Revolution, he wrote that rich nations like Britain were "the Most Tyranacal, Cruel, and inhuman oppressors of their Fellow Creatures in the World, these make all the confusions and distructions among the Nations of the Whole World." Here, he echoed those first insights into British life and no doubt reminded himself of the scandalous inequalities he had seen in London. At the same time, he pined for some aspects of city life; in 1775, he wrote to a London merchant, "O that I had old Cloaths from London, if London was not more than half so far as it is, I would Come over to beg old Cloaths." Meanwhile, the Mohegan land case would not be decided in his people's favor during his lifetime; indeed, it would be more than two hundred years after his death that his people would finally see their rights to land and nationhood recognized by the United States.[46]

For Thayendanagea, the disappointment had come while he was still in London, with Lord Sydney's final decision to make only limited compensation for the losses of war, and it continued after. In his later life, Thayendanagea would see his people's land base shrink again and again as British settlers moved into the territory around the Six Nations reserve. Meanwhile, his reputation in Britain would take a dramatic turn in 1809, two years after his death, with the publication of Thomas Campbell's *Gertrude of Wyoming; a Pennsylvanian Tale,* an epic poem in which Brant appears as a rapacious warrior responsible for the deaths of hundreds of American soldiers at the

Battle of the Wyoming, a conflict in which he had not in fact participated. The "Monster Brant" was a radical new role. In the English imagination, the man who had attended masked balls, inquired into antiquities, and become a Freemason was thus reduced to a demonic figure out of colonial nightmares. Meanwhile, in North America, the Mohawk and other Haudenosaunee nations would find themselves increasingly at odds with settlers and would continue in the centuries to come to assert their direct relationship with the Crown rather than the Canadian government, as we shall see in a later chapter.[47]

For Atajuq and his family, the trip to London was an unmitigated tragedy. In May of 1773, Cartwright wrote that all were "well pleased in the expectation of soon seeing their native country, their relations and friends again; and I very happy in the prospect of carrying them back, apparently in perfect health." But as they left the estuary of the Thames on May 13, Qavvik became violently ill. Stopping for supplies at Lymington, Cartwright had a surgeon confirm that it was smallpox, and within the next three weeks, all four of Qavvik's relatives died. Ikkanguaq, Tuglavingaaq, and Atajuq were cremated; their ashes were buried in sand dunes outside Plymouth alongside the unburned body of Ikiunaq. By all accounts, Cartwright was devastated. But in many ways, it was Qavvik who suffered most of all, having been "reduced to a skeleton." The winter after she returned, Cartwright reported that the Inuit of southern Labrador were almost entirely wiped out by the disease, which was "retained and communicated in a most wonderful manner."[48]

This was perhaps the greatest urban footprint in Indigenous lives, not just in London or Labrador but around the world. The combination of animal domestication and widespread urbanization across Europe, Asia, and Africa had led to the development of epidemic diseases against which Indigenous peoples in the Americas and elsewhere had little or no natural resistance. It was this urban reality that had likely cost the lives of the Algonquian people who disappeared into the city, that had killed one of Tomochichi's retinue, and that had prevented four of the five Inuit from making it home. In London, meanwhile, for all the improvements of the Enlightenment—new if imperfect understandings of disease, inoculation, and advances in urban design—disease remained one of the most intractable and threatening of urban realities. What scholars have called ecological imperialism, the means by which biology facilitated Europe's imperial and colonial incursions in places like the Americas, the Pacific, and New Zealand and Australia, had its roots in the city.

Against this larger backdrop, though, Indigenous men and women made sense of London, despite the challenges they and their contemporaries, from other foreign travelers to the city's elites, faced in comprehending the urban landscape. Far from mere confusion, Samson Occom, Atajuq, Thayendanagea, and the others found ways to overcome their bewilderment. They critiqued the city's class divisions, asked hard questions about its ecology, and played on ideas about savagery at masked balls. Their stories give the lie to Rousseau's racist claim that Indigenous people were but stupid, passive recipients of enlightenment, and to Samuel Johnson's argument that "savages" had nothing to teach the English. Their stories also do not end in the late eighteenth century. Through their connections to culture, the dynamic persistence of their political institutions, and their connections to traditional territories, the Mohegan, Inuit, and Mohawk peoples survive into the present, a survival that, in the minds of many observers, was never dreamed. The confusion, then, was—and continues to be—a colonial one.

A Lost Museum, 1793

Sparry bodies, eagle stones, Muscovy mica, ponderous earths;
garnets of twenty-six sides, violet fluors, Brazil rubies, Peru emeralds.

Eora people are singing, Eora people are dreaming,
Eora people are stick-firing the land,
Eora people are seeing the ships come in. Eora people
are greeting the newcomers, Eora people
are spearing the newcomers, Eora people
are dancing and singing.

They are the people of Bennelong and Yemmerrawannie,
hosts in 1793 to a new colony of iron hoops and farthings,
convicts and tinderboxes, first fleets, oaks and governors.

This is New South Wales. From here, Yemmerrawannie and Bennelong,
servant and diplomat, sail for London in 1792,
aboard the *Atlantic* and eventually across the Atlantic.

Balls of mountain pitch, candle-coal, camphor wood, cork-bark;
an uncommon shaped walnut, tamarinds in the pod, steeple fungus.

Museums have their origins in cabinets filled
as much with vanity as with curiosity.
Ashton Lever, son of a Lancashire sheriff,
amasses twenty-eight thousand things, shows them in Leicester Square.
Bankrupts himself in 1786.
No one will buy, neither Russian empresses nor British museums.
A man named Parkinson wins the collection at lottery, moves it to Southwark.
Still known as the Leverian, it is also named
Holophusicon, meaning "whole, natural."
Gather all of it in.

The Leverian Museum.

The Leverian Museum, or Holophusicon, as it appeared near the end of the eighteenth century.
(By an unknown artist; © The Trustees of the British Museum, all rights reserved)

Warted gorgon, crested madrapore, cinnamon coral, sea feather;
lantern-fly, orator mantis, bird-catching spider, spectacle snake.

Yemmerrawannie and Bennelong live in fashionable
Grosvenor Square. Archived in receipts, their new London wardrobes:
  green coat, salt-and pepper-coat, blue and buff-striped waistcoats;
  worsted breeches, cravats, buckles;
  silk, muslin dimity, spotted quilting, cambric, and spectacle.

Vulture, penguin, woodcock's egg, swallow's nest in conch shell.
Skull of hippopotamus. Skull of elephant. Teeth of fishes.

On the Surrey side of Blackfriars Bridge
under a great Rotunda, apartments of shelves, corridors of cabinets,
the words of Milton and Pope inscribed on the chamber walls:
These are thy glorious Works, Parent of Good.
All Matter quick, and bursting into Birth.
Also matter dead and vultured.

Scythian lambs, East India rice, Chinese tinderbox, American paper-money;
Scotch dirk, powder horn, Queen Anne farthing, miniature of Cromwell.

The audience of a museum is always
another sort of collection.
Had the singular good fortune while there
to see the two New Hollanders who arrived
about 6 months ago, diaries one man, not knowing
he is also an exhibit, he and the ticketed
ladies and gentlemen and schoolchildren, museum displays all;
  museums display all, including themselves;
  museums of museums.

Eel spear, fish gig, rude bow, long drum;
skin of sea-otter, bracelet of dog's teeth, hat of spruce root, cloak of feathers.
To the Immortal Memory of Captain Cook.

Indigenous objects, Indigenous eyes—
Who sees and what is being seen?
Objects of earth emerging up into cases,
  birds and animals flying and crawling down into shelves,
  other peoples' dreamings behind glass.

All things birthed into being and blossom, captured and collected,
quickened by taxonomy and looking back at the looker.

Bennelong and Yemmerrawannie will not be the collected ones.
Instead, they collect cambric, the Tower, Holophusicon, diarists.

And then, amid the sparry bodies and miniatures:

> *Cockatoo, jabiru, lizard, three curious snakes.*
> *Yellow-winged creeper, turquoisine parroquet, purple pecten.*
> *Bark basket, fish hooks, spear-thrower, spear.*

Skins and shells from home, familiar feathers and woods,
     known Dreamings.
Memories of good harvests in the water that brought the fleet,
of sharp wood through a governor's shoulder,
captured and encased pieces of home, like scalps in a Craven Street parlor.

They go out the doors they came in, into Blackfriars Road,
collect more spectacles, especially of the stage:
     The *Suspicious Husband, Doctor Faustus, The Accomplished Fools.*

> *Whistling arrow, flaming sword, iron hoop found in an oak tree;*
> *the writing of a woman without arms.*

Holophusicon is dispersed, sold in 1806. Reverse-taxonomied,
     stones rattling into cupboards, rubies and emeralds embracing into heirlooms,
     feathers and skins fading into drawing rooms,
     curiosities curating to who-knows-where.
The Rotunda changes hands, changes meanings:
     reformists and waxworks, pub and diorama,
     music hall and cockfighting ring, warehouse.
The flaming sword of the Blitz cuts pieces out of the building,
sets it on the path to its undoing.

The men go into the ground in their own time.
Yemmerrawannie that same year,
far from home, in a Kentish churchyard, chest infection.
Bennelong gives him a second name: Kebarrah, initiated man.
Bennelong twenty years later, at Kissing Point in Sydney, of age and new neighbors.

An unknown artist's portrait of Bennelong of the Eora. (Courtesy of the Mitchell Library—State Library of New South Wales, call number P2/511)

One lies under sandstone and grape hyacinths, steeple;
the other in an orchard, now a suburban garden.
Ponderous earths.

Where the Rotunda once stood, office block.

A coda:
A generation after their visit, their voices are put to paper,
an imprecise echo of stick against stick and voice against voice,

dedicated to Charlotte, Princess of Wales.
In sixteenth notes and two-four time;
a song to lovers, collected and collecting;
Eora people, dancing and singing:

Barrabula barra ma, manginè wey enguna
Barrabula barra ma, manginè wey enguna
Barrabula barra ma, manginè wey enguna
Barrabula barra ma, manginè wey enguna
Barrabula barra ma, manginè wey enguna.[1]

5. That Kind Urbanity of Manner

Navigating Ritual in Māori and Kānaka Maoli London, 1806–1866

They that go down to the sea in ships, that do business in great waters;
These see the works of the LORD, and his wonders in the deep.
For he commandeth, and raiseth the stormy wind,
which lifteth up the waves thereof.
They mount up to the heaven, they go down again to the depths:
Their soul is melted because of trouble.
—Psalm 107:23–26 (KJV)

In 1791, a young Hawaiian man collected the city. He had spent a total of two years in London, arriving in 1789 aboard a fur-trading ship named *The Prince of Wales*. His name was Kualelo, and he was a native of the island of Moloka'i in the archipelago of Hawai'i. While the details of Kualelo's life in London are mostly lost, one account gives us a sense of the young man and his relationship to the city. On their way to join the crew of *Discovery*, captained by George Vancouver, the ship's botanist and physician Archibald Menzies noticed Kualelo's reaction to the receding London skyline:

> It was a fine Morning when we left London & engaged a Boat, that in leaving the Metropolis he might have a larger scope for exercising his observations & curiosity on both sides of the River. . . . He did not possess his usual elevation of Spirits, the different objects he passed which had formerly attracted his attention he would now & then look back with a dejective countenance & observe that he would see them no more! This was his observation more than once with respect to St. Pauls Cathedral *Harre nove Eatua* [*hale nui akua*] as he called it, which in his language signifies "The great house of

God" on whose structure & elevation he had often gazed with admiration & Astonishment. He took care to provide himself with perspective views of it as also of Westminster Abbey & Greenwich Hospital &c so as to be able to give his countrymen some idea of those stupendous buildings.[1]

Like any visitor to London, Kualelo sought mementos, in pencil and in watercolor and lithographic, that would remind him of his time there and that would document his experiences for his people. He was partaking in a particularly urban ritual.[2]

In the decades after Kualelo's visit, London became a place driven by ritual. It always had been, but as scholars of the early nineteenth century have noted, British society experienced in those decades a social revolution in which an ever more formal culture "acquired taboos, introduced strict rules of propriety, and became reticent about sex and the emotions . . . revolting from the customs of their elders." Temperament and taste both changed, informed by evangelicalism, reform-mindedness, and a repudiation of the cultural excesses and coarseness of the eighteenth century. The word most often used to describe this new reality was "manners."[3] This culture of manners centered on London. As one etiquette guide from 1836 decreed, "*in all cases, the observances of the Metropolis (as the seat of refinement) should be received as the standard of good breeding.*"[4] Several years later, a similar tract asked, "London is the grand centre whence all change must first emanate . . . for where shall we find so many congregated means of refinement as in London?"[5] Simultaneously lauded and lambasted by authors from Jane Austen to Charles Dickens, ritual, in the form of manners, comportment, sentiment, and protocol, began to transform Georgian values into what would eventually come to be known, often in caricature, as Victorian culture.

Such urban practices were also understood in the language of civilization that had emerged out of imperial and colonial encounters, so it is no surprise that in the minds of etiquette writers and other patrollers of custom, British manners compared favorably to those of other societies, with Indigenous peoples near the bottom. "We do not profess a preference for the unclad or half clad barbarism of a Choctau or Ojibbeway, over the tasteful decencies of civilized life," wrote one arbiter of custom. "A skin handsomely tattoed [*sic*] and rubbed in with gunpowder, may be admired," it continued, but civilized, urbane dress was more desirable "than that of the most fastidious Brummel among the Indian braves."[6] That said, proper treatment of a foreigner was required of a gentleman; as an 1816 etiquette manual argued, "the general deportment . . . of a man of rank in this country towards a foreigner who he casually meets, is marked by more civility than he employs towards a gentleman who is neither a foreigner nor a man of fashion."[7] At the crossroads of urban refinement and British racism stood restrained comportment.

These sorts of ritual, manners, and protocol ruled a new kind of London: a Pacific London, with networks of exploration and exploitation reaching out into parts of the planet the British had before only known through half-truths and aspirations. The stories here focus on travelers from two places in particular: Aotearoa, "Land of the Long White Cloud," which the newcomers would call New Zealand and which is home to the various Māori peoples; and Hawai'i, whose people call themselves Kānaka Maoli. Like other Indigenous visitors before them, they drew great attention and left significant archival wakes in their passing. Oscillating between accounts of Māori travelers and their Kānaka Maoli counterparts, we see Polynesian men and women deftly navigating the shoals of London ritual. If the city was a place steeped in etiquette and manners, Indigenous peoples had their own systems of ritual and protocol as complex as those of the Regency and the early Victorian city and brought these with them. Their journeys linked Indigenous rituals—the recitation of genealogy, the instantiation of a welcoming song, the donning of a cloak of feathers—with rituals of London life: the machinations of the House of Lords, the etiquette around a formal dinner table, a toast in a dockside tavern. Kualelo collecting mementos of the city was only the beginning.

Of ironmongers' shops near the wharves: *Pai ana uta, nui nui toki.* "Very good country, plenty of iron." Of coaches in the streets of the city: *Pai ana whare, nui nui haere.* "Very good house, it walks very fast." Of lame men along the docks: *Kuare tangata.* "Good for nothing man." Of the city itself: *Nui nui tangata, nui nui whare, iti iti ika, iti iti potato.* "Plenty of men, plenty of houses, but very little fish, very few potatoes." And to the people he met: "How do you do, my boy!" while shaking everyone's hands.[8]

The man named Mahanga, who made these observations, had grown up among the Ngāpuhi, an *iwi* (tribe) of the North Island of New Zealand. The Ngāpuhi were the most powerful group in the region, holding sway over a large swath of the northern part of the island. Mahanga was an *ariki* (noble) of one of the most powerful peoples in all of Aotearoa. This status no doubt made him a good candidate to join the crew of one of the many British ships plying Ngāpuhi waters, and in 1805, he became the first Māori person known to have visited England. From his first appearance on the docks of an increasingly industrialized Thames, Mahanga's presence was a spectacle. "It was extremely inconvenient to take Moyhanger to public exhibitions, or even to walk with him in the streets, on account of John Bull's curiosity," wrote John Savage, the man who had overseen Mahanga's passage. The city was a spectacle in return. "I accompanied him to St. Paul's cathedral," Savage continued, where "he dwelt with infinite pleasure upon the monuments of our great men."[9]

Mahanga cast a shrewd eye on London society. Upon being introduced to the Whig MP William Fitzwilliam at his home, Mahanga was really only interested in assessing the earl's status by counting the chairs in his dining room.[10] He also had an audience with George IV, which he described to the ship's captain Peter Dillon:

> I was much disappointed: I expected to see a great warrior; but he was an old man that could neither throw a spear nor fire a musket. Queen Charlotte was very old too. . . . Queen Charlotte asked me to give the war-dance of New Zealand. When I did so she appeared frightened: but King George laughed, saying ha! ha! ha![11]

This was the very first performance of a *haka* (war dance) in Britain, the first Māori assertion of masculinity, prowess, and *mana* (authority deriving from his *whakapapa*, his "genealogy"). Ultimately, though, the journey conferred little benefit to the ariki. Instead of the muskets he coveted, he was given only tools. Upon returning home, he sought to translate his experiences into increased social status but was unsuccessful. In the end, he had to leave his own *marae* (communal home and ancestral gathering place), and accounts describe him being treated as insane, or even criminal, because of the London scenes he recounted.[12]

Three years later, in 1809, another Ngāpuhi ariki came to London. Or, more to the point, he *almost* came to London: Ruatara was never allowed off the *Santa Anna* as it sat at anchor in the Thames. He had already suffered violence at the hands of fellow sailors and the privations of sealing stations in the deep southern seas; when he expressed a profound interest in visiting King George—no doubt having heard stories of Mahanga's journey—Ruatara was told that no one knew where the king lived. Meanwhile, his health suffered: missionary Samuel Marsden described him as nearly naked, coughing up blood, and deeply depressed before being given into the care of London physician James Mason Good aboard a new ship. Ruatara spent a total of fifteen days in agonizing proximity to the city he so sought to explore. This experience, however, was tempered with a new intimacy; as historian Anne Salmond has argued, the relationship between Ruatara, Marsden, and Good was a mingling of the men's *hau,* their vital energy, with Ruatara teaching Marsden his language and sharing the creation stories of his Ngāpuhi people. Unlike Mahanga, Ruatara returned with increased mana, becoming one of the most influential figures in his people's region through his relationship with the missionaries, serving as benefactor and protector to Christianity's first toehold in the region.[13]

A few years later, off of Edgware Road in Marylebone, a very different sort of encounter took place. There, a young Ngāpuhi man named Maui taught English children the lessons of scripture. The relative of an important ariki, Maui had been sent to Samuel Marsden's school for Indigenous children in Parramatta, New South Wales. Upon completing his studies, he served on whaling ships, including one that arrived in the Thames in May of 1816. The ship's captain sent the "friendless stranger" to the Missionary Society in Salisbury Square, whose members voted to provide for his care. An account of Maui's life, published in the Missionary Society's register, described—self-servingly—the young man's deep piety and how Maui spent his free time drawing elevations of London buildings, creating images like those Kualelo had purchased a generation earlier. Mostly, he longed to return home as a missionary of the gospel, but this was not to be. He fell ill on Christmas Day 1816 and died three days later. "Mowhee is dead," lamented the missionary society's account, "but his work is not yet done. Let his Grave address his Countrymen. Who can tell, but they may yet hear and believe!"[14]

Other Māori journeys to London, less well documented, took place in

Maui as he appeared in a London missionary newsletter, 1816.

the first quarter of the nineteenth century. In 1807, only two years after Mahanga's arrival, yet another young Ngāpuhi man, Matara, met with George IV and the royal family, learned English, and, according to one account, "dressed and behaved like a gentleman."[15] In 1816, the same year that Maui arrived, two other young Māori men from Samuel Marsden's school in Parramatta, Tuai and Titeri, spent time in London. After visiting the Tower, Titeri wrote, "I see plenty guns, thousands. I see lion and tiger, and cockatoo; I talk to cockatoo he know me very well." Seven years later, in 1823, two Māori men described as chiefs among the Ngāpuhi, Kiatara and Amahau, performed on stage at the Royal Coburg Theatre, now the Old Vic. Both would die within weeks. The following year, a man named Te Pehi Kupe of the Ngāti Toa iwi caused something of a sensation by giving out "signatures" based on his *moko* (facial tattoos), and in 1829, two unnamed Ngāti Maru men were also performing for fascinated audiences.[16]

A visit in 1820, however, best illustrates how a sojourn in England could shape Māori realities back home. It involved Hongi and Waikato, two Ngāpuhi ariki who were eager to attract miners, blacksmiths, agriculturalists, and soldiers to their homeland in order to achieve advantage over surrounding Māori communities. While in London they resided at an exclusive Montague Square address, entertaining dukes and earls, the Lord Mayor and the chancellor of the exchequer, members of Parliament, and various clergy, and having their portrait made by painter James Barry. They also met George IV, with Hongi, who had five wives, expressing his surprise that the king needed Parliament's permission to divorce. Not long after, something of a melee erupted at the House of Lords as members jostled to see the two fashionably dressed and heavily tattooed strangers. On their return voyage, gifts they had received in England were sold in Sydney to pay for some three hundred to four hundred muskets, which were then taken home. Thus began a profoundly destabilizing series of conflicts known today as the Musket Wars, in which thousands of Māori people died and the Ngāpuhi deepened their hegemony over large stretches of the North Island.[17]

The stories of Mahanga, Ruatara, Maui, Hongi, and the others seem to have little in common, except that they are Māori stories. Most of the men were Ngāpuhi and most were ariki, but the kinds of urban spaces they encountered were profoundly different from each other—King George's receiving rooms, the crowded Thames docklands, missionary houses near Edgware Road, and the stages of the West End could hardly be more distinct. But despite their diversity, each had sought to increase their own personal power—or the power of their iwi—through engagements with the British, whether by joining whaling crews, converting to Christianity, or seeking audiences with the British monarch. New political, economic, military, and religious relationships offered possibilities not just in relations with the foreigners, but with neighboring Māori peoples. In each case, London played a central role, whether as the ultimate port of call for the whaling industry and the naval arsenal, as the home to missionary societies' motherhouses, as a place of gift giving or succoring of the ill, or as the seat of royal presence and parliamentary authority. These journeys linked marae and metropolis, and they were the first steps toward a Pacific London that was shaped by shared ritual.

In the first years of the nineteenth century, it seemed as though Hawai'i was poised to become the center of the world. Set squarely in the middle of the Pacific, it was a natural stopping-off point between the Americas and Asia, a fact that both the United States and European powers quickly acted on at the turn of the century. Only a few short years after being "discovered"— fatally—by Captain James Cook, Hawai'i was becoming a crucial hub in the Pacific fur trade, and it was a place undergoing dramatic, even traumatic, change. The idea of a unified Hawaiian archipelago was a new one; the islands had only been united in 1810 by the military and diplomatic campaigns of Kamehameha I, and this political transformation took place at the same time that massive epidemics were sweeping the archipelago, transmitted by ships moving between ports such as Guangdong and San Francisco. Perhaps the greatest transformation of all, however, was the collapse of the 'Aikapu (sacred eating) system that had ordered everything from gender relations to the balance between the *ali'i*, the "elite of the kingdom," and the *maka'āinana*, the "people of the land." From the seemingly simple act of elite men and women eating together to what would become a wholesale transformation of land tenure in the islands, everything, it seemed, was changing.[18]

At the heart of all this was an ali'i named Liholiho who had become Kamehameha II with the death of his father in 1819. That same year, Liholiho, under guidance from senior women, sat down to eat with them, transforming tradition and catapulting his family into almost complete control of the islands. Liholiho would also continue his father's aim of establishing a partnership with the British to keep American, French, and Russian interests at bay. According to one observer, Liholiho described these changes as "polishing," bringing his own people closer, both strategically and culturally, to the British.[19] But Liholiho was no collaborationist, nor was he breaking tradition with his ancestors in pursuing these changes. Indeed, Hawaiian tradition holds him up as an exceedingly intelligent man who drew on his ancestors in his decision making. Asked once why he was so knowledgeable, he is said to have responded, "Na wai ho'i ka 'ole o ke akamai, he alanui i ma'a i ka hele 'ia e o'u mau mākua" (Why shouldn't I know, when it is a road often traveled by my parents?).[20]

And so, in 1823, Liholiho gathered around him a delegation that would make the first Hawaiian voyage to Britain since Kualelo's in 1789. The group included Liholiho's senior queen, Kamāmalu, herself a daughter of Kamehameha I; an important ali'i named Boki; Boki's wife Liliha; the overseer of the sandalwood trade; the commander of the Hawaiian navy; and a steward, three servants, and two interpreters.[21] The goal of the mission, according to the missionary Hiram Bingham, was "to gain information, political and commercial, to gratify curiosity, to achieve by the tour something great . . . to increase his wealth and power." He also specifically desired an audience with George IV. In preparation for this, Liholiho had his ship loaded with the symbols of royal mana: feather cloaks known as ʻahuʻula, which connected individual aliʻi with their gods.[22] Other sacred and kingly objects included tall plumed staffs called kāhili, fine garments made of kapa (mulberry bark) cloth, and western-style suits and satin dresses. While Liholiho, Kamāmalu, and their retinue would be on a new road—a sea-road to London—they carried with them the power of their ancestors, a wealth of knowledge, and a clear agenda.[23]

Like virtually all of the Indigenous visitors before them, the presence of Liholiho and his retinue caused chaos. "The crowds of idlers who throng the front of his house from morning to night were so large," wrote one newspaper, that "no coach could approach the door of the hotel but it was instantly surrounded on all sides by a rabble of the open-mouthed curious, all trampling and scrambling over each other, and poking their prying noses into its windows . . . to the very great annoyance of the customers of the house, the injury of its business, and the scandal of the whole neighborhood." Such scenes were replicated whenever they went out on the town, and shops began selling images of the visitors. Interest went far beyond the rabble; at their lodgings at Osborn's Hotel at the Adelphi on the Strand, nobility in the city for the season visited them, with women as high in status as Lady Liverpool and the Duchess of Northumberland presenting gifts to Kamāmalu. Meanwhile, the visitors saw the sights of the city: the palace and gardens at Fulham, the children's wards at Chelsea Hospital, and a performance of Pizarro at Covent Garden.[24]

Amid all this attention, there were detractors. The Times, for example, noted that the women's clothing looked more like "robes de chambre" and that they were tall, fat, and of the "darkest copper colour," while The Examiner sniffed that Kamāmalu smoked cigars "with as much goût as some of our modern dandies." But the worst commentary came from upper-class women who circulated at parties. Mary Berry had met Kamāmalu and Liliha at a soiree at the home of the foreign secretary, George Canning. "It was with

Liholiho (Kamehameha II) and retinue at the Royal Theatre in Drury Lane in 1824, by J. W. Gear. (Courtesy of the National Library of Australia, Rex Nan Kivell Collection, no. NK4869)

difficulty that the Minister and his company could preserve a proper gravity for the situation," she wrote, noting that it didn't matter, since the Hawaiians' minds were "not civilized enough either to notice or to suffer" the lurid staring. A Mrs. Arbuthnot, meanwhile, recalled in her diaries that she felt Kamāmalu was "a man in woman's clothing" and that Boki was nothing but a "bruiser."[25]

Such portrayals, however, were in the minority. Throughout their time in London, the royals were afforded significant levels of respect and were described in most of the media as participating flawlessly in the rituals of urban life. George Anson Byron penned a typical account: "The decorum of their behavior was admirable during their residence in the hotel. Not one instance occurred of their overstepping the bounds of decency or civility in their intercourse." Elsewhere, he wrote that the group was "decorous and self-possessed" in contrast to the "well-dressed mob" that often crowded in on them. "The King," Byron wrote, "knew how to hold his state, and the erees [aliʻi] to do their service, as well as if they had practiced all their lives in European courts. . . . The queen particularly felt gratified with that kind urbanity of manner which distinguishes her royal highness." While attending the theater, the group's behavior was "greatly admired; no awkwardness, no inattention on their part . . . they knew they were in the royal box, and that it had been prepared and appointed for them." The level of scrutiny was intense; newspapers noted the visitors' emotional reactions to specific scenes in operas and plays, commenting that their responses were always exactly correct: silence, applause, laughter, or tears as the libretto or script warranted.[26]

It might be tempting to understand these accounts simply as Londoners condescending to foreign guests. Whether this is true or not is largely irrelevant, if what we are interested in is what Liholiho, Kamāmalu, Liliha, Boki, and the others thought they were doing. When attending a reception at Northumberland House, for example, Kamāmalu's mix of English and Hawaiian clothing could only have been expressions of her confidence in her own status in both milieu, rather than an aping of London fashion or a ridiculous mash-up of styles. Retinue member Kekūanāoʻa, meanwhile, attended the event in full Hawaiian regalia, including carrying a kāhili to symbolize alakaʻina (leadership). Other accounts emphasized their "great and stately indifference," or the fact that they seemed "to have learned the Court etiquette of not showing astonishment, however they might feel it."[27] As he would write to his younger brother, "We are having everything we desire."[28]

Despite the changes in practices back home, some of the traditional strictures and attitudes came through during the time in London. During a visit to Westminster Abbey, for example, Liholiho and Kamāmalu were, according to Byron, "much pleased." But their reactions were more complicated than simple pleasure. They were also "impressed with great veneration for the place where they knew the remains of so many great men were deposited . . . hearing that the ancient kings of England were buried there, they said it was too sacred, and no argument could prevail upon the king to enter it."[29] For two leaders from society where even talking too much about one's progenitors was deeply frowned upon—mai kaulaʻi wale i ka iwi o na kūpuna (do not dry out the bones of the ancestors) went the proverb—entering someone else's ancestral burial ground was beyond the pale.[30]

That the royals sought to distance themselves from the foreign dead seems now like something of a foreshadowing. Back in Hawai'i, priests had made note of a lunar eclipse that took place during June of 1824, when Li-holiho, Kamāmalu, and the rest were exploring the city. Such omens often meant the death of an ali'i. Sure enough, not long after their visit to the Abbey, Liholiho noted in a letter to his younger brother that he and his queen were sick. They had fallen ill with measles. Newspaper coverage was rapt, with detailed daily reports of the progress of their illness. Kamāmalu suc-cumbed first, on July 8, and only six days later, Liholiho died, his last words recorded as being, "I shall lose my tongue, I shall lose my tongue. Farewell to you all, I am dead, I am happy." As for the rest of the party, one press account lamented, "it is impossible to describe the sensation the distressing event has caused throughout the whole of the King's suite."[31]

Even in dying, though, the king and queen of Hawai'i had kept their mana intact; in the eyes of English observers, they had faced their deaths with appropriately civilized sentiment. When his wife died, Liholiho had at first intended to pursue his grief "in the manner of His country, and to shew the marks of defernce [sic] which are usually paid to the dead there," but acquiesced "with good sense and patience" to suggestions that her body be removed from their chambers. He had, in the eyes of press observers, been "remarkable for the mildness and affability of his demeanour" and for his "firmness of mind" despite his profound grief. Lest we think that this was simply a reading of English desires onto Liholiho's behavior; Hawaiian tra-dition holds that Kamehameha II was known for, above all, both his intelli-gence and his patience.[32]

In the funerals of the king and queen, English and Hawaiian protocols of sorrow and rationality came together to create a hybrid ritual space. Lil-iha would play a central role in this part of the story: at first overcome with grief at Kamāmalu's death, the noblewoman soon took charge of preparing her body for burial. Afterward, the English ritual of embalming took place, performed by King George's own surgeon, who later wrote that "the process was performed in the most delicate, and respectful manner possible, so as to give no offence of the feelings of any who were present. After it was fin-ished, all . . . were particularly pleased on being informed . . . that the whole ceremony was conducted as is usual when any of the Royal Family of this country are embalmed."[33] Similar procedures took place after Liholiho had followed Kamāmalu.

At their lying-in-state, traditional Hawaiian practices continued to determine the protocols. First in a room at Osborn's Hotel, and later in the crypt at St. Martin-in-the Fields on Trafalgar Square, the king and queen lay in state in scenes that were both imposing and heartbreaking: two lead coffins, covered with red velvet, surrounded by red and yellow 'ahu'ula and tall kāhili, the floor strewn with red rose petals, and the whole scene lit with candles. Byron described it as "a kind of decoration of death which so pleased the Eriis [ali'i]," but it obviously attracted others, as well; guards had to run off several men who attempted to break into the crypt and steal the royal bodies. Above all else, the funerals of Liholiho and Kamāmalu were, in the eyes of London, fit for royalty. As *The Times* reported, "the whole was conducted with a simplicity, regularity, and solemnity, consistent with the most rational taste." Public opinion seemed to find deep empathy with the Hawaiians. Before he himself died, Liholiho had received cards of condolences from nobles and gentry alike, showing concern for the new widower, and newspapers reported that much of London society was "inconsolable" to learn that they both had died.[34]

After the funerals, things moved quickly. Boki had been named as successor to Liholiho while the party remained in England, and he took the lead role in audiences, including with George IV. On meeting the king, the party was "touched and astonished" at the expressions of sympathy offered by the monarch on the loss of the two sovereigns, and he was joyful at his promises to protect the Kingdom of Hawai'i from foreign encroachment.[35] They finally arrived home under Byron's care—or "returned to the backbone," to use a Hawaiian idiom—to immense outpourings of communal grief.[36] But the tragedy of their journey would not deter other ali'i from taking the same sea-road to London in the decades to come.

Fourteen years after the deaths of Liholiho and Kamāmalu, in 1838, and far from the Adelphi and the theater district, a young Māori man raised his glass in a tavern in the docklands. Nahiti toasted his compatriots, men he knew well, a group of sailors and gentlemen who were about to embark on a settlement campaign in his own Ngāti Toa homeland at the southern end of the North Island. His story, like those of his Māori predecessors and the Hawaiian royals, would center on his ability to navigate the rituals and protocols of urban life.

Nahiti had left Ngāti Toa territory two years before for France, but by late 1837 he had arrived in London to, according to one source, "obtain knowledge of the manners and customs of civilized nations." During his two years in the city, he would become something of a celebrity; one newspaper reported that he was "the subject of great interest among the nobility, the religious, scientific, and literary societies." He participated in a "converzatione" over dinner with the Duke of Sussex, a kind of social gathering that one early-nineteenth-century man-about-town described as, "a circle of talent as well as fashion." Nahiti was also examined by the Earl of Devon, met judges at the Central Criminal Court, and visited the House of Correction; his host on many of these occasions was Edmund Halswell, a magistrate and member of the Royal Society.[37]

Like Liholiho and Kamāmalu before him, Nahiti was described in the press as seamlessly fitting himself into such rarified social settings. Despite his moko, the facial tattoos that clearly set him apart from the English, his comportment impressed observers. "His English apparel does not appear to inconvenience him," announced one newspaper, "and he adapts himself easily to our good manners." *The Times* went so far as to notice that Nahiti's fashionable black suit was worn with "as much apparent ease as a Bondstreet dandy." Over the course of those two years, he had made quite an impression: he was described as "decorous and gentlemanly, adapting himself with facility to the customs of the country, neat in his dress and polite to everybody." He made his way about London unaccompanied, spoke English well, and in the words of one observer, expressed an "unwavering adherence to truth in the most trifling matters, as well as for an amiableness of character that scarcely ever permitted him to speak ill of any one."[38] His navigation of the streets and squares was evidence of a quick mind and an ability to read the signs and ceremonies of urban life. Like Thayendanagea decades earlier, Nahiti was not so much an outsider to the city as a participant in it.

Out of such experiences came a kind of intimacy with at least some Londoners. In the months approaching his departure for home, Nahiti be-

came associated with a clique of entrepreneurs who had formed the New
Zealand Company, perhaps seeing the group's plan to settle in the distant
land as an opportunity to return home. But for the members of the company,
who saw themselves as creating a community of "respectable Englishmen"
in contrast to the convicts and sailors whose presence had already led to violence, Nahiti was a crucial human resource, and they quickly signed him up
as the translator for their venture.[39]

This relationship led to the toast at Lovegrove's West India Dock Tavern in Blackwall on the eve of the ship's departure for Aotearoa. That evening, the company chairman, William Hutt, stood, mug of ale in hand, to
draw attention to the man "who was entitled to a considerable share of their
notice." He described Nahiti's time in London, listing his experiences with
high society—some of whom, including the Earl of Durham, were there at
the tavern—and stated that the young Māori man would return home as an
equal officer of the company. "In conclusion," reported *The Morning Chronicle,* Hutt "proposed the health of the chieftain Nayti," and the toast "was
drunk good humouredly by the company, and the compliment . . . received by
the chieftain with much propriety of meaning." Nahiti then returned thanks
in his own language, "which appeared to be perfectly well understood by
those accustomed to hear his conversation."[40]

In this moment, a certain kind of intimacy between Londoner and
Māori was expressed in a *whaikōrero* (formal oration), which perhaps included a short ritual chant, an acknowledgment of his own ancestry, and
statements of goodwill—a practice that Māori scholar Poia Rewi has called
a "ritual of encounter."[41] Or perhaps it was something much simpler, a toast
after the fashion of those he had no doubt heard over and over in London.
Either way, the moment had arisen out of Nahiti's own ability to negotiate
the rituals of elite society in the capital. Without forgetting the reality of
Māori-newcomer relations during this period—the New Zealand Company
would ultimately bring thousands of settlers to the islands, precipitating
new wars—it is impossible to ignore the apparently genuine affections that
came out of these face-to-face relationships and the rituals that had deepened
them. According to one of Nahiti's contemporaries, the young Māori had
"carried with him the regard of all who knew him," even if such regard also
depended on the notion that the Māori as a people were "a race whose na-

tional qualities only require to be cherished and cultivated . . . to raise them to that grade in the scale of humanity to which they are, at no distant day, evidently destined to rise." It is in this complex combination of respect and racism that Nahiti's story sits, albeit uncomfortably.[42]

Upon his return home, Nahiti, like Mahanga before him, was unable to translate the social capital he had built up while in London into increased social status among his people.[43] But during those two years in London, Nahiti, for all his eagerness to return home and his clear identity as a Ngāti Toa person, found a sort of place within London society in his own encounter with "that kind urbanity of manner." His own words say it best: writing from Plymouth, his last port of call before leaving England, Nahiti expressed the feelings he had for his London hosts:

> My dear Sir,
> I am very much obliged to you for giving me a watch;—I hope I shall think all about you;—I shall take great care of it;—I am very much pleased to see in the paper about more ships come to New Zealand;—I like my ship very much;—very good people on board. . . . Remember me to all my friends, and believe me
> Your friend,
> NAITI.[44]

"There was the Sun just rising above the hills and the waters . . . were brilliantly sparkling and the whole thing was nearly perfection itself," the man wrote. "But when the Earthquake came on it was awful. There were houses thrown down . . . and the grumble of the bowels of the earth . . . it was enough to make one faint. . . . The smoke curling up—in volumes, and people running to & fro in the houses," he continued, and "the ships were swallowed up in the harbor. You could here [sic] the roaring of the breakers and the heaving of the sea."[45]

The great spectacle of the earthquake that had destroyed Lisbon in 1755 was one of the most lavish and technologically complicated entertainments in all of London, a simulacrum of unprecedented sophistication. And the man who wrote those words—who also called the whole thing "indescribable"— was a connoisseur of London society and sights, a royal figure who knew

Alexander Liholiho and Lot Kapuāiwa with missionary G. P. Judd, 1850. (Courtesy of the Hawai'i State Archives)

what he liked and scorned what he didn't. His name was Alexander Liholiho, and he was the heir to the throne of Hawai'i.

Between 1824, when Kamehameha II and his retinue visited London, and 1849, when Alexander Liholiho and his younger brother Lot Kapuāiwa—who would eventually rule as Kamehameha IV and V, respectively—came to the city, much had changed in Hawai'i. European traders and American missionaries had made significant inroads into the kingdom's economic, social, intellectual, and political landscape. One outcome of these new pressures was a massive reordering in the 1840s of the ways in which land was owned and managed, known now as the Māhele. Described by Hawaiian historian Jonathan Kay Kamawawiwoʻole Osorio as "the single most critical dismemberment of Hawaiian society," the Māhele saw the Hawaiian crown and the aliʻi—under pressure from outside interests—take control of the majority of Hawaiʻi's land, transforming the makaʻāinana into *hoa ʻāina* (tenants) and establishing a new capitalist property regime that would ultimately benefit European and American interests and leave the common people with less than 1 percent of the lands allotted to them.[46]

In 1850, just as the Māhele was transforming the landscape of Hawaiʻi, both literally and figuratively, Alexander and Lot took a circuitous route to England, spending time in places as far-flung as Monterrey, Mexico; San Diego, California; Kingston, Jamaica; and New York City. They traveled under the tutelage of the American missionary G. P. Judd. In their journals of their time in London, the two young aliʻi expressed a clear sense of royal presence, which determined how they saw and understood the city. On their arrival, *The Times* had noted that "the two young gentlemen, who, from their exterior and manners, are fully entitled to the name, . . . speak English thoroughly, with pleasing correctness, giving every evidence of good manners and education," and predicted that they would be treated with respect. The prediction, by all accounts, would come true.[47]

The two young men were taken to some of the most prestigious and elite places in the city. In April, they were presented to Prince Albert at Buckingham Palace, where they discussed the troubling presence of the French in Hawaiʻi, the islands' chief exports, and the prospects for trade with China. A few days later, they attended a service and took communion at the Chapel Royal, where they heard a performance of Henry Purcell's "They That Go Down to the Sea," and attended a "réunion" at the mansion of Viscount and Viscountess Palmerston in Carlton Garden, along with some three hundred guests that included ambassadors, members of Parliament, and the Speaker of the House of Commons. During the rest of their stay, they took in what must have seemed like every sight the city could offer. The Thames Tunnel, Millbank and Newgate Prisons, Bedlam, Drury Lane Theatre, the House of Commons, Westminster Abbey, Madame Tussaud's, the Docklands: from their itinerary, it seems as though they must have had very little time to themselves. Indeed, at one point, finally alone in a carriage, the young men sang "words that had been made at the Islands" to each other, Alexander later wrote.[48]

While they enjoyed at least some of these sights—Alexander called a panorama of Paris "indeed a sight"—others were less than impressive. Alexander wrote of the Zoological Gardens, for example, "I was much disappointed with the animals. . . . They did not come up to my expectations of size or strength." He was also disappointed with the queen's kennels, and the East Indian House Museum offered "nothing that we had not seen before." And when Prince Albert asked if the royal teenagers had seen anything of note in their time in the city (four months at that point), Alexander replied, "not very much."[49]

There was one exception to this: when the brothers encountered objects and people associated with their own kingdom. At the Tower, for example, Alexander noticed a feathered helmet that he thought had come from home, while Lot wrote of two ʻahuʻula the brothers saw at Windsor Castle. Among the collections of the British Museum, "Sandwich Island Curiositys such as cloacks &c, some native idols, &c.," Alexander wrote, were the only things they hadn't seen elsewhere. And far from wanting to see these things returned to Hawaiʻi, or comparing them unfavorably with other objects held by the museum, Lot wrote that "we had the best lot of things in the house." In addition, of particular note were things, places, and people associated with the earlier visit of Kamehameha II, their ancestor and predecessor. At the Armoury, they made note of ʻahuʻula and feathered helmets that had been presented by Liholiho, and elsewhere they viewed "an old house where the King had stopped when he was in England." And at Osborn's Hotel, where both Liholiho and Kamāmalu had died, the brothers "saw an old maid there that knew them & waitted on them She showed several rooms where they occupied when they were here. She knew Father inquired for Madame Boki [Liliha]."[50]

Sometime later, after a visit to Paris, Lot wrote upon their return to London that "the folks here recognized us."[51] While he no doubt meant simply that they had become a familiar presence in London society, there was another kind of recognition going on: that of sovereignty. Kamehameha IV and his younger brother appear to have been understood as true foreign royals and dignitaries rather than as representatives of some "savage race." The visit of Alexander Liholiho and Lot Kapuāiwa, then, was something quite different from many past sojourns by Indigenous people. Meanwhile, they held on to their own sense of sovereignty and resisted British authority over their kingdom. Perhaps nothing illustrates this more than when the young men took in the great paintings hung in the hospital at Greenwich. "Also saw a portrait of Captain Cook and his death scene at Kealakekua," wrote Lot in his journal, continuing, "this is one of the best scene we saw."[52]

In the painting, they look something like a family, or perhaps two families. The setting is a drawing room: piano in the center background, portraits on the walls, colorful carpet on the floor. In the right half of the painting, three women and a man are seated together and another two men stand behind them. Two of the women are in pale dresses; the third wears a dark green dress, a woven shawl, and ornaments in her hair. The man sitting with them wears a black suit and a white, high-collared shirt, while the men behind wear long cloaks made of either fur or feathers. On the left, a group of ten men and women sit or stand, clothed in bark and flax and feather and fur. At the center, on either side of the piano, two men: the first in mid-speech, gesticulating and wrapped in a cloak; the second resting one hand on the piano and the other on his hip, listening proudly. All seem calm, and a few smile and look at each other. It is a scene that suggests friendship or at least a happy introduction. It is 1863 in City Road.

In the years since Nahiti's 1839 whaikōrero, other Māori had come to London. The same year that he departed for his home with the New Zealand Company, the Māori wife of settler Charles Wilkinson drew attention upon her arrival in the city, including a meeting with the Lord Mayor. Another Ngāti Toa man, Pirikawau, made two poorly documented visits, in 1843 and 1854, resulting in his becoming the translator to New Zealand Governor Sir George Grey. In between, Tamihana Te Rauparaha, the son of a powerful war leader, came to London; the young ariki would go on to chronicle the life of his father in one of the first published pieces by a Māori author. Hoani Wiremu Hipango, a Māori leader who had allied himself with settlers in the Whanganui district, arrived in 1855 and was shocked to see violations of the Sabbath all across the city.[53]

The Maori visitors of 1863 at the John Wesley House in City Road, in an oil painting by James Smetham. (Courtesy of the National Library of Australia, Rex Nan Kivell Collection, no. NK138.ANL)

This string of travelers symbolizes not just a growing connection between Māori people and London, but also a deepening of colonization in their territories. The Tiriti o Waitangi (Treaty of Waitangi), signed in 1840, dramatically transformed relations between Māori and Pākehā peoples, setting into motion confusions and conflicts over the treaty's wording and meaning that continue to resonate today. One of the responses to the treaty and to accelerating alienation of Māori land was the Kīngitanga, or King Movement, in which some iwi sought to create a pan-Māori monarchy parallel to that of the British Crown, much to the consternation of Pākehā settlers and other Māori alike. Meanwhile, British settlement of the islands continued apace.[54]

This was the context for the Māori visit to London of 1863. The portrait of these people, made at the headquarters of the Wesleyan Missionary Society, was only one example of their high profile during their time in the city. Most of them were Christian converts, young people with names like Huria (Julia) and Horomana (Solomon).[55] Two others were war leaders, and the elders among the group: Te Hautakiri Wharepapa and Reihana Te Taukawau. In all, there were six different iwi represented in the group, but such divisions would be downplayed during the journey. "We were told," recalled one member of the group after their return home, "to put aside our quarrels, our bad words & all drinking & sin and live all together good & eat together & be together."[56] And in truth, there was likely a growing sense of togetherness at work here; although most if not all of the travelers had rejected the Kingi movement, which was uniting iwi across the North Island, they, like many other Māori people, were beginning to see the benefits of a pan-Māori movement in response to British presence. In their case, it meant a stated connection—even a kind of loyalty—to Wikitoria Te Kuini o Ingarani (Victoria, Queen of England). The man who chose them was an on-again-off-again missionary named William Jenkins (the Māori called him Toko Tikena, "Pole Jenkins," because of his height). Horrified by the wars that had already rocked Aotearoa, Jenkins wanted to bring "respectable" Māori to Britain to further peaceful relations between the two peoples.[57]

Whatever their reasons for joining Jenkins's venture, when the group arrived in London in the spring of 1863, Haromana, Wharepapa, and others were to have experiences while in the city that were like none they had ever had before. Upon their arrival, they were first housed at the Strangers' Home in Limehouse, a modern facility established for non-European sailors and which the Māori called Te Whare Mangumangu (Negro House). Later, they would move to a house in Marylebone's Weymouth Street, and finally to the decidedly more upscale Grosvenor Hotel in Belgravia. Throughout their time in the city they were, according to Jenkins, "vulgarly—as well as genteely mobed [sic]," and often could not see many of the sights because of the crowds that surrounded them. But they did manage to see, in addition to the usual landmarks, the bullion room at Bank of England, the arsenal at Woolwich, and the horticultural gardens in Kensington. Reihana recalled the experience after his return home: "We looked at the roads of London[;] the ground could not be seen through the multitude of people," he told a group of missionaries. "If it had rained it would not have touched the ground but would soak on the heads of the Pākehā[;] dark, dark, dark, the ground could not be seen.[58]

Always, the group's members were expected to comport themselves to, as Jenkins put it, "maintain the respectability of the party and to conduct our meetings in a manner which should secure the approval of a Christian audience." They were reminded of this by others as well; upon arriving at the East India Docks, they were met by an old missionary who warned them against being overly Māori in their self-presentation. "If it is for Christian purposes you will be welcome, thrice welcomed," he proclaimed. "My family, be sure that you do not fall into the mud." And throughout their visit, they often lived up to such expectations. Whether at formal lectures on Māori culture, meetings with the bishop of London, or the gathering at Wesley House where they had their portrait made, their deportment, according to one newspaper, "manifested the intelligence and propriety of a superior race." In their table manners and other matters of etiquette, they were "becoming quite aristocratic in their manner and bearing" to the extent that they would "perfectly astonish the ladies and gentlemen they visit." Such civilized virtue also appeared in a letter that group member Kirihini Te Tuahu wrote to Queen Victoria after they met with her on the Isle of Wight: "Is there no love, indeed, gushing up in my breast toward the Prince [Albert]? Blessed art thou who hast passed behind the hills! Firm shall I stand, as a sacred sign to the Queen. Alas! That is all." But perhaps the most explicit example of Māori Victorianism came when group members Hare and Hariata welcomed a baby boy into the world on October 26. They christened him Albert Victor at St. Paul's Tottenham; the queen sent a gold cup and a knife, fork, and spoon, while naming herself Albert's godparent; and Hare wrote in return, "Our tribe—your power is over them—your kindness shall be our theme to them."[59]

But for all the displays of Christian piety and civilized conversation, there were also moments where members of the group were incontrovertibly, and publicly, Māori. During a visit to the spectacle of the Crystal Palace, for example, when the Italian singer Carlotta Patti finished a performance, Wharepapa struck his *taiaha*—his ceremonial staff carved with symbols of his whakapapa—on the ground several times, demanding that she continue singing. Which she did. At another performance at the London Musical Society, group member Tere Pakia gave one of her hair feathers to a female singer, receiving a gold hair ornament in return. And during an audience at Marlborough House with the Prince and Princess of Wales, the group gave the royal couple gifts of *taonga*, cultural objects of great significance: an *ihupuni* (a mat made of dogskin), a *kaitaka* (a mat made of *harakeke*, the native flax), a whalebone staff representing whakapapa, jade jewelry, and even a piece of land.[60]

But from the beginning, there had been hidden cracks in the delegation. Even as Jenkins was choosing the participants, many had questions about the nature and purpose of the journey. One ariki, for example, had asked, "What is the straightness of this going?" And Reihana recalled the ways in which Jenkins had placed limitations on just how Māori the fourteen could be: "We were told . . . make good talk; speak, and we also there had to talk to Emigrants . . . [;] on board ship we heard of . . . war dances and then behold now he take us to a Chapel House & says; talk good." The tensions continued, and heightened, during the tour. For example, Reihana and other members of the group complained about the unnecessary expense of staying at the Grosvenor Hotel. Other pressures seem to have come from outside the group; Paratene Te Manu told a biographer years later that he and the others had heard in London that "if we remained there we would be killed by the white people." The most critical fault line in the journey, though, had to do with whether the fourteen Māori would be paid for their services and performances. They would not. This would lead to the most explicit rebuke to Jenkins, and to the fracturing of the group itself.[61]

This would be made possible by the presence of another Māori group in the city. Far from pious and polite Christian converts, these were per-formers who capitalized on ideas about Māori savagery that had existed ever since first encounters with Europeans but which deepened during the wars of the 1840s, 1850s, and early 1860s. They were the "Māori Warrior Chiefs," who had first performed to huge audiences in Australia before opening at the Alhambra in Leicester Square the same season as Jenkins's group was on the lecture circuit. Described by one critic as "haka ing in low places," the eight men and one woman were, according to one newspaper, "The Greatest Success and the Most Sensational Novelty of the Season." Mostly Ngāpuhi, the individual performers were regularly named in the press and described using terms like "illustrious" and "very great" and with "ancestors of renown," but their performances trafficked in the exotic, warlike savage. Most importantly, though, they made money at it, and members of Jenkins's group knew this. And so, in late 1863, three of them defected to the Warrior Chiefs. Jenkins was incensed. "The natives have *not behaved well*," he fumed in his journal. "*Ingratitude* of the *blackest kind* has been shewn by them while we have been treating them like Princes." As the conflict became public, the press called the entire venture into question. "It is pretty clear now," noted

The Daily News, "that these Maories never ought to have been brought to England."[62]

It had seemed, then, that there were two ways of being Māori in London. One kind of Māori gave lectures and met with the queen; the other kind gave "war dances" on the popular stage. One engaged with the rituals of genteel and pious London; the other with those of its rowdy, vulgar counter-city. And when a participant in one defected to the other, it was a sign that the civilizing process was working in the wrong direction. But there was a third way, one that was ineluctably Māori and that confounded the duality of the savage and the civilized, the proper and the popular. In a taiaha struck against the Crystal Palace floor, a gift between ladies, a haka at the Alhambra, or a letter to the queen, Māori men and women asserted their identities and engaged deftly in rituals, simultaneously Māori and urban, on their own terms. The painting of the group at the Wesley House, then, masks as much as it reveals; instead of tamed savages—the way many observers, including some of those in the portrait itself, might have seen them—they were women and men who made smart choices as they navigated the landscapes of the Victorian city. And they all, from young Albert Victor all the way to the Warrior Chiefs, made it home again.

Pacific London had been a relentlessly public London. From Kualelo's passage downriver to Nahiti's toast at the West India Dock Tavern, from lithographs of Liholiho and Kamāmalu to the thronging crowds around Reihana and his colleagues, Pacific travelers to the city, like their other Indigenous predecessors, found themselves in a maelstrom of publicity and at the mercy of a hungry, pressing public. The scene of Alexander and Lot, singing to themselves in a carriage during a rare bit of privacy, captures in relief—in both senses of the word—that a few fugitive moments of solitude and quietude were very, very precious in Indigenous London. And no one was more public than a queen.

Emma Kalanikaumaka'amano Kaleleonālani Na'ea Rooke of Hawai'i was the widow of Alexander Liholiho, the young man who had visited London in 1850 and who had reigned for nine years as Kamehameha IV before dying of asthma in 1864. In her widowhood, she was at least as popular as her brother-in-law Lot Kapuāiwa, who had ascended the throne as Kamehameha

Queen Emma of Hawai'i. (Courtesy of the Library of Congress, Prints and Photographs Division, LC-BH82-4885B)

V, and she was routinely described as the "dowager queen" of the Kingdom of Hawai'i. (She also had connections with the British Crown; Queen Victoria was godmother to Emma's son Albert Edward, who lived only for four years.) Working on behalf of the king, she left for London in 1865 with a small retinue and with two goals in mind, or, as one British newspaper described them, "two distinct but compatible forms of usefulness." The first was the continued deepening of Christianity in the islands; the second was a continued assertion of political independence and sovereignty for her kingdom. The former was understood in terms of Victorian female piety; the latter, described as emanating from her status as a representative of a civilized nation. Accounts of her time in the city almost always emphasized both aspects of her identity; one, for example, described her as "withal a lady" who "delights in exercising a quiet, unassuming benevolence," while another drew attention to her "graceful and dignified carriage, her manners and habits being those of the aristocracy of Europe." In all, she was received as a "gentle pioneer of religion, civilization, and morality," and was even cast in sharp contrast to her ancestress Kamāmalu.[63]

From her base at Claridge's Hotel, Emma moved through the Christian spaces of the city, making gifts of prayer books written in the Hawaiian language, while also taking in sights such as the Royal Academy and the Tower. As always, this Indigenous visitor was the target of widespread public curiosity; after one trip through the city in an open carriage, for example, she complained in her diary that the passage "exposed me, to the passing omnibuss, cabs, & pedestrians, who gazed with wonder upon us." On another occasion, she and some friends "sallied out incognito . . . for 2 hours sight seeing in the cheep shops of London, & a delightful time we had . . . as if a load had quite been taken from our back."[64] And, as always, Emma had opinions about the city and its inhabitants. For example, St. George's Hanover Square, where she attended the "worst service I have heard," was a "very ugley" building, and she complained about the flirting, whispering, and passing of notes that the saw during church services. She described the Prince and Princess of Wales as "nothing more than a big boy & girl, no conversation." But she also caught glimpses of home reflected in the urban landscape; at one point in her diary, she wrote of St. James's Palace being wreathed in *ua noe,* a "fine, misting rain."[65]

Emma was engaged in work of sovereignty and evangelism, meeting constantly with various aristocrats and missionaries, and what comes across most in her diaries, what she spends the most time describing in detail, are the rituals of a Victorian, if also Hawaiian, femininity. In addition to the ritual of urban consumption—"we selected, some veils, bonnets, canzoozs, basquines, circulars, handkerchiefs . . . saches, gloves, shoes jett [*sic*] ornaments, bl[ack] fans," she wrote—Emma also engaged in the intimate assertions of manners and sentiment that were so central to women's social practices during this period. "Mrs Newmans, formerly Mrs Lee," she recounted, "welcomed me with tears of affection which was pleasant to a stranger in a strange land

amongue strangers she embraced me in her little arms & kissed me repeat-
edly on my cheeks and head, her tears flowing the while." Another guest at
Claridge's, a Mrs. Lyall, Emma penned, "is a very nice person & tears stood
in her eyes almost the whole time she was here." These moments of intimacy
both relied on her status as queen but also expressed a particularly Victorian sensibility and set of emotional rituals. She could also be a harsh judge
of others; she complained bitterly, for example, about one of her ladies in
waiting, whose arrogance and ignorance of manners "is most disgusting, &
mortifys me not a little . . . most uncouth, unladylike . . . horrible, horrible."[66]

Despite the contrasts drawn between Emma and Kamāmalu, the two
Hawaiian women—like the women in Jenkins's Māori party—were understood as virtual paragons of nineteenth-century London manners. Poised,
proper, and in most cases pious, these women were notable because of
the ways in which they engaged with the rituals and protocols of the city.
Whether attending the theater, accepting Victoria as the godmother of their
child, exchanging tears with a fellow devout Christian, or chastising an unladylike servant, Emma and the others enacted values that were simultaneously Indigenous and British. When she returned to Hawai'i in 1866 after
several months in London, she had made such an impression on the city that
her future exploits—including standing (unsuccessfully) for election to the
throne of the kingdom in 1874—would be followed in the British press. All
of this was possible because of her deft use of the protocols of the city to
further her and her people's aims.

Neither the return of Jenkins's Māori group in 1864 nor the departure of
Emma in 1866 necessarily marked a watershed in terms of Māori and Hawaiian presence in London: others would come. King Kalākaua, who had
defeated Emma in 1874, made a trip around the world seven years later, including a stop in London, during which he was feted as a celebrity and sovereign king. In 1884, the leader of the Māori Kingi movement and Waikato
tribes, Tāwhiao, visited the city to much acclaim, even if he was often cast
as little more than a savage in the press. And others still—along with Hawaiian ali'i—participated in the Golden Jubilee of 1887, one of the ultimate
rituals of Victorian empire. Meanwhile, Aotearoa and Hawai'i were, for the
moment at least, on different paths. One was a British colony, subject to Vic-

toria and her functionaries of empire. The other remained an independent nation with close ties to the British, and had consulates in dozens of countries around the world—including one in Cornhill and later in Great Winchester Street—until the American overthrow of the Hawaiian monarchy in 1893 and subsequent illegal annexation in 1898.[67]

At the core of Pacific visitations to London was ritual, expressed in manners, etiquette, protocol, and comportment. In the case of ritual, both Kānaka Maoli and Māori visitors had been remarkably successful at navigating and negotiating the complexities of London's ritual life. Ritual was a space where profoundly different cultural traditions and practices could come together in unexpected ways, offering avenues of agency that did not exist before, and in the case of Indigenous London, linking places like Hawai'i and Aotearoa to the metropolis in ways both ephemeral and profound.

Rituals, however, can also go wrong; they are just as often spaces of misapprehension, misunderstanding, and mistake. Perhaps the most graphic and prosaic illustration of this does not have to do with war and peace, with death at the Adelphi or a haka at the Alhambra. It has to do with the head of a philosopher. When Jeremy Bentham died in 1832, he left behind a massive corpus of writing and thought. He also left behind, for lack of a better term, a massive "corpus," in the form of his own body. His wish was that his corpse would be made into what he called an "auto-icon," a physical survival of a now dead person, which would have an afterlife of sorts. In the case of Bentham, this meant being propped up at meetings of the trustees of the University of London and being put on display in a glass case in one of the university's corridors to much tourist notoriety.

The story of Bentham's auto-icon, however, is also a Pacific story. Throughout the nineteenth century, European intellectuals, collectors, and others had been fascinated with *toi moko*, the Māori practice of preserving through a form of mummification the heads of renowned enemies, loved ones, and other important personages. Numerous heads had appeared in museums throughout Britain and the continent, a particularly ghoulish component of the larger drive to collect ethnographic and other "specimens" from around the world. Bentham and his colleagues were also intrigued by toi moko, and when Bentham died, his friend Thomas Southwood Smith, under instructions from Bentham, took it upon himself to attempt the process with Bentham's remains. The attempt failed miserably. The result was ghastly: shrunken skin across the bones of cheek and chin, thin colorless hair straggling from the back of the skull, teeth bared within a dry rictus of a mouth. The worst part was the eyes: glass, cold blue, giving something of life to what was otherwise a desiccated, horrible thing. Although the head was on display for several decades alongside the rest of the auto-icon—and was often spirited away in college pranks, only to be returned—twentieth-century squeamishness saw Bentham's head locked away from view for good and replaced with a wax replica. It remains hidden today, its unseeing eyes staring out from inside a dark box—perhaps the perfect example of a ritual gone wrong and an apt metaphor for the blind, oft-hidden thing we call empire.

A Hat Factory, circa 1875

Above a sea of chimneypotted and stovepiped men,
four gargoyles perch in the Oxford Street skyline.
Neither lions nor demons nor saints: beavers. They look down from
Henry Heath's factory, where seventy men sew and block
Victorian manhood.

Newly carved and ensconced, the beavers are already epitaphs
to a dwindling trade, with styles already turning to silk
as arteried waters go bereft of furbearers,
as long chains stretching from the city
to the lands of the Ojibwe and Cree and Dene
creak under fashion's appetite.

In a single year:
One hundred and twenty-four thousand beavers.
Every city whim a fur desert makes.

And so turn it back.
Turn back the hands of time and commerce,
unmake.

> *Felting is a process*
> *by which animal furs are made to cohere and form a kind of cloth,*
> *without the aid of weaving or any similar process.*

Take the stovepipes and cylinders and uncurl them,
mend them back into fine, soft skins of black-brown velvet.
Immerse them, return them to the mercury baths,
let them reclaim the guard hairs and become almost-themselves again.
Give the hatters clear air and good minds,
end the muttering and trembling that gave their name to madness.

Detail of Henry Heath's Hat Factory in Oxford Street. (Photograph by Sven Klingen, used with permission of the photographer)

The principle of Felting
was not understood until the microscope
was applied to the examination of animal fibres. It was then found
that the fibre, whether of wool of fur, is surrounded
by a vast number of minute teeth, projecting away from the central stem.

Carry the pelts to the docklands,
to the river,
and from there to the sea, the hungry sea.

Skins disembark in Canada, stream back along the streams
running fast with newfound damless freedom, travel into territory
and return to home waters surrounded
in new uncincisored growth, birch and alder

risen up green and yellow-green and silver-barked
in the wake of the dammers' sudden absence.

> *As these teeth are very sharp*
> *and are turned in one direction, they present*
> *an obstacle to the motion of the fibre in that direction,*
> *but enable it to glide easily*
> *on the opposite one; just as an ear of barley,*
> *when placed stalk uppermost within the cuff of the coat sleeve,*
> *will soon work its way*
> *up to the shoulder by the motion of the arm.*

Follow the skins home into these home places
as they work their way into the places of old songs and new corporations.
Of posts with names like Cumberland, Ellice, Pitt, Edmonton.
Of scrip and hangdog trappers, traplines
handed down through families. Indigenous
knowledge on the land, winter paths and summer streams.

> *When a quantity of such fibres of fur are rubbed and pressed,*
> *and the fibres made to curl slightly by the action of warmth and moisture,*
> *they twist around each other,*
> *and then interlace so tightly as not to separate.*

Gently place the skin back on the meat,
white fatty inner layers against red-pink muscle,
fur wrapping limbs, a mask dropping over the face
to become beaver once again, dark beady eyes
ready to watch from water's edge, paddled tail
ready to warn—
crack!—
against the mirror of water.

Unjudder the body,
calming it against the thrashings of the snare
and returning it to the freedom of the mud path
between forest and dam pond.
Musk emerges in the waiting for life,
comes to the nostril dense and sexual, the scent of
the lodge and the rut.

Elders will tell stories of the hunt:

> *How the trees float down the water because of the beaver.*
> *The person feels like the beaver is going so fast it feels like tin rattling.*
> *It feels like the beaver just came out of this place.*
> *The first year I started to kill beaver*
> *It took me one whole year to know his ways.*

It is this knowledge of rattling years that built Oxford Street,
this house of beavers, this *amiskowestih,* this *amikwiish,* this *tsàkèè.*

In the new millennium:
four gargoyled faces against the Oxford Street sky, not lion or demon or saint.
They preside over the franchise chemist, the sex shop, the bank, and the Bennetton,
tchotchke kiosk and hair salon, Foot Locker and newsstand.
The Hat Factory, now luxury flats.

> *Successful system of Head Measurement*
> *ensures the luxury of a well-fitting Hat*
> *adapted to the form of the wearer's head.*
> *Henry Heath, manufacturing his own goods, can guarantee—*
> *1st, Their Quality;*
> *2nd, Excellence of Finish;*
> *3rd, Style.*

So few obstacles to motion, this trade
in skins and spaces and styles.
Oxford Street and the far north interlaced so tightly
and woven into fabrics of near extinction.
In gargoyles, the signs of London's hunger.

But halfway across the world,
more than a century later,
the healing has begun.
When the city turned to silk instead of skin,
the dammers returned to the northern rivers.

Now the waters rest in beavered ponds,
faces upturned toward the sky,
waters moving down toward capital seas.[1]

6. Civilization Itself Consents

Disciplining Bodies in Imperial Suburbia, 1861–1914

Oh! it really is a pretty little garden,
And Chingford to the eastward could be seen;
Wiv a ladder and some glasses, you could see to 'Ackney marshes,
If it wasn't for the 'ouses in between . . .
If yer eyesight didn't fail yer, yer could see right to Australia,
If it wasn't for the 'ouses in between.
—A music hall song by Edgar Bateman, 1894

Almost exactly four months after Colonel George Custer's shocking defeat at the Battle of Greasy Grass, a group of Indigenous men and women appeared onstage at the Theatre Royal in Covent Garden. Colonel MacDonald's Troupe of Trained Sioux Indians made something of a splash among the trapeze artists, comic ballets, and popular singers that entertained diversion-hungry audiences that night. At the same time, their performance suggested a new approach to "savages." A journalist for *The Era* wrote,

> It has more than once been said that the only effectual way of arguing with a North American Indian is to shoot him, and the so-called civilized brutes . . . have done their best to "improve him off the face of the earth." Colonel Charles Edward Stuart MacDonald is of a different way of thinking . . . [;] he has undertaken to show that when brought under civilizing influence these Indians can hold their own in intelligence and skill with those who have long boasted of their superiority.

No Indian war dance here; instead, a display of proficiency with bayonets. In place of a reenactment of a buffalo hunt, "marchings and facings, and wheelings and chargings, and firings and rallies and assaults." And all of it was done not in traditional regalia, but in Algerian-inspired Zouave uniforms that had become all the rage in military performances throughout Europe and North America. Between the Royal and other venues, such as Hyde Park's Crystal Palace, upward of fifty thousand members of the public attended viewings of the Trained Sioux Indians.[1]

Three and a half decades later, poet and essayist Arthur Symons published *London: A Book of Aspects*. In it, he waxed rhapsodic about the city's magnificence and the English air that tempered its fogs and smogs. But he also warned against the changes that had taken place in recent years. "London," he wrote, "was once habitable, in spite of itself. The machines have killed it." The similarity between the "hurrying and clattering machines" of the streetscape and the "creatures that we see now in the machines," the city's people, spoke to an "automobilization of the mind." The city's expansion into what would eventually be known as Greater London brought with it the enervating horrors of urban growth: "we are tunneled under until our houses rock, we are shot through holes in the earth if we want to cross London," and in the suburbs from which men traveled every day to work, "the women are shouting . . . [;] they want to get their shopping done and get into a motor-car or motor-omnibus." To live in London, Symons declaimed, was "to live in the hollow of a clanging bell, to breathe its air is to breathe the foulness of modern progress." In contrast to this frenetic cityscape were the splendors of wild and pastoral nature and of bodies unbound by the city's ligatures. Encounters with "a tree, a dimly jeweled frog, a bird in flight" had been replaced with the smokestacks and viaducts of modernity. "Does anyone no longer walk?" he asked. "The verbs to loll, to lounge, to dawdle, to loiter . . . are losing their currency," he warned. "They will be marked 'o' for obsolete in the dictionaries of the future [and] will fade out of existence like the Red Indian." Later that same year, he experienced a mental breakdown and published only rarely until late in his life. One must wonder if the new London he so despised had finally gotten under his skin.[2]

At first glance, these two moments—an ethnographic display of military regimentation from the third quarter of the nineteenth century, and an antimodern jeremiad from the first years of the twentieth—would seem to have little to do with each other. Certainly, both involved North American Indigenous people (real or metaphorical), and both were deeply shaped by narratives of civilization and progress. But perhaps more importantly, both happened in a specific place and time: the late Victorian and Edwardian city, where particular kinds of urban development created new anxieties about London and its empire.

These strands came together at a series of large-scale Indigenous spectacles in the late nineteenth and early twentieth centuries. A Seneca runner, a group of Aboriginal Australian cricketers, a Māori rugby side, and Lakota Wild West Show performers all riveted London, and their presence there tells us much not just about Indigenous visitors but about Victorian and Edwardian—and imperial—culture. More specifically, these athletes and performers linked Indigenous and urban spaces through a modern, imperial culture of the disciplined body, which stretched from the suburbs of London as far as the Great Lakes, Australia, New Zealand, and the American Great Plains, emphasizing manliness, physical prowess, and "civilized" morality. The Indigenous athletes would be caught up as subjects of this culture, experiencing its effects both at home and in London. At the same time, within the spectacles of pedestrian races, cricket pitches, rugby matches, and Wild West shows, there existed moments of resistance that drew attention to the fragilities of London and its empire, even at its urban apogee.

In the second half of the nineteenth century, London leapt over itself. When the German traveler Karl Moritz had gazed out from St. Paul's in the late eighteenth century, he had seen places like Paddington and Islington laid out among green hills beyond London's edges. By the end of the nineteenth century, those same villages and many others, like Hampstead and Stratford and Tottenham, had been incorporated into an altogether new kind of landscape: the modern suburb. Meanwhile, entirely new communities, such as Maida Vale and West Ham, sprang up almost out of whole cloth as the city spread inexorably outward. This was the land of the middle class: rows of terrace houses and semidetached homes, green parks and gardenlike cemeteries, shopping streets and omnibuses. It was an escape from the overcrowded, filthy city into a vision of *rus in urbe*, a careful mix of the pastoral and urban in which Londoners could access the benefits of the city and yet quickly find themselves in the blessed countryside.

At the same time, suburbanization brought with it new problems. It was always tied to the increasing industrialization of the city, which meant that the city's growth only entrenched it within the world of factories and pollution. The "automobilization" that Symons decried in 1903 was a real thing; as soon as the first line of what would become known as the Underground was built in 1863, it was immediately crowded to bursting with harried commuters traveling through dim and dingy tunnels beneath the city, while omnibuses and trams rattled across the city morning and evening, carrying men to work from the suburbs. As the city continued to expand, older suburbs were taken over by the working and lower classes, creating the kinds of social conditions that had inspired middle-class flight in the first place. There was no escape.[3]

In fact, for all its charm and gentility, suburbia provoked anxiety among many Londoners. In 1885, for example, physician James Cantlie gave a lecture at the Parkes Museum of Hygiene about the "degeneration" of suburban Londoners over the course of the nineteenth century:

> What I want to prove, if possible, is that a mere collection of human beings is enough . . . to render the air in such a condition that the families living in such an atmosphere here dwindle and disappear from inability of continuance. I want to find out if there is such a thing as "*urbomorbus*" or "city disease" . . . hence I chose to study London.[4]

Cantlie's concerns, like Symons's, reflected a broader malaise regarding the ways in which modern, suburban life could enervate the body and lead to, in short, extinction. In other words, was the progression of British society toward ever increasing levels of urbanization, wealth, and comfort in fact leading toward a demographic dead end?[5]

This hand-wringing also had to do with the question of masculinity. The suburbs, it turned out, were the domain of women; when the men went to work, the result was a feminized landscape that threatened the order of things. In his 1905 work *The Suburbans*, journalist Thomas Crosland spelled out the danger in clear terms:

> This absence of responsible male population throughout the day may be reckoned a much more serious matter than appears at first sight. It tends to render what is already suburban in essence more

suburban still. Practically it gives over the household and all that dwell therein to the unquestioned rule of woman, which is not good.[6]

The fears of men like Cantlie and Crosland centered on the precarious nature of masculinity amid civilized, suburban modernity.

What was at stake, beyond the realm of suburbia, was the very empire itself: an unfit man was an unfit imperialist. The connections were all too clear. Cantlie lamented, for example, that while older generations of Britons had built the empire, the softness of younger generations raised in London's suburbs spelled potential disaster. "It is beyond prophecy," he cautioned, "to guess even what the rising degeneration will grow into, what this Empire will become after they have got charge of it." And while suburban growth was initially understood as a venue for masculine pioneers such as urban planners and the middle manager, by the later nineteenth century, as Todd Kuchta has written, suburbia came to be understood as the realm of "ineffectual colonizers, threatening savages, and powerless slaves." It was as though London was colonizing itself straight into global irrelevance.[7]

One solution to the suburban and imperial crisis of masculinity came in the form of sport. Few cultural practices captured the ambitions and anxieties of imperial Britain more than games such as cricket and rugby football. As Richard Holt has noted, "nervous strain" on the middle and upper classes—"the enfeebling effects of long hours at the office"—presented a challenge to urban British society, and sport could be an answer to the problem. Games were not only about physical fitness but about moral and intellectual preparation for the rule of others; the prosperous British middle and upper classes saw sport as an essential tool in creating leaders that would be free of that prosperity's negative influences. The goal, always, was to temper and discipline inherently violent male impulses and direct them into useful enterprises. One such enterprise was empire. As a correspondent to *The Times* wrote, "wherever the Englishman goes he carries that bat and the goal posts . . . [;] the first leisure in an invaded colony is sure to bring forth its cricket match or its athletic sports. . . . It forms a bond of sympathy between the various parts of the Empire of which, perhaps, the strength is as yet imperfectly realized."[8]

As Bateman's music hall lyric suggested, then, the expansive suburbanization of Victorian London was not unconnected to imperial places such
as Australia. At least in the mind's eye, one could practically see to Australia and other colonies over and through suburbs like Hackney and Chingford. The question, though, was whether Londoners, and in particular male
ones, were disciplined enough to sustain those connections between places
through imperial rule. This was the question on Arthur Symons's mind as he
fretted about the state of modern life in London. He worried that the city's
men would "wither and dwindle," with devastating results for Britain's place
in the world.[9] And one answer to his and others' questions about the imperial
fitness of suburban London could be found in the presence of Indigenous
visitors to the city, and in particular, Indigenous athletes who came to London in the late nineteenth and early twentieth centuries. Their bodies would
be set against British bodies in the suburban spaces of London, measured
up, and sometimes found wanting, sometimes found threatening. The story
of this disciplining of bodies begins with one of Symons's "Red Indians," a
hugely famous man known as Deerfoot, right in the heart of Hackney.

The special train was running every fifteen minutes, and still it could barely
keep up with the thousands on their way to see the spectacle that September
day. Hundreds boarded at Fenchurch Street, and hundreds more in Shadwell
and Limehouse. From there the train crossed Regent's Canal and steamed
past the gasworks and market gardens of Bow, where it picked up still more
passengers. At last it stopped at the Hackney Wick Station, where the throng
disembarked, pouring down off the platform into the racing grounds of the
White Lion Inn. Some gathered in the stands, others climbed up onto the
railway embankment, and some even shinnied up trees—anywhere they
might get a view of what was to come. Several thousand strong, the audience
was a sea of men surrounding a cinder track. They were ready for a show,
and they would not be disappointed.

First came Edward Mills, an athlete known to his loyal followers as
"Young England," his small, taut body in tip-top condition. The audience
cheered loudly for Mills, but it was his opponent who drew their most rapt
attention. Nearly six feet tall, he entered the oval and stalked around the

DEERFOOT,
THE SENECA INDIAN RUNNER,
IN ONE OF HIS CELEBRATED MATCHES.

A lithograph of one of Hutgohsodoneh's races. (Artist unknown; courtesy of The Old Print Shop, Inc., New York City)

track. From toe to head, "Deerfoot" could not have been more different from Mills, who wore a knitted woolen sweater, short pants, and the running shoes common to his sport. In contrast, Deerfoot wore moccasins, red drawers covered in metal bells, and a red and gold headband sporting a feather. On top of it all, he wore a wolf's skin. When the starting gun rang out, the crowd burst into cheers and yells, and the two men catapulted themselves onto the cinders. The audience, most never having seen a man like Deerfoot before, "looked on in amazement" as the stranger pulled ahead of Mills. In the end, Young England won by five yards, but both men received a standing ovation.[10]

This man who lost the race but stole the show was only "Deerfoot" when on the course. His English name was Louis Bennett, and he was a member of the Seneca Nation of western New York, among whom his name was Hutgohsodoneh, "He Peeks Through the Door." Between the fall of 1861 and the spring of 1863, he electrified audiences throughout Britain and Ireland with his feats of athleticism, most notably his ability to run great distances at high speed. It was his London performances, though, that would draw the most attention, in terms of both numbers present and coverage in papers around the nation. At these events, observers gave voice to ideas about the nature of English and Indigenous bodies and what constituted bodily health and constitution, prefiguring critiques of suburban life and its relationship to empire.[11]

Pedestrianism's name does not quite do it justice. While it did have its origins in a more general strolling—as sport historian Richard Holt has written, "Victorians were prodigious walkers"—and in the idea of walking great distances in the bucolic English countryside, by the middle of the nineteenth century, what constituted pedestrianism had become something quite different indeed.[12] It had become a raucous sport in which individual pedestrians sought fame and fortune in a marketplace of showmanship that appealed to broad swaths of British society. Like today's professional wrestlers, pedestrianists, or "peds" as they were often called, developed flamboyant personas, carrying such monikers as the Crow Catcher and the Gateshead Clipper. Among the middle and upper classes, such displays were typically considered vulgar. Deerfoot's presence would change that.[13]

By midcentury, pedestrianism was also largely an urban and suburban phenomenon. In the 1850s, running grounds had appeared all around the outskirts of the city, in places as far afield as Finsbury Park in the north and Wandsworth in the south. Others popped up in places like Brompton and Bow, satisfying the ever increasing popularity of the sport. Almost without exception, these running grounds were associated with public houses, whose proprietors benefited directly from ticket sales and wagers. This was the case with the White Lion, whose owner, James Baum, had opened a pedestrian course in 1857 next to the Hackney Wick Station. In the early 1860s, the grounds were still at the edges of the city; to the west lay new streets and terrace houses, but to the east lay the uncultivated and undeveloped marshes of the Lea River. So while Hutgohsodoneh lived at the very urban Spotted Dog in the bustling and unsavory Strand, his actual performances, and the places where he was seen by the most people, were on the suburban fringes of the city.[14]

At places like these, Hutgohsodoneh was a long way from home. He had been born into the Seneca people, traditionally understood as the keepers of the western door of the Haudenosaunee's great metaphorical longhouse. By the early nineteenth century, however, such relationships were being sundered, thanks to the expansion of American settlement. Under pressure from the New York government and land development companies, the Seneca and other Haudenosaunee peoples ceded some 95 percent of their lands, and on the handful of land remaining in reservations, overcrowding and political factionalization became central issues, as did the increasing presence of Quaker and other missionaries and American-style schools, which emphasized a program of "civilization." Hutgohsodoneh's own community of Cattaraugus was caught up in all this. Born into the Snipe clan, he first appears in the historical record in the early 1850s, when he began to make a name for himself at races throughout New York. Sometime in 1860, he came to the attention of British promoters visiting the United States, and soon he was tapped to make a tour of Britain.[15]

Upon his arrival, some English observers doubted whether he was an Indian. "He is of Indian blood," complained one newspaper correspondent, "but for generations his ancestors have been civilised. Paint, feathers, and wampum are not his natural habiliments." The writer went on to refer to the whole Deerfoot phenomenon as "nothing but a tremendous sell," with its subject "about as real as Barnum's woolly horse." Another paper offered a review of Hutgohsodoneh's performances that referred to pedestrianism's audiences as "too credulous," imagining that "in seeing him, he beholds the savage." (Then again, audiences had been tricked before: not long before Deerfoot's arrival, a Wandsworth runner sold to the public as a Tonawanda Seneca turned out to be an English crossing guard.)[16]

More observers, though, saw Deerfoot as the real deal. After reporting the fact that he slept under his wolf skin on the floor of his Spotted Dog room, a correspondent for *The Era* noted that "the Indian has shown himself to be anything but an imposter."[17] Not long after, a writer for the same paper lauded him as a "genuine American Indian, with a skin as bright as polished pine," and went on to detail his physiognomy in terms that can only be described as forensic:

> He is one of the finest specimens of the American tribes that have appeared in England, being much above the usual altitude, with the dorsal muscles so fully developed, that he, when running, appears to be round-shouldered, the muscles in the lumbar regions being equally well-matched with the former; his thighs are a mass of muscles, especially the extensors, while his lower extremities are rather light in appearance, but without an ounce of superfluous flesh on his calves.[18]

Whether too civilized to be truly Indigenous, or too Indigenous to be civilized, Hutgohsodoneh's body was a worthy subject of debate.

It was the contrast between his body and those of his adversaries, though, that both highlighted his uniqueness and drew attention to the possible shortcomings of English bodies. As one paper noted of that first race against Young England at the White Lion, "the feet of one of the redskins . . . being pitted against those of a pale face, caused so much excitement among the lovers of such sports that several thousands of persons assembled." However, the contest, the paper warned, might not have been fair: Mills, it noted, was "a pigmy by comparison." Accounts of Hutgohsodoneh "towering over his tiny opponent" or showing pectoral muscles "larger than in most British peds" drew attention to the possible inferiority of his English opponents. While Deerfoot's competitors might be described as "manly," sport commentators warned that "it must be a 'pale face' of first class, and in good faith, too, that can hope to contend against him." This is not to say that Hutgohsodoneh couldn't stand to improve himself; numerous accounts reported his undisciplined "rocking and rolling" running style, and one in particular noted that "it was the general opinion of all present that he could lose a stone of flesh and be all the better for it."[19]

Whether he was authentically Indigenous or not, sufficiently disciplined or otherwise, Hutgohsodoneh's presence electrified London audiences. It also transformed them. By the end of September, three weeks after his debut, the price of admission to the grounds at the White Lion had doubled, and so had the crowds. But they had also changed. "The company at Hackney Wick," wrote *The Era*, "numbered hundreds who do not usually patronise such sports." At the West London Cricket Ground in Brompton two weeks later, scores of upper-class men were present, having, according to one newspaper, "deferred their visits" to the horse-racing course at Newmarket in order to see Deerfoot for themselves. By the end of November, crowds as large as ten thousand came from "every grade of society." But the most shocking element of these enormous audiences was the fact that they included women. "Among the fair sex Deerfoot has greatly ingratiated himself," noted *The Morning Chronicle*, "and he has been somewhat embarrassed with the numerous cases of 'love at first sight,' but women worship notorieties, of whatever dime or colour." These new participants swelled the ranks; by the week before Christmas, crowds at Hackney Wick reached up to fifteen thousand. And this was not a bad thing; *The Era* commented that it would "give an impetus to pedestrian sports, a sport which all can practise." In this, pedestrianism might finally become a legitimate part of the civilizing project. Strong legs and lungs made a strong city, nation, and, by extension, empire.[20]

Things could go wrong in the world of pedestrianism, however. The illegal practice of race fixing had shut down many a pedestrian course in the years prior to Hutgohsodoneh's arrival, and before long, he found himself caught up in it as well. By the fall of 1862, rumors and then legal accusations flew that Deerfoot's track record—victory after victory after victory, despite his early losses—was a result not of his skill but of theater: the competitors who toured with him were losing on purpose to bring in more money. The judge in one of the cases ruled that the whole thing "was an exhibition, not a race." Things could also go wrong on a more individual level: at one race, incensed by the goading of a particularly garrulous racegoer, he attacked the man as the crowds around them shouted "Shame! Shame!" at the Seneca runner. But even after these setbacks, an especially dramatic victory at Brompton brought back the positive notoriety he had enjoyed in the early days of his tour.[21]

In the end, Hutgohsodoneh ran some 130 races over the course of eighty-seven weeks—an average of one every four and half days. He won most of them, but the grueling schedule took its toll. After the great success of Brompton, he began to decline, and by the time he left Britain in 1863, he had clearly run himself into the ground. He returned home to Cattaraugus, though, as a relatively rich man, and bought a farm where he would live the rest of his life. When he died in 1897, he was interred on his farm in Cattaraugus County, but four years later his remains were relocated to Forest Lawn Cemetery in nearby Buffalo, where he was laid to rest alongside famous Seneca leaders such as Red Jacket and Ely Parker. And in London, he would be remembered through occasional retrospective newspaper accounts, and a burlesque about him would be performed at the Britannia Theatre in Hoxton. Hutgohsodoneh also left another kind of mark on the sport of pedestrianism itself. In the decades to come, the showiest and most flamboyant peds would be known as Wild Indians.[22]

The Wimmera can be a homeland or a hard place. Located in the western part of what is now the Australian state of Victoria, hemmed in by mountains to the south and desert to the north and west, it has been home for the Wotjobaluk, Jardwadjali, and other Aboriginal peoples for thousands of years. Underneath today's veneer of agriculture is a landscape of eucalypts and mallee scrub, of sacred histories known as Dreamings, and the gatherings known as corroborees. It was into the Wimmera that three young settlers—Jane, Isaac, and Frank Duff, all under ten years of age—disappeared in 1864. They had wandered away from their family's homestead into the dry, tangled bush, and after several days, it was assumed by most local settlers that they were dead. Others held out hope, hiring Wotjobaluk trackers to find them. Before long, the children were returned to their grateful parents and one of the trackers, Jungunjinanuke, also known as Dick-a-Dick, quickly became famous both locally and nationally, and the story of Victoria's "babes in the wood" has been a staple of the nation's frontier mythology ever since.[23]

Four years later, Jungunjinanuke stood before seven thousand roaring Londoners, facing a line of Englishmen, each of them holding a stone-hard cricket ball in his hand. The men raised their balls, took aim, and threw. Ball after ball flew, fast and violent, at Jungunjinanuke. One observer described the scene:

> Possessed of a narrow shield and triangle, he defended himself against a shower of balls incessantly pelting him from a distance of about twenty yards. He fended off many that must have struck his head and other parts of the body, with wonderful adroitness by

means of these primate instruments, while others he avoided by a leap or bend.[24]

The Englishmen had each paid a shilling for the privilege of participating in a game one observer called "Throw 'em Ball." In the end, the Wotjobaluk man won the day: not a single ball had hit home. He took all the money for himself. The crowd erupted.[25]

Jungunjinanuke did not come to London to be a target in some sort of perverse imperial dodgeball. Instead, he arrived as part of a team of skilled athletes. Except for their captain, an Australian settler named Charles Lawrence, all were Aboriginal men. They included Jungunjinanuke; six other Wotjobaluk; a Jardwadjali man named Unaarrimin, or Johnny Mullagh; and two additional men, one likely from the Budawang of the southern coast of New South Wales, and the other, possibly Eora or Dharug, from Sydney. Together, they composed the first foreign cricket team to play in Britain, and even before their arrival, they were celebrities. The weekly *Bell's Life in London*, for example, drummed up interest ahead of their first appearance in the city, calling them (mistakenly, if we recall Bennelong and Yemmerrawannie) "the first specimens of the Australian native we have seen in this country."[26]

The public debut of Jungunjinanuke and his teammates came on May 27, 1868, at the Kennington Oval in south London. The largest cricket venue of its day, it was located in a neighborhood marked by overcrowding, poverty, and disease, and the green turfs of the Oval stood in sharp contrast to their surroundings. Home to the Surrey County Cricket Club, one of the most influential and successful teams in Britain during the middle of the nineteenth century, the Oval served as something of an antidote to the urban squalor around it, attracting audiences from a wide range of economic classes and connecting older neighborhoods just outside the eighteenth-century boundaries of the city to the new suburban ones that had sprung up in the nineteenth.[27]

On that May morning at the Oval, crowds began gathering early in the day, eager to see the "form of the Blacks" as they practiced. When the players emerged from the dressing room for the match, kitted out in uniforms, the crowd began to cheer loudly. Jungunjinanuke and his fellow cricketers gave three shouts and a "war whoop," and the game was on. Unaarrimin drew particular attention for his skills at bat. The match lasted two days, with

The Aboriginal Cricketers of 1868. (With permission from the National Library of Australia, no. 340227)

Surrey, who would go on to become the Aboriginal team's sponsor, winning on innings by seven runs. Despite their loss, the visitors succeeded in making themselves the stars of the show; indeed, it was Jungunjinanuke's idea to play that game of Throw 'em Ball with members of the audience. A true showman, he knew how to turn a loss into a win.[28]

Similar displays of Aboriginal skill took place throughout their tour. Journalist W. B. Tegetmeier, for example, described the boomerang prowess of one of the players, noting, "it is impossible to conceive anything more beautiful than its movements." On several occasions the group also performed what one observer called "a sham fight": wearing opossum skins and lyre-bird headdresses, the men stood in lines facing each other, throwing spears at times up to one hundred yards to the crowds' astonishment. Such performances were attended by figures such as ethnographer Augustus Pitt-Rivers, who visited the Oval while writing a manuscript on the history of technology, using what he saw as evidence for the nature of "primitive" societies.[29]

Many attendees of the team's games no doubt saw nothing more than savages in their midst; derisive comments must have flown among the throngs. One did appear in the London press:

> Arrayed in skin of kangaroo, and deck'd with lanky feather,
> How well you fling the fragile spear along the Surrey heather.
> And though you cannot hope to beat the Britishers at cricket,
> You have a batter bold and brave in Mullagh [Unaarrimin] at the
> wicket.[30]

Meanwhile, the Marylebone Cricket Club—the most powerful and influential in the country—initially refused to play the visitors at Lord's Cricket Ground. And Frank Gerald, who had been there at the Oval on the opening day of the tour, and whose uncle had been involved in the gold rushes that brought squatters to places like the Wimmera, described the players as "jabbering around . . . like monkeys" and "just like a lot of children, which indeed they were." In all, as Anthony Bateman has argued, the notion that they might actually win was "hard to be conceived."[31]

In fact, Unaarrimin and his teammates were decent cricket players. Fred Gale, a cricketer himself, reminisced some two decades later, "all of them were fine fieldsmen . . . [;] they would grab a ball like a cat nailing a mouse, with the left hand, pass it like a flash of lightning to the right, and they could throw very straight and well." Referring to Jungunjinanuke's game of dodgeball, Tegetmeier wrote that "their wonderful quickness of eye and precisions of muscular movement must be greatly to their advantage in the game." And a decade after their visit, cricket writer Charles Box described them as "straight and upright . . . conveying a fierce military aspect . . . and a physiognomy, taken altogether, by no means unintellectual . . . [;] in all of them there was a manly and dignified bearing."[32]

"Straight . . . upright . . . fierce . . . manly . . . dignified": such language might have been used to describe the English cricketers against which the "blacks" played. Having exploded in popularity in the 1850s, cricket carried with it ideas about the meaning not just of the game but of the bodies that played it. Most importantly, cricket was informed by what historians have called "muscular Christianity," a creed and set of practices that dominated Victorian thinking and emphasized "brute strength and power [and] prayer, upright living, discipline, and exercise," according to historian Keith A. P. Sandiford. This ideology promised, through bodily practices such as sports, a bright future. As school headmaster George Ridding wrote, "Give me a boy who is a cricketer and I can make something of him."[33]

Cricket also followed empire. Between the 1850s and the 1890s, the game became the most widely played and symbolically important sport throughout the British Empire. It was understood by both British and colonial authorities as part of a civilizing mission. As another headmaster would argue in the 1890s, "the pluck, the energy, the perseverance, the good temper, the self-control, the discipline, the co-operation, the esprit de corps, which merit success" were "the very qualities which win the day in peace or war. . . . In the history of the British empire, it is written that England has owed her sovereignty to sports." Spaces such as the Oval in Kennington, then, like similar kinds of spaces across the empire, spoke of an imperial, Anglo-Saxon masculinity intended to dominate much of the world.[34]

In the Wimmera, such domination had begun in the 1850s. As squatters, missionaries, and the Victorian provincial government moved into the region, they disrupted the ways of life of the Wotjobaluk and other local peoples. Outright violence, internal conflicts caused by Christianity, and attempts by the government to curtail and control Aboriginal people's movements destabilized many aspects of Aboriginal society. As a result of these dislocations, wage labor at the ranches soon became one of the primary sources of livelihood for many local men. Wage packets and range fences, the Sabbath and the church bell, "protection" boards and claimed legal jurisdiction all conspired to dispossess the Wotjobaluk, Jardwadjali, and other local peoples.[35]

Amid all of this came cricket. One of the most popular leisure activities on the ranches, the sport was soon dominated by Aboriginal players, even as its complex rules and formal protocols served to regulate Indigenous bodies and incorporate them into the empire. Indeed, it was often seen as the most effective way to do this. As one press account noted of the traveling team, echoing Ridding, "other measures have been tried and failed. The cricket ball has made men of them at last."[36] The combination of innate Aboriginal skill and the "sport of empire," then, offered not so much a contradiction as a plotline. Imperial bodies, whether in London or the Wimmera, could be—

must be—shaped through bodily discipline. The spectacle of Aboriginal Australian cricketers was London's empire and civilizing mission writ small.

That the Aboriginal visitors might win at cricket seemed all the stranger since, as *Bell's Life in London* claimed, they were members of "a race which is fast disappearing from the earth." And indeed, early in the tour, two players, Ballrinjarrimin and Jallachmurrimin, were sent home to Australia because of an unspecified illness. But it was the death in June 1868 of Bripumyarrimin at Guy's Hospital in Southwark that seemed to confirm impending Aboriginal extinction. The thirty-year-old was laid to rest in Victoria Park Cemetery, and Charles Lawrence penned an ode calling the deceased player "a hero intrepid and bold," echoing the game's imperial language.[37]

What the players thought of their experiences is completely opaque; no archival sources offer their perspective on their time in Britain. While scholars like Richard Holt have suggested that such matches could be a refutation of white superiority, there is no clear evidence of this. Whatever they thought, in the end the visitors lost more games than they won, no doubt confirming in the minds of many the fitness of British bodies over Indigenous ones, and as an economic venture, the tour was something of a wash, and not a single shilling went to the players. And when they returned to Australia, they faced a new set of policies designed to assert further control over Aboriginal bodies and minds, including the Act for the Protection and Management of Aborigines of 1869, which limited Aboriginal movement around Victoria, and the Aborigines Protection Act of 1886, which laid the foundations for what would come to be known as the Stolen Generations: thousands of Aboriginal children taken from their families in the interest of assimilation and "improvement." Individual members of the 1868 team carried on as successful cricketers, continued their work on area ranches, or simply disappeared from sight as far as the colonial archive is concerned. Jungunjinanuke, for his part, returned to the Wimmera to work on the ranches and at a local mission, eventually converting to Christianity. And as for Charles Lawrence, he became known as "the father of Australian cricket."[38]

The presence of ten Aboriginal cricket players in the city highlighted the tensions inherent in the imperial narratives that coalesced around the sport. More than in the case of Hutgohsodoneh just a few years before, Jungunjinanuke and his fellow players elicited explicitly racist sentiment, at the same time that they provoked clearer articulations of the power of sport in an imperial context. And the bodily and moral discipline built into the game of cricket reflected tensions both in London and in Australia. Those tensions would grow over the next two decades and then be on full display as a new team of Indigenous athletes, the precursors to today's famous rugby All Blacks, would make their debut in London.

"Ake ake kia kaha!"

The newspapers called it a "whoop" and a "war cry," but it was nothing of the sort: this was a haka. And this was a specific sort of haka: a *ngeri*, crafted not to engage in vocal warfare but to strengthen those who sang it, both spiritually and psychologically. Its lyrics "Forever forever be strong!" rang out not among friends and family and ancestors on a marae somewhere in New Zealand, but in front of a crowd of thousands at Rectory Field at Blackheath, among the southeastern suburbs of London, in the fall of 1888. Some wearing cloaks made of feathers and others wearing capes made of the fibers of the muka plant, the singers were young Māori men who had come to Britain to compete in rugby matches against British teams. Their chant echoed Mahanga's back in 1805 and would resonate for generations to come, even as its performers found themselves entangled in the civilizing missions of both London and their own homelands.[39]

The haka at Blackheath that October day had its origins in the efforts of two men—one Pākehā, the other Māori—to create a sensation in the form of the first New Zealand rugby team to tour internationally. The first, Thomas Eyton, would become the team's promoter and treasurer. He had served for a time in the Armed Constabulary, the legislated colonial militia that had emerged out of the "Māori Wars," before joining the civil service. While visiting England for Queen Victoria's Golden Jubilee in 1887, Eyton saw several rugby matches and he was not impressed. "It seemed to me," he would later write, "that the play I saw was not vastly superior to that I had seen in New Zealand." Seeing a clear opportunity, he began planning for the creation of a team that would eventually make its way to England.

Eyton's vision came at a good time; rugby had become one of the most popular pastimes in New Zealand since the first proper match was played

The New Zealand rugby team of the late 1880s, photographed in England. (Courtesy of the John Oxley Library, State Library of Queensland, Neg: 160512)

there in 1870. By the late 1880s there were twelve formal rugby unions in the colony, and the sport was closely linked to a developing sense of local identity. It was also an antidote to the changes taking place in New Zealand as colonial society became more urban. Rugby became a way for Pākehā men to craft a strong, masculine identity that referred back to the strenuous exertions of the New Zealand frontier while also containing that manhood, and the violence that was so central to it, within the limits of respectability—something rugby historians Timothy J. L. Chandler and John Nauright have called a "civilizing process." All of this was in contrast to the creeping urbanity of places like Wellington and Auckland, where, as one local magazine noted, "we are rapidly developing a town dweller whose stature and physical strength we ought to improve." As in suburban London, sport was a way to inoculate British subjects against racial and imperial degeneration.[40]

It was not, though, just a matter of enlisting Pākehā players. After seeing the teams play in England, Eyton wrote that "if a team from this colony—especially Māori or half-castes—could be taken to England, and brought to up-to-date form, such a venture would prove a success in every respect."[41] As he set to achieving this goal of an all-Māori team, he soon crossed paths with another man who was already on the job, and for whom the game of rugby meant something quite different. Joseph Astbury Warbrick, a twenty-six-year-old man of mixed Māori and European ancestry, from the Ngāti Rangitihi in Rotorua, had already been recruiting other young Māori men to create a full team. Many of the recruits came from missionary-run institutions like the Te Aute School and St. Stephen's Native School, where Warbrick had been a student. At schools like these, Māori boys from elite families were groomed to become leaders in both sport and civil society, with a clear eye toward "amalgamation" of the races. But while rugby might have been understood by schoolmasters and teachers as a way to "improve" the Māori out of existence, for Māori people themselves, rugby could have quite a different meaning altogether. As numerous scholars of New Zealand and Māori sport have argued, rugby was a way for Māori men to assert mana. And while boys and men of mixed ancestry, like Warbrick and his classmates, were understood by the British to be pawns in an assimilating process, Māori communities generally perceived them as part of the Indigenous social fabric and rarely were concerned about intermarriage or "race-mixing," except where it led to conflicts over land.[42]

So while Eyton saw the Māori players as something of an exotic attraction that was sure to bring in British pounds, for the Māori athletes themselves, such a venture could mean something else entirely. Despite their different motivations, Eyton and Warbrick joined forces to create what would be the colony's first international touring team, with Warbrick as captain and Eyton as promoter and treasurer. The other members were mostly drawn from Ngāi Tahu of the South Island and Ngāti Rangitihi of the North Island, and from the student bodies of the St. Stephen's and Te Aute Schools. Five were Pākehā, but these received little to no attention in the press and were folded into a team that was routinely described as simply Māori. With their high profile, the twenty men would become ciphers for the welter of discourses about masculinity, race, the frontier, and urbanization that were circulating in late-nineteenth-century New Zealand.

Similar anxieties were circulating in Britain as well. As in New Zealand, organized rugby in Britain was about manly restraint replacing outright violence, and the regularization of the sport was, to borrow Eric Dunning and Keith Sheard's term, a kind of "embourgoisement," an instilling of middle-class values over a game that was increasingly popular with the lower and working classes, especially in the north of England. Indeed, it would be these class and regional fissures that would lead to the schism of the sport into different leagues in 1871. The tempering of male violence, such a useful balancing force against urban "overcivilization," became a form of civilizing in and of itself.[43]

All of these strands of civilizing missions and fraught urbanity, with their origins in both home country and colony, came together at Blackheath in the fall of 1888. From the moment they arrived, the Māori players had been celebrities and were placed under a particularly imperial kind of scrutiny, as evidenced by one account from *The Daily Telegraph:*

> We have been invaded, and the Māori is upon us. . . . Yet the timid may take heart of grace. . . . It is but another of those ever-welcome colonial invasions in which our fellow subjects from across the sea come to wage friendly war with us in some of our national sports and pastimes. . . . The Māori have certainly progressed since Captain James Cook . . . found the finely painted and neatly tattooed ancestors of our visitors eating each other in the bush.[44]

Drawing on both the British nation's triumphalist history of exploration and on lurid ideas about cannibalism, the account managed to be both titillating and jocular. Perhaps most important, as Māori scholar Brendan Hokowhitu has argued, the team was largely perceived as being made up of "tamed savages." Still, descriptions of them often focused on their raw physicality; *The Times* reported, "in physique they look an especially formidable lot of players." Indeed, as Hokowhitu has shown, war and sport were the two arenas in which Māori men were perceived as equals (or, at times, even superiors) to the British. Meanwhile, other portrayals of the team slipped into the overtly racist; one cartoon in the *Illustrated Daily News* used a grotesquely caricatured Sambo-like figure in a grass skirt, carrying a war club across ground littered with skulls and bones, to represent the team's arrival in London.[45]

Sometimes, the team's own behavior could confirm observers' suspicions about Māori savagery. In the spring of 1889, for example, a match at Blackheath was interrupted when, outraged by a referee's call, several members of the Māori team stormed off the field, prompting the press to note the ways in which they had not fully internalized the civilized qualities of the game. One paper, for example, noted that the men must have obtained their knowledge of the game "in a bad school" where "their knowledge of all that is unfair surpassed their acquaintance with the legitimate game." By and large, though, the team was portrayed sympathetically by the press, particularly after they were completely snubbed by the Rugby Union, who declined to offer any hospitality to the "dusky colonials" after they had completed their tour.[46]

All told, from the fall 1888 game where they chanted "Ake ake kia kaha" for the crowd of thousands, to their disappointed departure in the spring of 1889, the team played a total of seventy-four games. They won forty-nine of them, having, in the words of a poem published in one newspaper, "flabbergasted Surrey and scrumpulated Kent." Of the London matches, at Richmond and Blackheath, the men won all but one. In all, the tour had been a success, not unlike those of Hutgohsodoneh and the Aboriginal Australians in the 1860s. Joe Warbrick's assessment of the tour was more complicated; interviewed for a Melbourne newspaper on his way home, he spoke quite harshly of the British: "As long as they [we] were losing they were jolly good fellows in the eyes of the crowd. But as soon as they commenced to win they were hooted and the papers were full of the weakness of the home side and the rough play of the visitors." And of England more generally, he pointed out that "England is, I should say, the rich man's paradise and the poor man's Hades," recalling the critiques of other Indigenous visitors. As for the other members of the team, their later lives moved in many directions. Some disappeared from the historical record, others continued as rugby players or became guides and surveyors, and still others went on to become members of the Māori Parliament. Meanwhile, the team's black uniforms, emblazoned with a silver leaf of the ponga tree fern, became the basis for the now-famous All Blacks, just as the haka of 1888 echoes in the ones performed wherever the New Zealand team plays.[47]

At breakfast one morning, Heȟáka Sápa smiled, fell out of his chair as if dead, and began to dream. In his dream, the roof of the house where he was staying began to spin and stretch, and a cloud came down and carried him away across a great expanse of water, and Heȟáka Sápa knew he was going home. He came to another land and watched a big town, then streams and green land passed quickly beneath him. He began to see places and people he recognized: a river, sacred hills, and his mother and his people gathered in one place. Suddenly, though, the cloud reversed direction:

> There were streams and green land and towns going backward very fast below me. . . . Then there was only water under me, and the night came without stars; and I was all alone in a black world and I was crying. . . . Soon the cloud stopped over a big town, and a house began coming up toward me . . . [;] when it touched the cloud, it caught me and began to drop down, turning around and around with me. It touched the ground, and then I heard the . . . voices of frightened people.

Heȟáka Sápa, an Oglala Lakota holy man more commonly known as Black Elk, had just, in the form of a dream, reenacted his journey from the Pine Ridge Reservation to the cities of Europe, including London.[48]

Black Elk was one of scores of Oglala Lakota people who traveled to London beginning in 1887 to perform as part of Buffalo Bill's Wild West Show. Expert horsemen and skilled performers, the Lakota visitors appeared before crowds far, far larger than those experienced by Hutgohsodoneh, Jungunjinanuke and his teammates, or the Māori team organized by Warbrick and Eyton. Crowds of tens of thousands attended each performance, twice a day for six months, with a total of some 2.5 million tickets sold—and that was just in London. Along with the difference in scale, the presence of Lakota men in the city provoked even more intense anxieties about the civilized bodies of the metropolis. The narratives of overcivilization and degeneration found their full flower in accounts of the Wild West Show and exemplify the extent to which Indigenous people could serve as a mirror to urban life. At the same time, like previous Indigenous travelers, Lakota men had their own reasons for participating in the shows, and through the experiences of three men in particular—Heȟáka Sápa, Ógle Lúta (Red Shirt), and Ota Kte (Luther Standing Bear)—we can catch glimpses of what the experience meant for the men in question.[49]

In 1887, when the Wild West Show originally appeared in London, the Lakota were not supposed to be the star attraction. Rather, the American

Unidentified Wild West Show performers pose in a London park. (Courtesy of the Denver Public Library, Western History Collection, call. no. NS-190)

Exhibition, of which it was part, was set up primarily to highlight the United States' modernity. The urban spectacle of the exhibition was literally built atop and amid a place that had recently undergone its own urban revolution. Over the course of the nineteenth century, the district of Kensington had gone from a landscape of manors and market gardens to an urban borough of almost a quarter million residents, with much of the development spurred by the Great Exhibition at the neighboring Hyde Park. This was largely a middle-class neighborhood, full of draftsmen and other middling professionals: exactly the kind of suburban men who were on the minds of so many social critics. As for the site of the American Exhibition itself, it was located on derelict ground between railroad tracks that brought commuters to the city.

The spectacle of Buffalo Bill's Wild West Show was on an unprecedented scale: as just one example, more than seventeen thousand carloads of rock and earth were brought to the site to re-create the Rocky Mountains, and in Buffalo Bill's own words, "the rapidity with which we had transported our stuff from dock to depot, and depot to grounds, and made our camp . . . had an immense effect." The real show, of course, was the Wild West Show. It included all the elements of the American West that had captured imaginations around the world: cowboys, Mexicans, Annie Oakley, and more. But it was the Indians who stole the show every time. From a mock buffalo hunt to simulated attacks on wagon trains, stagecoaches, settlers' cabins, and ranches, the Lakota horsemen riveted audiences with a reenactment of the United States' westward expansion.[50]

To say that Londoners were fascinated by "Red Indians" is an understatement, and the millions who attended the show included some of the most influential and powerful figures in British society. Henry Irving, the most popular actor of the era, served as something of a mouthpiece for the 1887 show: prior to its opening, he told his audiences that "the most interesting episodes of life on the extreme frontier of civilization in America are represented with the most graphic vividness and detail. . . . No one can exaggerate the extreme excitement and 'go' of the whole performance. It is simply immense."[51] Actress Ellen Terry, Irving's female counterpart, also attended the show, receiving an eagle feather from Red Shirt himself. Even Prime Minister William Gladstone and many members of Parliament came. The most important visitors to the show, though, were the royal family. Black Elk, also a member of the 1887 show, recalled the queen's speech to the performers in May of that year:

> I have heard about some people that were in America and I heard they called them American Indians. Now I have seen them today. America is a good country and I have seen all kinds of people, but today I have seen the best looking people—the Indians. I am very glad to see them, if I owned you Indians, you good-looking people, I would never take you around in a show like this. You have a Grandfather over there who takes care of you . . . but he shouldn't allow this, for he owns you, for the white people to take you around as best to show the people.[52]

Victoria's clear ambivalence about the Wild West Show was likely shared by at least some observers, but clearly these were in the minority: the show would return in the 1890s and 1900s and play to equally large audiences.[53]

The high drama and romance of the Wild West Show, so carefully cultivated, could not have stood in starker contrast to the reality for Lakota people on the Pine Ridge and Rosebud Reservations, from which the vast majority of Wild West Show performers were recruited. The show had begun before the great wars associated with American expansion into the northern plains had even ended, tangling up reality and representation. With the wars won by the Americans—with the occasional exception like the Battle of Greasy Grass—Lakota and neighboring peoples found themselves restricted to bleak and ever shrinking reservations. During his 1887 tour, Red Shirt described the situation to a *Western Mail* reporter: "Our buffaloes are nearly all gone, the deer have entirely vanished, and the white man takes more and more of our land," he explained, going on to say that his people would starve were it not for the government's meager rations.[54]

The Wild West Show season of 1891–92 in Europe offered an even greater contrast between romance and reality. It included Ghost Dancers—most notably Tȟatȟáŋka Ptéčela (Short Bull), a leader of the Brulé Lakota at Rosebud; and Matȟó Wanáȟtake (Kicking Bear), a Miniconjou Lakota soldier. Both had been imprisoned at Fort Sheridan in the territory of Wyoming for their roles in the Ghost Dance, a millennial movement that inspired terror in settlers and government officials alike and which had largely ended with the infamous massacre of at least 150 Lakota men, women, elders, and children at Čaŋkpé Opí (Wounded Knee) on the Pine Ridge Reservation in 1890. Along with twenty-one other Ghost Dancers, Kicking Bear and Short Bull were released from Fort Sheridan to participate in the Wild West Show. Cody outlawed the Ghost Dance in his show's camps and refused to reenact the massacre, at the same time promoting (falsely) a child participant as the "last survivor of Wounded Knee."[55]

For many observers, there were clear connections between the stories of places like Wounded Knee and those of Britain's own empire. As historian Joy Kasson has noted, the Wild West Show "displayed American military and cultural adventurism in a way that seemed familiar to Europeans at the high tide of imperialism." British audiences of the period were steeped in images of far-flung places and foreign wars through plays, popular adventure novels, and staged re-creations. Meanwhile, Cody's persona as a sportsman, hunter, and scout fit with imperial values of the day, the same ones that circulated around sport: stamina, bravery, individualism, fairness, and mastery. The Wild West Show, Kasson writes, "evoked a world of risk and dominance, of virility and exoticism, that formed both the amusement and the serious business of empire." Perhaps most important, British enthusiasm for Cody's venture arose from a confidence in Anglo-Saxon superiority shared by both the United States and Britain.[56]

At the same time, the obvious success of the American imperial project, so clearly evidenced in the Wild West Show, presented a problem for British audiences—and London ones in particular—that was cast in language that would have been familiar to James Cantlie, Arthur Symons, and others. While many accounts of the show highlighted the friendship between the United States and Britain, others saw competition between the nations that Britain was in danger of losing. The London *Observer* explained that the Wild West Show performers spoke of a time before modern life had made people like the British "civilized and effeminate," while another paper noted that "we are, perhaps, suffering a little from over-culture just at present." Member of Parliament Lord Charles Beresford, meanwhile, wrote that "there is a want of congruity in the companionship of an illustrious British officer who fills an important position in the Government with a gentlemen chiefly famed as an adroit scalper of Red Indians." As historian Louis Warren has argued, such statements belied a deep fear of racial degeneration, in keeping with the kinds of antisuburban critiques launched by men like Symons. Once again, it was clear: a modern, urban, and ultimately soft man was no man for empire. And while such descriptions often focused on the white performers, it was their proximity to Indigenous people that articulated their distance from the urban civilization of London. As *The Sunday Chronicle* described, "these dusky Indians, with their unearthly streaks of colour on their faces, and their, monotonous, and hollow cries as they ride past . . . remind us of the earlier forms of savage man whence we have evolved, not by any manner of means always in the right direction." *The Times* was most succinct, however, in its discussion of the issue: "Civilization itself consents to march in the train of Buffalo Bill."[57]

These spectacles of empire and the very real effects of imperialism on Lakota people did not mean that the Lakota did not have some options. As L. G. Moses and others have argued, participation in Wild West Shows was an important way for Lakota men to leave the reservation, at least for a time, while earning money and continuing to pursue the activities—most notably horsemanship and battle skills—that were so central to Lakota masculinity. It was also a way for them to resist the national project that sought to solve the "Indian problem"; indeed, both the missionary societies that ran reservation schools and the U.S. ambassador adamantly opposed the Wild West Show.[58]

Meanwhile, Lakota people expressed their agency in very concrete, intimate ways while in London. Luther Standing Bear, who performed in the show in the first decade of the twentieth century, described an encounter he had while performing in London for Edward VII: "I had a beautiful lance, and as the dance proceeded I worked over toward the King's box. There I shook the lance in his face and danced my very prettiest, you may be sure." Standing Bear also described the ways in which he and his compatriots took in the city as observers. From their quarters in Kensington's Olympia Theatre—which had, coincidentally, opened in 1806 with a show of horsemanship entitled *The Indian Chief*—performers could take in the sights of the city. At Westminster Abbey, Red Shirt had a vision of angels; around the same time, he saw a performance of *Faust* at the Lyceum starring Henry Irving. Other performers visited the Tower or simply wandered Kensington freely, including visiting a Congregational Chapel where they sang "Nearer My God to Thee" in Lakota. Of the city itself, though, Black Elk pointed out the same shortcomings that Joe Warbrick had noted: "I could see," he told his biographer, "that the Wasichus did not care for each other the way our people did . . . [;] they had forgotten that the earth was their mother."[59]

When Black Elk, Red Shirt, Luther Standing Bear, and their fellow Lakota people wandered the city, they would have seen themselves portrayed in the ubiquitous advertising that brought audiences to see them. One published ditty from the day illustrated the urban footprint of Cody's public relations machine:

> I may walk it, or 'bus it, or hansom it: still
> I am faced by the features of Buffalo Bill.
> Every hoarding is plastered, from East-end to West,
> With his hat, coat, and countenance, lovelocks and vest.
> Plunge in City or fly suburbwards—go where I will,
> Bill and Bill's 'Billy-ruffians' appear on the bill.[60]

This one poem highlights the ways in which London's suburban landscape intersected with the Wild West Shows. As in the cases of Hutgohsodoneh, Jungunjinanuke, and Joe Warbrick, suburban and Indigenous histories were never far apart. In fact, they were the same story.

How much thought did everyday Londoners give to the fact that they even had an empire? Did a working-class man in the East End have daily experience with the workings of, say, the Raj in India? What about an upper-class woman in Kensington—did she ever pause to think of the West Indies? And did those clerks and accountants commuting from Finchley and Tooting care a whit for the global processes and conflicts that today we name as so central to British history, even as they administered its stocks and futures? Historians have long debated these questions, and the argument has largely been settled in favor of those who see empire as fundamental to the lived experience of domestic Britons: tea sipped over a calico tablecloth and a meal of kedgeree, adventure novels of dark continents, even the very notion of an Anglo-Saxon identity. All were constructed in conversation with the far-flung imperial net that centered on London. Empire was also built into the very landscape of the city, in colonial offices in Victoria Street, in the imposing edifice of the Bank of England in Threadneedle Street, or in the thoroughfare spectacles of soldiers returning from the Boer War. If at times invisible, empire shot through the warp and weft of London life, culture, and politics. From those "'ouses in between" of the music hall song, it was indeed possible to "see right to Australia" if one bothered to look.[61]

Bodies were part of this entanglement of the domestic and the imperial. It is well known that the Victorian period was remarkable for its emphasis on the policing of female sexuality, movement, and political roles, but men were being disciplined as well, by the workweek and the rulebook among other things, illustrating the deep relationships between places like New York and Hackney, Australia and Kennington, New Zealand and Blackheath, and the American West and Kensington. It was in the spectacle of encounter between Indigenous and British bodies, in the form of sport, that empire was literally performed in the public spaces of London, and then linked to urban stories of degeneration and civilization. And even though Indigenous athletes like Hutgohsodoneh and Joe Warbrick were at times lauded by the press and the public, at other times they were, like Unaarrimin and Ota Kte, the butt of racist jokes and fantasies of vanishing races. Even as London turned its civilizing mission on itself with the proprieties of manly sport and fears of downward racial mobility, it was Indigenous people like Jungunjinanuke who would experience the greatest challenges of urban empire. In their lives, and on their bodies, the terrors of discipline—boarding schools, racial policy, stolen generations—made their greatest marks.

Particular kinds of cities, at particular moments in time, inspire particular kinds of stories. In the late Victorian and Edwardian eras in London's history, stories about the city focused not just on its imperial grandeur but on the new threats it presented to masculinity, order, and Britain's global prospects. These anxieties about bodies, cities, and empire came together around sporting events in which Indigenous people served as ciphers for British ideas and desires. But for men like Red Shirt, the Warbrick brothers, Jungunjinanuke, and Hutgohsodoneh, such events offered opportunities: to get off the reservation, to pursue prestige and profit, and to engage in traditional pursuits. In doing so, they also challenged the stories about civilization that swirled around them.

The last Wild West show came to London in 1914. Its mastermind was not Buffalo Bill; rather, this was a close copy organized by the impresario Imre Kiralfy, and it took place not at Kensington but in Shepherd's Bush, a suburb farther to the west. "The White City" was built on the site of the 1908 Olympic stadium—where Hopi runner Louis Tewanima had competed in the marathon and Tuscarora Frank Mount Pleasant in the triple jump and long jump—and featured all of the spectacles one would have expected from Cody's Wild West Show nearly thirty years earlier. "Thrilling fights" led by "hostile Indians who resent the march of civilization," a Sun Dance and "Indian Chiefs at Home," and several celebrity Indians whose individual stories were part of the promotional materials—and who included, all these years later, Red Shirt. Even more than in earlier iterations, this Wild West Show trafficked in imagery of the vanishing race; its official guide described the drama of extinction:

> Not many generations ago, where now great cities carry on their
> multifarious life . . . lived and loved another race of beings. . . . Not

many years hence the inquisitive white man, as he stands by some western city, will ponder on the structure of their disturbed remains and wonder to what manner of person they belonged. They will live only in the songs and chronicles of their exterminators.[62]

Like so many other accounts of American history—whether an indictment or a celebration—Kiralfy's White City Wild West cast Indigenous peoples and cities as mutually exclusive. The story line was clear: just like the Senecas, Aboriginal Australians, Māori, and Lakotas, all Indigenous peoples would fade into the past, overwhelmed by modernity. Never mind that Indigenous performers were there to participate in that very same modernity by appearing in the arena at Shepherd's Bush; they were imagined by observers as little more than shadows of the "real Indians" of the past. This is the core narrative of what we all too often think of as Western history: a clear break between Indigeneity and modernity. And in 1914, a storm was coming that would bring a damning new modernity to urban and Indigenous people alike, as they all went down in global war.

A Notebook, 1929

Do you see this?

He pins black cloth over his greatcoat,
leaves his room in Warner Street and trundles his olding bones
down to the Strand
where Australia House corners the thoroughfare.

The black cloth speaks indictment. Covered
in toy skeletons, it drapes his stooping shoulders,
                    penny toys that speak of dark things.

Do you see this? he cries, his beard straggling and white.
This is all Australia has left of my people.
This is all Australia has left of my people.

Crowds are rushing by on the pavements,
ignoring, turning away, scorning—
Do you see this? Do you see this?—
until a bobby scatters him and his beard back to Clerkenwell
or arrests him for nuisance,
clears the Strand of the story of a people driven into darkness,
            the accounting of genocide.

He returns to Clerkenwell,
enters the day in a small red book,
catalogs its abuses and his own outrage.
Reads accounts of the massacres in the bush in the papers.
        Blackmans Butcher land England, he writes.

Anthony Fernando has come a long way to Australia House,
from farther than Clerkenwell.

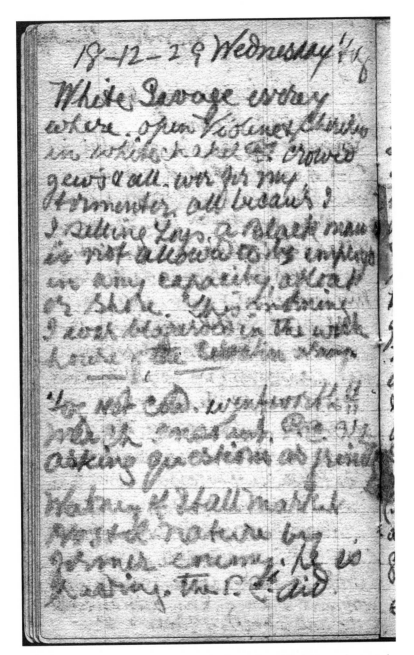

The notebook of Anthony Fernando. (Notebooks, Anthony Martin Fernando, Australian Institute of Aboriginal and Torres Strait Islanders Studies, ACT, MS 4904, vol. 2, p. 19, 18-12-29)

From Woollomoolloo, son of a Dharug woman
      —his *guiding star*—
and a man from Goa, from Sri Lanka, from even farther perhaps.

But Anthony is not only of New South Wales, not only
an Aborigine circling at the edges of Australian society.
His life is spent as a traveler: Austria, Switzerland, Rome,
a pilgrimage of outrage, a peroration for anyone who will listen.
Every moment I spend in thinking &
serching some one who would take up the caus
of Natives of Australia but I am generally
made a Laughing
Stock

Then to London:
Australia House, Speaker's Corner.
Do you see this?

Work in the city is an unsuccessful string of markets.
Trays of toy birds and fish and policemen,
and hatreds strung all along the days.

Barking, Leytonstone, Whitechapel, Hoxton, Limehouse.
Emaciated children taunt and chase,
pelt him with rotten pears, rotten tomatoes.
Mothers pull them away from the dark skin, sidelong glances
their own indictment.

> *Go to your country you bk bastard wash your face dirty Sod*
> *Samboo be off Now Nigar you get out or else get off Black thing*

Battersea, Hampstead, Mile End, Stratford, Petticoat Lane.
Refused meals in restaurants, turned away from trams and buses.
Christmas 1929: *Every where seen Drunken Glee, open imorality*
I was abused by men & Women & Children more today than usual.

> *Get the hell out of England you black Beast you are the dirt*
> *Your type should be killed Indians should be extermanated*
> *Black Bastards aught to be linched they don't allow them in America*

Italian, Indian, the other Indian, African, Arab,
anything but Dharug, anything but Aborigine, anything but Human.
No matter who I changed to they were at me like fly's to the milk.

And always, the diary, the litany.
Do you see this?

Clerkenwell is only an interlude; he is always on the move.
An infirmary in Bow:
I am Exhausted from coughing. Feverish. All my nerves in Trembel. No rest.
The whole of my body is a contunual tumbel
I have no means whatever from this Land of Savages.
The Salvation Army in Middlesex Street, bed 236,
soaked in piss from the bunkmate above. *A Black*
man is not safe even in bed from the White Schum
I eat very littel food of this place
for they are not norishing

The Black man must not defend himself, he writes in the red books,
but he does: a pistol drawn against a fellow market seller,
followed by a hearing at Old Street:
Look at my rags. I can't make ends meet.
All you hear is 'go away, black man, go away.'
Do as you like with me, but the Natives of Australia
must be looked on as human beings.
Remanded at the Old Bailey, *the iron has entered his soul,*
writes one visitor, and he is *consumed like the prophets of old.*
From the prison into the custody of a former employer—
I gave him not only a chance to chain my limbs
but put a halter around my neck

As the years move, he will descend into desperate violence.
1935: stabs a fellow lodger in the arm in Islington.
1938: throws boiling water over another in Shoreditch.
In court he recounts the story of his people in Australia,
                of massacres at Forest River and Alice Springs,
                hangings and stolen children,
of the *cultivated savagery* of the British and their colonial cousins,
and of London itself.

Years on, 1942,
in an old men's home in Ilford after the war,
he will remember:
remember the kindness of an Essex farmer
who rescued him from the last court, his thousandth man.
I am still in the land of the living and that is about all,
he will write to Douglas Jones.

1949, as he approaches death,
he remembers those red books
of Clerkenwell and Middlesex Street and Bow,
passed on to the final man who listened.
And young Cressida Jones, his
dear little Ding Dong of Valley Farm

At the end, 1949,
the heart and mind failing, the lungs filling,
he remembers

> his *guiding star,*
> and children's toys turned into the People's bones.

Do you see this?
Do you see this?[1]

7. The City of Long Memory

Remembering and Reclaiming Indigenous London, 1982–2013

When we shall have acquainted our People with what we have seen,
our Children from Generation to Generation will always remember it.
—Oukah Ulah (Cherokee), 1730

We are long-memoried people, and we remember what happened the
last time the world was flat.
—Jodi Byrd (Chickasaw), 2011

In 1892 Long Wolf, a Lakota performer in Buffalo Bill's Wild West Show, died of pneumonia in London at the age of fifty-nine. Like other travelers before him—the missing Algonquian people of the seventeenth century, Atajuq and his family in the eighteenth, and Maungwaudus's family members in the earlier nineteenth—the ecology of the city took its toll, sending Long Wolf to his grave much earlier than might otherwise have been the case back on a South Dakota reservation.

Just over a century later, a group of Long Wolf's descendants gathered at that grave in Brompton Cemetery in West London, amid the tombs of famous Londoners, such as suffragist Emmeline Pankhurst and numerous writers, politicians, and colonial officials. The Oglala Lakota had long told stories of their ancestor but did not know the location of his grave until an amateur historian from Britain contacted them after she had located the site. After a long journey from South Dakota to London, they conducted a ceremony that should have been done all those years before, closing a circle. As family member John Blackfeather told the press, "I've been hearing about Long Wolf since I was a little boy. It's sort of like a fairytale story. He's someone I never knew, but my mum talked about—and here I am 60 years later." Long Wolf's daughter Lizzie had been twelve when her father died, and her granddaughter, Blackfeather's mother, had carried the story across the twentieth century. And so finally, that day in 1997, they were able to sing for their kinsman:

> *Takala kun miye ca*
> *Ohitiye waun kun*
> *Wana henamala yelo.*

> My people take courage
> A warrior I have been
> Now I am no more.

Horses then pulled away from the grave, carrying his casket draped with an American flag, and Long Wolf began the long trip home to the Black Hills.[1]

Repatriation is reconnection, a radical reordering of the spoils of empire, in which Indigenous and other peoples have asserted their rights to cultural patrimony and ancestors. As in the case of Long Wolf, it is the closing of a circle that reaches from Indigenous territories to the metropole and back again. London, like other cities that have collected bodies and objects, has been the focus of repatriation efforts on the part of Indigenous communities and others around the world, with the British Museum, the Smithsonian, and other institutions beginning in the last years of the twentieth century to return ancestors and sacred objects, thanks to the activism of those to whom such people and things truly belong.

But aside from the story of Long Wolf—an example of repatriation widely discussed in the London press—this chapter is not about the repatriation of sacred objects and ancestral remains from the descendants of the Holophusicon. Rather, it is about another kind of repatriation that has taken place in the city, particularly in the latter part of the twentieth century and early years of the twenty-first: the remembering and reclaiming of the city and of Indigenous travelers by descendant communities. In this entanglement of memory between the city and its Indigenous history, activism, ceremony, and reenactment are central to the story. Indigenous communities, particularly from Canada, have continued to assert relationships to the Crown through journeys to London, in a tradition that goes back to earlier journeys by Indigenous diplomats. Other communities and individuals have come to the city to commemorate and honor specific travelers, many of whom did not make it home. And last, the development of a Māori community in London attests to a lived Indigenous presence in the city, even if other travelers such as Pocahontas remain primarily metaphors in a new, allegedly multicultural city. Together, these stories illustrate the ways in which memory has entangled London in Indigenous history, even as the city has tended to forget its own empire. It is about the interleaving of past and present, in which the two commingle through both acts of memory and the bonds of community.

"The trouble with the English," the author Salman Rushdie has famously written, "is that their history happened overseas, so they don't know what it means."[2] Indeed, over the course of the twentieth century, it seemed that Britain largely forgot its imperial history; by the time repatriation moved around the world, becoming a significant movement among Indigenous peoples and others, London had for the most part mislaid the empire that brought such things and people to it in the first place. Over the course of what John M. MacKenzie has called a "sixty-year implosion," in which Britain lost almost all of its colonies, Britons struggled with the empire's legacies, including with the very recognition that those colonies existed. In the late 1940s, for example, one study showed that only half of those surveyed could name a single British colony.[3]

For those who did pay attention, the loss of the empire could cause great consternation, as the values that had influenced the disciplining of imperial and Indigenous bodies in the late nineteenth century—ideals such as duty, stoicism, self-restraint, and gentlemanliness—seemed to be eroding in parallel with the empire itself. By the 1960s, the empire, when it was talked about at all, was done so with a sense of both shame and avoidance. Diplomat Merwyn Jones, for example, declaimed in 1968 that Britain had oppressed people around the world, noting, "it has never been considered, or at times it has been explicitly denied, that they are human beings like ourselves." As late as 1997, when Hong Kong was handed over to China, attitudes toward Britain's imperial history were a confusing mix of pride, regret, and ignorance; as the historian Bill Schwarz argues, empire was "un-nameable, forgotten, invisible, unspeakable." So while the academic and political debates about empire continue in the twenty-first century, dominated by conservatives such as Niall Ferguson and Michael Gove, for most Britons it is a subject mostly located outside of living memory. "Memory and forgetting are not separate practices, but are interlinked, the one a function of the other," Schwarz has written. "There is never one without the other. But we also need to distinguish . . . between *a desire* to forget and *an inability* to forget."[4]

London is little different. Most histories of the twentieth-century city have virtually nothing to say about the relationship between the empire and its metropolis during that century, focusing instead primarily on narrower—if still crucial—civic issues such as municipal governance, environmental management, or social unrest. At the same time, though, the urban landscape remains littered with the detritus of empire. As MacKenzie has eloquently written:

> It may be that those who hurry down Whitehall seldom reflect on the extraordinary imperial façade of the Foreign Office with its busts of heroes; that passers-by in Kensington Gore scarcely notice the statues of Livingstone and Shackleton that project from the walls of the Royal Geographical Society; and that visitors to the Victoria and Albert Museum are only dimly aware of the imperial origins of some of its collections. Moreover, even if familiar and overlooked, statues and war memorials everywhere speak of an imperial past.[5]

So although the empire might have, in the words of historian John Darwin, "sailed away to the Coast of Nostalgia" (if it was remembered at all), the city held within its fabric the tangible evidence of what had once been so central to its identity. But if for Britons generally and Londoners specifically the empire has largely been lost to memory, for many Indigenous peoples the city lies neither out of sight nor out of mind. Rather, it remains contested ground.[6]

The Crown lives in London and so, then, does Indigenous history.

In the 1970s, Great Britain and Canada initiated a process by which the Canadian constitution would be patriated to North America and undergo a series of powerful revisions and reorientations in the interest of Canadian sovereignty. However, Indigenous people in Canada were not being consulted in the process, so they turned to the Crown for help. Over the course of the late 1970s and the early 1980s, First Nations from across Canada sent representatives to London to draw attention to the many treaties that the Crown had signed, many long before Canadian confederation. In July 1979, some three hundred chiefs—a total that was perhaps more than the sum of all other Indigenous visitors in this book combined—came to the city with a clear and crowded agenda that included meeting with MPs, interviews with the press, and most important, the hope that Elizabeth II would meet with at least some of them. Carrying with them copies of numerous treaties going back to the eighteenth century, they sought to make explicit the connections between past and present.[7]

Perceptions of the huge First Nations delegation were mixed and at times even derisive. One Canadian politician described the journey as "live theatre" but not much else, and *The Globe and Mail* seemed surprised that "there wasn't a bead, feather, or moccasin in sight. The two Indian chiefs sitting stiffly behind the conference table wore neat businessmen's clothes and used neat businessmen's language." One political cartoon, meanwhile, showed MPs with arrows shot through their bowler hats, next to a news-stand crowing "RED INDIANS AT WESTMINSTER." Other observers, however, could see the connections with London's deeper past. "Indeed, the sun never sets on the old Empire," noted Parliament's official news organ. At the same time, it continued, "we cannot hold out much hope for these Red Indians making the British Parliament look back to its great Imperial past[;] it is a reminder of our history. And what splendid names there are, from such fa-mous tribes as the Cree, the Sioux, the Mic-Mac, and the Ojibway under the great leader chief Noel Starblanket." As for the business suits, and proving that he would not be relegated to the romantic or imperial past, Starblanket himself pointed out, "We went there in business suits because the Indians mean business."[8]

Other delegations and transatlantic encounters would come in the en-suing years, as the wrangling continued over the patriation of the Canadian constitution. In a single month in 1981, for example, members of the House of Lords met with National Indian Brotherhood and Indian Association of Alberta (IAA) leaders in Canada to see "the privation and political ma-nipulation to which the Indian people are daily subjected," while an IAA consultant attended the Labour Party's national convention in London and other First Nations lobbyists met with officials elsewhere in the city. *Indian News* described another group that joined the efforts that month: "Amidst the throbbing of sacred drums, a 15-member delegation from the Federation of Saskatchewan Indian's [*sic*] (FSI) cultural college journeyed to London in full regalia. According to troop leader Earnest Tootoosis, the FSI isn't worried that the traditional dress will reinforce the Indian stereotypes. Instead," the article noted, "the Federation hopes to assist the lobbies already in London by adding a cultural flavor."[9]

The efforts of Indigenous Canadian leaders in the 1970s and early 1980s were part of a longer trend that stretched across the twentieth century. In 1973, for example, Cree politician and author Harold Cardinal, who had famously coined the term "buckskin curtain" to describe the deep divides between Indigenous and settler peoples in Canada, traveled to London and gave a speech to the queen in response to the Liberal Canadian government's deeply misguided attempt to "revolutionize" race relations by bringing to an end the Indian Act.[10] Four years before that, the young Mohawk activist and model Kahn-Tineta Horn—"a voice out of Britain's colonial past" according to one press article—had made something of a splash in London by giving speeches calling on the British to support her people's treaty rights, including, for example, the right to move unimpeded across the national borders that crossed through Indigenous homelands.[11]

Such journeys had taken place in the early twentieth century as well. In 1930, for example, a group of Canadian Indigenous statesmen took tea in full regalia on Westminster Terrace as part of their lobbying efforts. When Mohawk leader Levi General, also known as Deskaheh, sought an audience with the League of Nations in 1921 in order to bring attention to his people's concerns and claims, he made sure to stop in London. He would make several trips to the city, during which he confronted Department of Indian Affairs functionaries and made unsuccessful appeals to George V to hear his case. And a generation before Deskaheh, fellow Mohawk John Ojijatekha Brant-Sero, a descendant of Thayendanagea, first visited England as a performer and lecturer in 1891, offering orations in the Mohawk language and making presentations to various learned societies, such as the Imperial Institute. Eventually he settled in London, continuing to perform but also writing to newspapers to draw attention to Mohawk loyalty to the British cause in various colonial wars and to the ongoing presence of and challenges faced by his nation.[12]

We can see these twentieth-century travelers as part of an unbroken tradition of Indigenous political journeying from Canada to the home of the Crown to pursue diplomatic relations. All the way back to Ojibwe activists like Gakiiwegwanabi in the 1830s and the Four Kings of 1710, Indigenous men —and sometimes women—had traveled to London as representatives of their nations, insisting on direct relationships between their peoples and the Crown and emphasizing the long history of Indigenous alliances and diplomacies. In this way, Canadian Indigenous leaders did not so much reclaim the city as they continued to claim it, in a pattern that had existed for more than three hundred years.

Those claims continue in the twenty-first century. Whereas Parliament and the Crown have, since the nineteenth century, consistently punted Indigenous affairs back to Canadian turf, thus abrogating the initial treaties, Indigenous leaders' efforts during the late 1970s and early 1980s did have an effect: the Canadian constitution of 1982 included explicit acknowledgment of Indigenous rights and title. What that has meant in practice, however, remains open to question and is the source of continued and contentious legal and political machinations, which almost always refer back to Britain's colonial entanglements with Indigenous nations.

In 2013, for example, a group led by the Federation of Saskatchewan Indian Nations came to London to commemorate an event that had happened two and a half centuries earlier. The Proclamation of 1763 had come at the end of the Seven Years' War, intended to bring an end to the violence that had marred so much of European expansion into Indigenous homelands by creating a line. Behind the line, settlers could live safe from Indigenous reprisals over the dispossession of land. Beyond the line, the Crown would have total authority over the expropriation of Indigenous lands. Over time, Crown officials claimed, the line would slowly move to the west in orderly stages, responding to colonial population pressures and the always present threat of conflict. All of this was an ideal rather than a reality. Independent settlers continued to cross the line. Others would demand it be moved and complain of the Crown's seeming complicity with "savages" and its apparent preference for Indigenous diplomacy over the needs of the "civilized" and Christian. The Proclamation of 1763, though a critical turning point in the history of North American relations among European colonial powers, and between Indigenous and European polities, solved very little and in many cases only added to the complexity and confusion that was settler colonialism.[13]

It has also remained, at least in the minds of settler officials and courts, the basis of Indigenous title in Canada. As such, it has been a prime target for the lobbying efforts of Indigenous activists, and the emissaries who arrived in the fall of 2013 drew attention to its importance through a series of commemorative events and lobbying efforts. Organized by the Federation of Indian Nations of Saskatchewan, the delegation had a full schedule that included a reception at the Canadian High Commission, a pipe ceremony at Guards Chapel in honor of Indigenous veterans who had taken up arms in defense of the Crown, and a viewing of archival documents associated with the Proclamation at the British Library. They also met up with representatives of Idle No More London, an activist group that expressed solidarity with the Indigenous grassroots movement of the same name that was then sweeping Canada.[14]

The Proclamation of 1763 commemoration journey also allowed its members to connect with their Indigenous predecessors through a walking tour based on the research that makes up this book. In the plaza at Horseguards, they heard of Eiakintomino's appearance in St. James's Park and about how attempts by British authorities to enlist Indigenous visitors in colonization schemes had rarely prevented violent conflicts between colonial powers and Indigenous nations. Earlier in the tour, they had stopped in Covent Garden to discuss the Four Kings and the Mohocks and to look at the house where Thomas Arne had written "Rule Britannia." They heard Samson Occom's words of dismay at the confusion of the city, stood on the porch of St. Martin-in-the-Fields to ponder the funerals of Kamehameha II and Kamāmalu while pearly kings and queens gathered on the street below, and faced the site of Durham House where Thomas Harriot and Manteo had devised the Ossomocomuck orthography. As one of the delegation members noted, learning about these earlier travelers—via one of the walking tours that appear in the appendix of this book—linked the 2013 delegation to a broader Indigenous history. "They're like our ancestors," she told me.

Meanwhile, in Canada, the United Nations rapporteur on Indigenous affairs was meeting with Indigenous leaders to assess the state of Canada–First Nations relations, and the Idle No More protests were being held across the country to remember and speak out against the ongoing colonialism that the Proclamation of 1763 represented. Canada's Conservative government, led by the right-wing prime minister Stephen Harper, had little to say on the anniversary. As for the group of travelers I met with, their journey to London and their appeals to British authority were in direct defiance of the Canadian government's own claimed sovereignty over Indigenous peoples and their mendacious claims of goodwill. As Perry Bellegarde of the Little Bear Reserve noted in a presentation at the University of London, "They don't like us being here." And "here" meant, ultimately, the city, the seat of imperial power. Such journeys of commemoration and ongoing activism affirmed deep connections between past and present, between the "center" and the "periphery," and between Indigenous peoples and London. And they spoke to the ongoing realities of colonialism.

In the late twentieth century, however, a new kind of commemoration altogether began to take place in the city. In these moments, the focus would be not on the relationship between Indigenous nations and the British Crown, but rather on the relationship between the living and the dead, and in particular, on those who did not return home.

Some sixty years after Anthony Fernando stood before Australia House in his coat covered with tiny skeletons, another Aboriginal man stood in the same place, protesting the same things. Born Harry Penwith among the Wurundjeri people, he had taken on his great-grandfather's name Burnum Burnum (Great Warrior), connecting his ancestral past to his activist future. By the 1980s, he was the most well known advocate for Aboriginal people in Australia, and in 1988, he brought his campaign to Britain. First, he landed at Dover, planting a flag and making a formal declaration calling for a *koompartoo* (a fresh start) between the two peoples. He promised that no British heads would be placed on display in museums, that no wells would be poisoned, and no sterilization programs enacted, that Europeans would be kept alive as ethnographic curiosities. Then he headed for London.[15]

Burnum Burnum became something of a minor celebrity during his time in the city. In addition to his appearances outside the Australian High Commission just off the Strand, he also performed at a concert at Lambeth Town Hall, quieting the unruly audience of punks and radicals with an account of his people and calls for peaceful resolution to profound atrocity. Perhaps most important, though, it was his visit to the outlying suburb of Eltham that not only captured the press's attention but sutured together his own life with that of one of his predecessors: Yemmerrawannie, the Eora man who had been brought to London in 1792 but who had died before he could return home. Alongside a parish priest, Burnum Burnum led a memorial ceremony for Yemmerrawannie that must have been the first time in nearly two centuries that anyone had acknowledged in any meaningful way the Aboriginal man's life and death. In doing so, Burnum Burnum expressed the shared experiences of Wurundjeri and Eora peoples with the realities of British colonialism and connected those experiences across time.[16]

Burnum Burnum's ceremony at St. John's in Eltham was not the only such event conducted by Aboriginal visitors in 1988. The same year that the Wurundjeri activist visited Yemmerrawannie, a group of Aboriginal cricket players attended a graveside service for Bripumyarrimin, the cricketer who had died while on tour in 1868. Led by John McGuire, the team members planted a gum tree and laid a wooden plaque. The original monument to Bripumyarrimin had been destroyed sometime in the late nineteenth century as Victoria Park Cemetery fell into disuse and became the haunt of "loafers" and "razor-boys." In the twentieth century, all the other monuments were removed and the cemetery was turned into Meath Gardens Park, a patch of green surrounded by council flats. Bripumyarrimin's grave became the only one still marked in the entire expanse, out of the half a million people said to be buried there.[17]

The plaque laid by McGuire and his teammates was itself eventually vandalized, but in 1996, another ceremony took place at the grave during which a more expensive and robust metal plaque was installed, reading

> In memory of King Cole, Aboriginal cricketer who died on the
>   24th June 1868
> Your Aboriginal dreamtime home. Wish you peace
> Nyuntu Anangu Tjukapa Wiltja Nga Palya Nga.

The grave of Bripumyarrimin in Meath Gardens Park, with a plaque commemorating him at the base of an Australian eucalyptus tree.

The ceremony was led by Aboriginal poet and longtime London resident Rikki Shields, who read a poem dedicated to Bripumyarrimin called "The Last Over."[18]

Five years later, yet another ceremony was held at Bripumyarrimin's grave. This time, the participants were a cricket team made up of Australian Aboriginal and Torres Strait Islander youths. Their manager, Grant Sarra, read out a statement that connected Bripumyarrimin's short life to the broader experiences of Aboriginal people in Australia. Sprinkling Australian soil around the gravesite, Sarra described the connections between Aboriginal people and their ancestral territories: "We come from the land and we go back to the land," he said. There, in the shadow of a gum tree, he and his compatriots engaged in an act of healing and reclaiming, in the hope that it would at last allow the long-dead cricketer to rest.[19]

A similar act of healing took place in 2006, this time created by the Mohegan people of Connecticut. In 1736, 270 years earlier, a Mohegan diplomat and sachem named Mahomet Weyonomon had traveled to London to present a petition to George II. Like Samson Occom thirty years later, Mahomet sought to protect his people's land base from constant encroachment by British settlers. Unlike Occom, however, Mahomet's journey was cut short; he died of smallpox before he could meet with the king, and he was buried at what is now Southwark Cathedral, known at the time as St. Saviour's. Thereafter, although he no doubt was at first mourned deeply among his people, over time the Mohegan lost track of his story, just as London seemed to forget that he had ever existed.[20]

Then, in the early twenty-first century, a group of researchers, including a Mohegan tribal member, uncovered a brief mention of Mahomet in *The Gentleman's Magazine*.[21] By bringing the find to the Mohegan tribal council, they set into motion a series of events that would eventually return Mahomet to the attention not just of the Mohegan people but of London more generally. Enlisting the skills of a British artist to carve a boulder from the Mohegan reservation into a monument for the lost traveler, Mohegan leaders made plans to travel to London to pay respect and conduct ritual on Mahomet's behalf. Then, just a few days before they left the United States for Britain, they received surprising news: through the dean of Southwark Cathedral, word of the impending ceremony had traveled to Buckingham Palace, and Queen Elizabeth now wanted to be involved. And so once again, Indigenous relations with the Crown would attract public attention in the metropolis.

Indeed, on their arrival, Mohegan tribal council president Mark Brown, council member and spiritual leader Bruce Two Dogs Bozsum, and tribal member Shane White Raven Long became, in the long-standing tradition of Indigenous travelers, celebrities. Their presence in the city drew the interest of the London media and the general public, who would turn out in the hundreds to observe the goings-on at the cathedral. While coverage of the event would traffic in stereotypical images of Native Americans—"Wigwam Ma'am," "Queen Buries Hatchet with a Host of the Mohegans," and "Me Big Chief Elizabeth" read some of the headlines, while most of the articles noted the "incongruous" and "unlikely" presence of Indigenous people in an urban

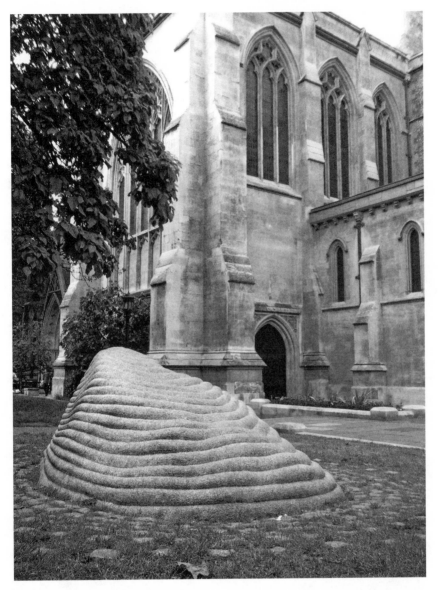

The monument to the Mohegan sachem Mahomet Weyonomon at Southwark Cathedral.

setting—the ritual itself would carry deep meaning for Brown, Bozsum, and Long.[22] In re-membering Mahomet—and London—the ceremony illustrated something tribal leaders had articulated soon after federal recognition: "We walk as a single spirit on the Trail of Life. We are guided by thirteen generations past and responsible to thirteen generations to come. We survive as a nation guided by the wisdom of our past. Our circular trail returns us to wholeness as a people. *Ni ya yo.*"[23]

Like the ceremonies for Yemmerrawannie and Bripumyarrimin, the rituals conducted at Southwark that November day in 2006 linked London's Indigenous past to an Indigenous present. Nothing symbolized this more than the moment at which Mark Brown presented Elizabeth II with a facsimile of Mahomet's original petition. And like travelers from what had become Canada, these Mohegan counterparts asserted a historic relationship with the Crown, even if such diplomacies were entirely symbolic in the United States legal context. This symbolism mattered: a people who had long fought simply to exist in their homeland had not only survived but linked their present to a much deeper past in the city where Mahomet had died all those years before.

Such ceremonies, if infrequent, highlight the ways in which London is still relevant to at least some Indigenous peoples. Like the memory of travelers who were lost for a time—in some cases for centuries—the historical relationship between the city and its Indigenous past could be recalled and reclaimed by descendant communities. The city, its very landscape a palimpsest, holds within it the possibility of a usable past for the Indigenous peoples whose long relationship with the center of imperial power continues to resonate into the present.

Yet another such resonance was crafted in 2013, deep in the heart of the Old City. In the twenty-first century, the cemetery at St. Olave Hart Street is but a shadow of its former self. Once within sight of the Tower but now obscured and closed in by office blocks, the church was founded sometime in the thirteenth century and was one of the few in the city to survive the Great Fire. In the nineteenth century, it became Charles Dickens's "St. Ghastly Grim," named so for the grinning skulls that sit atop the archway leading from Seething Lane into its churchyard, through a spiked iron gate "like a jail," to Dickens's thinking. Between 1563 and 1853, when city churches were closed to new burials, more than eleven thousand people were interred in the grounds of St. Olave's. It is unclear what happened to all those bodies, although the "bone hole," or charnel house, in the crypt below the church no doubt held many of them for a time before they were buried elsewhere.

Somewhere amid all of this lay two Inuit. The first was the unnamed inuk, captured by Martin Frobisher in 1576, who "bit his tong in twayne within his mouth" before dying. The second was a baby captured a year later. In 1577, on his second voyage, Frobisher was happy to report, "I have aboord . . . a Man, a Woman, and a Childe, which am contented to deliver for you." Although the two adults would be "of use for the possession of language," probably as translators—they quickly learned the English phrases "God geve you good marroe" and "farewel"—the baby was the true prize. Given the name Nutaaq (an Anglicization of the word *nutaraq*, "baby," in Inuktitut), the boy, who had been injured in the capture, was the first North American child brought to Britain. When his mother and the man died almost immediately on arrival in Bristol, Nutaaq was given a nurse and rushed to London, where he was put on display at an inn called the Three Swans. He died eight days later, before Queen Elizabeth could see him. The Cathay Company, which had in part funded Frobisher's expeditions, paid for the cost of burial at St. Olave's. His name, however, like that of the inuk buried the year before, does not appear in church registers.[24]

Almost three hundred years later, in 1850, the anthropologist and explorer C. F. Hall developed a standardized survey with thirty-six questions that he gave to Inuit he encountered during his journeys in the far north of what would soon be known as Canada. Question eight read, "Did some ships a great many years ago, come into Tu-nuk-jok-ping-oo-sy-ong and carry away some Innuits?" The response, he found, was always this: "Never heard of it." Even though some respondents had been abroad themselves, none of them seemed to know—or want to talk about—the Inuit who were taken away in centuries past.[25]

There are other kinds of remembering, though—of speaking new stories into the silence of the colonialism of forgetting through shared Indigenous experience. To honor the boy Nutaaq, a ceremony took place 436 years after his burial. Peter Morin, a Tahltan artist from northern British Columbia, had spent parts of the summer and fall of 2013 engaging sites of colonial and Indigenous history in the city through what he called "cultural graffiti." He lay down on the ground in front of Buckingham Palace in his regalia, singing into the earth. He placed a button blanket over the statue of Columbus in Belgrave Square, retiring him. He wept at the burial place of Pocahontas in Gravesend. He spoke back to the statue of Victoria at Royal

Holloway University. Of his work more generally, he writes about the ways in which the ritual of performance engages with place: "The Art is Ceremony. In cities, in towns, in villages in hearts. The Art is a method to engage with our breath."[26] Of the interventions in London specifically, Morin said,

> my body became a very interesting site while i was living and eating and breathing on the land over there. this impact site also became a portal for time travel. dreams inform my practice. i understand the dreams to be connection to ancestral knowledge and ancestors. an active force in our lives. i started having these dreams about falling deep into this land. looking for the ancient beings of that land. i also, at times, felt that my body was walking/wading through blood . . . deep deep blood.

Morin's account of his "cultural graffiti" speaks to the ongoing violences of settler colonialism in Canada and around the world, and the ways in which that colonialism emanated from the London landscape. "The graffiti act," he went on to say, "also became a way to speak back to the powers that define london and british north america. it was also a way for me to transfer tahltan nation ways of being into the infrastructure of the colonial machines. the graffiti act is a way to promote sabotage."[27]

Eventually, Morin turned his attention to Nutaaq. After a conversation we had about my research for this book, we developed a plan: I would tell the boy's story to a group of fellow activists, artists, and researchers, and Peter would lead a healing ceremony to bring some peace to the baby's spirit. The day before the planned ceremony, which would take place ironically on Halloween—when there is a thin place between the worlds of the living and the dead—Morin visited the verger of St. Olave's to let him know about what would happen. The verger's response was shocking. There would be no drumming or singing on church premises. No smudging. No speaking out loud. In fact, any ceremony that would be done would be done "in your head," silently. The reasoning: "We're in England now." Morin would later write that the encounter with the verger connected that moment in London to a much longer history of imperialism: "What stayed with me was his admonition—that i could perform any ceremony or song silently inside my head. my body felt this moment as a very colonizing moment. that i was being taken back in time to the first conversations between these 'preachers' and indigenous bodies and how they produced converts to this religion. sit silently in our pray house and your body can become ours."[28]

The next day, Peter and I were joined by five or six others, some Indigenous, some not. The restrictions laid out by the verger were very much on our minds. The ceremony we did do was a private matter that I will not describe here. Suffice it to say that we did speak to Nutaaq and some of us wept for him. And we did leave traces behind in the church. Perhaps the verger will find them someday.

Nutaaq might have been our focus that October day, but there was someone else on my mind the entire time we were there: Samuel Pepys. Diarist extraordinaire, one of the key witnesses to the Great Fire, and man of great perspicacity and myopia, Pepys is one of those people about whom we know almost everything. We know the intricacies of his political machinations. We know the quotidian urban landscapes through which he moved. And we know the minutiae of his everyday personal life: meals eaten, arguments with his wife, dalliances with the help. Buried 126 years after Nutaaq, Pepys is the historian's dream, and the difference in archival weight between these two individuals is the truth of colonialism. In a place described by one source as "a church living in the present with a past that is alive" and "a shrine of personality no Englishman can ignore," the cemetery in Hart Street is a site in which the past and present are deeply enmeshed with each other.[29] It is one of the many domains of entanglement in the city, where networks of knowledge, disorder, reason, protocol, discipline, and memory link London to Indigenous territories and back again. And lastly, it is a site where the colonial authority of the metropolis is asserted, even in the "postcolonial" age. *"We're in England now."*

At the same time, the stories of Burnum Burnum and Yemmerrawannie, the ceremony at the grave of Bripumyarrimin, the events at Southwark Cathedral, and Peter Morin's intervention at St. Olave Hart Street limn a pattern that challenges colonial authority. Together, they tell a story of survivance: of Indigenous survival and resistance into the present, of the deep connections between past and present—and between diverse Indigenous peoples who share the experience of colonization—that can stretch across centuries. "London can see the dead, and holds them close," literary critic A. A. Gill has written, but through remembering and reclaiming, Indigenous people hold these particular dead even closer.[30]

But there is another way to claim Indigenous London: not to remember the dead, but to create living community in the city. It is to that kind of story that we now turn.

In 1872, the French artist Gustave Doré made his London known. He had recently completed a tour of the city, and the resulting chiaroscuro images of railway arches and smokestacks and the urban poor remain iconic, nineteenth-century counterparts to the works of Hogarth, documenting the moral landscape of the metropolis. One of these pieces in particular tells a story of Indigenous London—or at least purports to. *The New Zealander* is an exercise in contrasts, not just between black and white but between the "civilized" and the "savage." In it, a robed figure sits in the foreground, surveying a city that has fallen into shambles. The figure is, putatively at least, a Māori; in the 1870s, "New Zealander" would have referred to an Indigenous person, not a Pākehā settler. So the story of *The New Zealander* is clear: by the time a Māori person finally arrived in London, the city would be in ruins. Though an inversion of the usual story—here, Indigeneity supplants urbanity, rather than the reverse—the overall narrative remains the same: urban and Indigenous realities cannot coexist, and must be mutually exclusive, linked to each other only in one's inevitable destruction.[31]

The problem with *The New Zealander,* of course, is that it is a lie. By 1872, Māori people had been coming to London for more than six decades, all the way back to Mahanga's visit in 1805. In the intervening years, many others had come as well: Maui, Hongi Hika, Nahiti, and others. Doré's work, then, is perhaps best understood as an illustration of the power of stories over the realities of lived experience: no matter how many Māori had come to London, and no matter how great their celebrity, the narrative utility and legibility of "the New Zealander" outweighed any actual accounts of Indigenous travelers; the metaphorical "native" was simply more compelling to Doré and his audience than any real one at the heart of empire.

The longer history of Māori journeys to London, however, challenges this story. Not too many years after its publication, for example, the

The New Zealander by Gustave Doré, 1872. ()

Waikato leader Tāwhiao would come to the city to attempt a meeting with the Crown—just like his Canadian counterparts. Meanwhile, Māori performers continued to visit London; in an echo of the "Māori Warrior Chiefs" of 1863, another troupe of men and women brought their haka to Britain in 1911 under the leadership of Makareti Papakura, a young Ngāti Tuhourangi entrepreneur and performer. Not long after, Māori soldiers on their way to (and, if they were lucky, returning from) the trenches of the First World War would pass through the city.[32] But there is an even more direct challenge to *The New Zealander:* the development of London's modern Māori community.

This other story begins in Putney. There, just before Christmas 1957, a young Ngāi Tai woman named Esther Rātā Kerr settled in after a four-week boat trip from New Zealand. She had come to join her sister, both of them drawn by letters from British relatives and the excitement and opportunity of the metropole. Before long, Esther's flat in Putney became much more than a New Zealand expatriate's home, however: it became the center of a nascent community of Māori people and their friends and allies. "It wasn't well into the new year that the phone started ringing," Kerr—now Esther Jessop—recalled in 2014. " 'Oh yes, oh yes, come over, come over.' And we decided that Tuesday night was a good night to meet. Saying to people, 'Look, just anybody, you meet anybody, it doesn't matter where they're from, if they're interested in Māori culture, bring them along.' And so before we knew it, we just had a flat full of people!" And the name for this flat, unofficially at least, was "Putney Pā." Pā is the name for the great stone hill forts that dotted the landscape of New Zealand, and it easily translated into the name for a gathering place in the great stone city.[33]

Finding other Māori in London was not easy in the 1950s and 1960s. "You'd be in Piccadilly, for instance," Jessop recalled, "and you'd see someone and you'd think, 'Are they Māori?' We used to walk by and say 'Kia ora!' and if they answered, 'Wow!' and if they didn't, 'Oh, must be Italian or Spanish.' So you met very, very few, if any, Māori at the time." But they did meet others, from opera singers and other performers to World War II veterans who had married Londoners and settled there. New Zealand House, the official face of the country in London, was particularly important to this nascent community of Indigenous expats, and it was there in the late 1960s that an organization was founded and a name was coined: Ngāti Ranana—literally, "the tribe of London." "We were a family, we were a *whānau*, where people could find brothers and sisters and the older ones, moms and dads, and children and little babies. So this whānau feeling happened right from the beginning, and today the *whanaungatanga* is very important to us. *Manaaki-tanga,* where we look out for one another, watch out for one another, and the *kōtahitanga*, 'togetherness.' Those are our three feelings which we just keep going."[34]

Over time, Ngāti Ranana and the larger Māori community of London created new traditions. One site for those traditions lay to the south of the city, in Surrey. There, in the gardens of a stately home named Clandon Park, a traditional Māori meetinghouse had stood since the 1890s, when it—or rather, she—was bought by New Zealand Governor William Onslow near Lake Tarawera. Over time, the ancestral structure, named Hinemihi, fell into disuse, save as an exotic ornament, but beginning in the 1980s, she was revived and reconnected to Māori people living in both Britain and New Zealand. Restored and unveiled in 1995, Hinemihi now sees annual Māori cultural celebrations and often draws more attention from tourists than Clandon Park itself.[35]

In 2007, Karl Burrows described the place that both Ngāti Ranana and Hinemihi played in his and his family's sense of themselves as Māori people in London. "When we first came to the United Kingdom," he wrote, "it was not a priority for us to be involved in Māori kaupapa . . . as this was something we could do at home at any time. However, it wasn't long before we came to Ngāti Ranana . . . to seek Māori companionship and sing again the songs of home. Not long after that, we were standing before Hinimehi." While Hinemihi's presence at Clandon Park can inspire sadness— "Hinemihi is lonely, longing for the voices and warmth of her descendants, her people," says Burrows—she nonetheless plays a crucial role for Māori in the metropole. "With people staying longer and settling in London, and my feeling the need to find more meaningful ways to express themselves, in what is quite a soul-less city . . . [i]t is where the community gathers for meetings, funerals, weddings, family reunions, and celebrations. . . . [O]ur words do not simply bounce off concrete walls but are absorbed, given meaning, and given body through Hinemihi's presence."[36]

Like Maui, Nahiti, and the others who came before her, Hinemihi is a traveler. She is also a *taonga,* a sacred being, who herself carries stories of movement and power. But she is not the only taonga in London, and local Māori relationships with her are mirrored by something else: the relationship with Māori objects to be found in institutions such as the British Museum. For young Māori Londoners, many of them in Britain for a two-year work experience, encountering taonga in the spaces of the city—feathered cloaks and more, the same sorts of things brought with, for example, the Māori visitors of 1863—is an opportunity for them not only to connect with home but to craft a Māori identity through connection to ancestral pasts. Māori youth in London are able to claim their heritage in, of all places, an institution that has all too often presented taonga as simply things extracted from cultures doomed to extinction. Efforts such as these, in the capital of the former empire, mirror processes that have taken place back home in Aotearoa since the 1970s, as the younger generations of Māori people became radicalized in response to urbanization and social dislocation. As Conal McCarthy has argued, relations with taonga were part of this, and "should not be interpreted as simply nostalgia for the past but a claim for the future." Māori scholar Amiria Henare, meanwhile, describes taonga as active agents in creating social relationships through time, suggesting yet another way that London is bound up in Indigenous realities through active processes of remembering and reclaiming.[37]

Instead of *The New Zealander,* then, another image might serve as a symbol of Māori London. In the 1990s, Māori artist John Bevan Ford was asked to mark the opening of a new Māori exhibition at the British Museum by creating a new work. The resulting piece is a powerful commentary on the place of institutions such as the British Museum in the history of the Māori peoples. But *Te Hono ki Ranana* (*The Connection with London*) is not only a recounting of cultural loss and the disappearance of taonga from their home territories; rather, it is a statement of reclaiming. In it, a woven Māori cloak, a *kaitaka,* hangs in the sky over a London skyline that includes the British Museum. The kaitaka is like one of London's low skies, but instead of scudding across the city, it embraces and enfolds it, making it Māori. *Te Hono ki Ranana* is a kind of repatriation.[38]

Other memories exist of Indigenous travelers to London. On a reserve in Ontario, Christian Mohawks worship using a silver service sent by Queen Anne following the return of the Four Kings in 1710.[39] In an oak-shaded square in the old town of Savannah, Georgia, a small monument marks the grave of Tomochichi, the Yamacraw mico whose 1734 journey to London remains an important part of the southern city's colorful history.[40] On the

John Bevan Ford's pigment ink print of *Te Hono ki Ranana* (*The Connection with London*), created in 1991. (© The Trustees of the British Museum, all rights reserved)

remote border between Québec and Labrador, the provincial government has named one of the high peaks Mount Caubvick after Qavvik, the lone survivor of the Inuit family who traveled to London in 1772.[41] Bennelong, who came to London in 1792 with his Eora kinsman Yemmerrawannie, is a central figure of the earliest chapter of Sydney's story, thanks in no small part to the exceptional nature of his journey.[42] In Hawai'i, meanwhile, remembrances of Kānaka Maoli royals' nineteenth-century sojourns in London inform a modern sovereignty movement that rejects the ongoing U.S. occupation of the islands.[43] And among the Cherokee, the famous delegation in 1762 that included Utsidihi inspired a commemorative journey by tribal members in 2012, resulting in the piece *London Calling 1762* by America Meredith—an image that locates Indigenous presence in an iconic St. John's Wood zebra crossing.

And then there is Pocahontas. Although a recent exhibition at the National Portrait Gallery included eighteenth-century two-time Mohawk

visitor Thayendanagea, the Four Kings, and Bennelong and Yemmerrawannie in its treatment of foreign travelers to Britain, it is really only the
seventeenth-century Powhatan noblewoman who has maintained anything
like a public presence in London's urban imagination.[44]

In 1851, for example, a publishing company took over the Bell Savage
Inn, where Rebecca Rolfe had famously stayed in the early seventeenth century. Her memory lived on in that place; John Cassell and his partners took
her as their colophon, her image appearing as an imprint in each of their
volumes. A century later, the company erected a statue of Pocahontas by
David McFall on a plinth in its new Red Lion Square location, her reclining
nude bronze body, tiger lily in hand and feather in her hair, recalling the
Powhatan visitor. When the company moved again in the 1980s, the statue
found a home in the firm's lobby, where tourists—particularly Americans—
continued to seek audience with her until she was sold to a private buyer in
1996, the year after the release of Disney's blockbuster *Pocahontas*.[45]

Indeed, the "native of the capital," as one 1995 article referred to her,
had reappeared now and again in the London press throughout the twentieth
century. In 1932, for example, local antiquarians embarked on a search for
her remains at St. John the Evangelist in Waterloo, where a dingy silver casket was said to contain the body of an "American Indian Princess" who had
originally been laid to rest in Gravesend. While the search in Waterloo was
fruitless, it nonetheless spoke to her continued place in London's imagination.[46] In the early 1960s, a musical comedy called *Pocahontas* enjoyed twelve
performances at the Lyric Theatre but suffered from negative reviews, including one noting that any historical veracity had been lost to the formulaic,
hackneyed conventions of pantomime. But audiences had obviously showed
up for something. Four decades later, the successful American author Patricia Cornwell announced plans to fund a new stained-glass window at
St. Sepulchre-without-Newgate—the church where the famed Virginia colonist John Smith is buried—that would feature Pocahontas. Despite meetings
with the Lord Mayor, the American ambassador, and the vicar of St. Sepul-
chre, the window never materialized, much to the chagrin of at least some
observers. Meanwhile, at the Museum of London, Pocahontas is represented
by a cigar-store Indian, and the museum famously showed earrings thought
to have belonged to her during an exhibition in 2005, while at its sister insti-

tution, the Museum in Docklands, one of the children's activity rooms in the basement is named the Pocahontas Room.[47]

This is an ephemeral presence, to be sure, but a presence nonetheless: from personal ads placed by a woman claiming to be a "Pocahontas look-alike" to an off-the-beaten-track guide to London that points explorers toward Blackwall Stairs "from which Pocahontas once sailed," the Algonquian noblewoman and diplomat remains a touchstone, if only a minor and occasional one, for London's encounter with the wider world. In one sense, then, the "native of the capital" belongs in London, her presence emerging out of London's entanglement with empire. As one writer in the *Evening Standard* put it, "She was one of many who moved here because of colonialism: 'We are here because you were there.'"[48]

It would be tempting—and indeed, expected—to then seamlessly incorporate Pocahontas into London's present-day multicultural identity, so rich with diaspora and diversity. Numerous scholars of British history have noted how, in the postwar period, Britain shifted its emphasis from empire to commonwealth, concomitant with an imagined progressive, liberal, and multiethnic self-image that masked and overwrote the sins of the colonial past. "Britain and the Commonwealth," Jodi Burkett has written, "needed to be clearly divorced from empire and its connotations of despotism, inequality, and violence. Constructing postimperial Britain required a level of distancing of amnesia about Britain's imperial past." This process had ramifications for London as well, particularly as the central city was largely emptied of a resident population and the urban landscape transformed into one of global capital and heritage tourism. According to John Eade:

> Within the global city . . . selling an image of place and people to outsiders becomes ever more crucial. . . . Powerful attempts are made to relegate the dominations of empire to the dustbin of history as the national capital becomes a provider of services to insiders and outsiders. The multicultural diversity of this imagined community establishes London's credentials as a tolerant melting pot where overseas tourists, investors, and professionals are welcome.

The result is a city that absolves itself of its imperial past through a vision of multicultural urbanity. Pocahontas—along with Epenow, Adgalgala, Nahiti,

Jungunjinanuke, and all the others—might easily be enlisted in this project, ticking a box on London's ethnic and racial checklist.[49]

There is something more complicated going on in Pocahontas's case, however, that speaks to how Indigenous peoples are all too often characterized in relation to urban places. At the same time that she has been incorporated into the city's story, she has also been "ghosted": transformed into a spectral presence that haunts London. This is not unusual; the process of turning Indigenous people into freighted specters of a vanished past has been a central project of place-making in settler societies, in which such accounts—for example, the mythic "Indian burial ground" as a site of paranormal activity and unsettling anxiety—serve as ways for settler populations to create vernacular languages of belonging. In telling stories of Indigenous ghosts, settlers claim territory as their own. This is particularly true in cities, where the imagined antonymy of Indigeneity and urbanity leaves little room for living Indigenous presence. Like those that estrange urban and Indigenous histories from each other, such narratives of extinction—or "lastings," as Ojibwe scholar Jean M. O'Brien calls them—serve to relegate Indigenous people to a disappeared past and to a position of only victimhood, except perhaps as revenants who unsettle and haunt the colonial imagination.[50]

In London, Pocahontas can also appear as a ghost, either figuratively or, in the case of psychogeographer Iain Sinclair's work, literally. When one of the characters in Sinclair's book *Downriver* finds himself drowning off the banks of the Thames not far from the city, Sinclair writes that all would be washed away "except the Indian woman. She was always there. Walking across the water towards him, daintily stepping from wave crest to wave crest . . . throat hidden in a ruff of sea-bone collar." As in so many other places, Indigenous ghosts serve the imaginer's ends; nowhere in Sinclair's imagining (or in her other urban representations) is there space for Powhatan survivance or collectivity in the form of Uttamattomakin and the other Powhatan travelers who accompanied her in 1616. Instead, in Sinclair's telling, her story is a pathetic one, and, oddly, one in which she did not even want to return to Tsenacomoco. Sinclair writes that she "could never be readmitted to the society of the forest. She was crossed, baptized in holy water. She was another." If the "plague dish" of the city had doomed her, so too does Sinclair's notion of the irretrievable Indigenous, lost to "civilization."

Disconnected from her own people's larger story and from the histories of other Indigenous travelers to London, the young Powhatan visitor becomes an isolated figure of tragedy, a singular and anomalous presence in the urban landscape. Pocahontas is a lonely ghost.[51]

Then again, things could be worse. In Disney's 1998 straight-to-video sequel *Pocahontas II: Journey to a New World,* the topic of her death is avoided altogether. Instead, after escaping imprisonment in the Tower, Pocahontas returns to Tsenacomoco with John Rolfe, literally sailing into the sunset to a swelling love song. This contrasts starkly with Terrence Malick's 2005 film *The New World,* which, despite its insistence on a romance between John Smith and the young Algonquian noblewoman, made an honest effort to capture the trauma of her death in England, crafting an evocative and elegiac twenty minutes that is the only meaningful filmic treatment—at least for now—of an Indigenous visitation to London.

Certainly, some London accounts of Pocahontas get the basic facts of her story right. A cycle of seven short poems published in 2007, for example, captures and rehearses the basic and well-known outlines of her life—the girl cartwheeling at Jamestown, the young woman burdened with crowds at the Bell Savage Inn, the cool observer of the Twelfth Night masque, and the young, dying mother at Gravesend.[52] But almost to a one, London's Pocahontas stories locate her firmly in a past that is vanished, at the same that she is emblematic of a multicultural genealogy for the city's modern realities and its imperial memory. Ephemeral as they are, they tell powerful stories about Indigenous peoples as noble foils to urban life and doomed savages within the implacable reach of empire: statues on plinths, bad plays, unhung windows, cigar-store Indians, ghosts.

For the descendants of the Powhatan people and for other Indigenous communities, however, Pocahontas's London history can have entirely different valences. In 2006, for example, delegations from nine Virginia Indian tribes—the Chickahominy, the Eastern Chickahominy, the Mattaponi, the Upper Mattaponi, the Monacan, the Nansemond, the Pamunkey, and the Rappahannock—traveled to England to commemorate the delegation of 1616 and its most famous member.[53] According to one statement from the allied tribes, the journey symbolized "the completion of the circle that began almost 400 years ago. . . . We will all come full circle with a new passion for our futures and new commitment to work together for the betterment of both our nations and our people." The high point of the tour was a pow-wow attended by thousands at Gravesend, and other stops included a visit to the Houses of Parliament and meetings with the Speaker of the House of Commons and the minister for Culture, Media & Sport. At these and other events, the tribes' leaders focused on a 1677 treaty, between their peoples and the Crown, that assured ongoing government-to-government relations and on the fact that none of the tribes enjoyed federal recognition—which meant that, in the eyes of the United States, none of them were Indigenous. Like so many travelers before and since, for the visitors from Virginia, a trip to London was more than sightseeing or semantics: it was a direct engagement with the protocols of the past and with the politics of the present.[54]

As in other Indigenous communities, stories held by the literal and fig-urative descendants of Pocahontas carried meanings that bore little resem-blance to those told by Londoners. Instead of antiquarian curiosity, facile multiculturalism, or spectral pathos, Indigenous accounts of Pocahontas's journey to London offer radically different views of what her life meant and represented—indeed, of what even happened. As Mattaponi historians Linwood "Little Bear" Custalow and Angela "Silver Star" Daniel describe in their book of tribal history, it is widely believed among Virginia Indians that Pocahontas was murdered by poisoning while in London, with the goal of preventing her from reporting back on what she had seen there. They argue that this claim goes all the way back to Uttamattomakin and his stri-dent critiques of English society. Meanwhile, Laguna Pueblo scholar Paula Gunn Allen claimed Pocahontas as an ancestor of sorts in her feminist and Indigenist revisioning of the Algonquian woman's life, arguing that she was a spiritual leader whose transatlantic journey not only changed the lives of those around her but also initiated a new epoch in world history. Both of these Indigenous versions of Pocahontas's story stand in stark contrast to those told by Londoners, in which Pocahontas features as a romantic, curious, and doomed footnote in the long history of the city's encounter with the larger world and its diversity. Instead, these accounts identify London as contested space in which an Indigenous woman, grounded in her community and na-tion and perhaps even threatening in her intelligence and power, was a vital agent in the making of the modern world.[55]

Instead of a facile, pleasing London in which Indigenous people appear as symbols of a vanished past or as footnotes in the inevitable march of
progress toward a multicultural city, we might imagine Pocahontas histories
and the stories of other Indigenous travelers as open-ended, and the urban
spaces of London as continually contested. The arrival of the multicultural
metropolis did not end empire; rather, it grew out of it and continues to be
implicated in the very structures of power, stretching far from the Thames,
and far back in history, which built it in the first place. This is certainly the
lesson of other "subaltern" histories of the city: Asian, black, and other
Londons continue to speak back to the capital of the empire and its all-too-
easy self-congratulatory stories of tolerance and diversity. If the city can in
fact encompass everything, then it must enfold its own colonial past and its
legacies.

The space between the ghosted Pocahontas and the ancestral Pocahontas is the space between metaphor and memory, between symbolic "savages"
and the real experiences of Indigenous people, both in their homelands and
during their travels to London. Memory, embodied through insistence on
political relationships with the Crown, through attention to the Indigenous
dead of London, and through the creation of diasporic communities, is one
of the grounds of this lived experience. Like knowledge, disorder, reason,
ritual, and discipline, the question of memory challenges the estrangement
of Indigenous and urban histories, bringing them together at a global scale.
The stories of men, women, and children who traveled, willingly or otherwise, from territories that became Canada, the United States, New Zealand,
and Australia capture this reality, challenging the notion that London has
no empire, has nothing to do with empire, and that that empire, if it ever
existed, is now past. Indigenous London remains.

Epilogue

The Other Indigenous London

In the 1860s, Hampstead was a retreat from the bustle and cacophony of the heart of Victorian London. As much a village as an urban neighborhood, Hampstead had just become more accessible to the masses thanks to the new North London Railway, which brought thousands of urban residents to the area and its green spaces. The poet James Thomson was one of those visitors; a melancholic Scotsman, he had lived in London for some time, and like so many others he found the city trying. His most famous poem, "The City of Dreadful Night," would be an elegiac jeremiad against the "dolorous mysteries" and "charnel air" of London. For Thomson, it was a city haunted by its past:

> Some say that phantoms haunt those shadowy streets,
> And mingle freely there with sparse mankind;
> And tell of ancient woes and black defeats,
> And murmur mysteries in the grave enshrined.

All good things, he continued, "have been strangled by that City's curse."[1]

Hampstead was a balm to all of this misery. In fact, Thomson would be inspired by a visit to the suburb to write a paean to the salubriousness of the village. A Sunday afternoon on the heath could, however, inspire thoughts of things other than simple pastoral virtues. Thomson's "idle idyll" with his friends also spurred his mind to wander ten thousand years into London's history:

> This place where we are sitting was a wood,
> Savage and desert save for one rude home
> Of wattles plastered with stiff clay and loam;
> And here, in front, upon the grassy mire
> Four naked squaws were squatted round a fire.

Soon, the "squaws" were joined by "sullenly ravenous" "braves" dressed in "war-paint," who fell upon the half-cooked meat that roasted over the fire. As Thomson shared his vision with his fellow park-goers, hearkening back even further to a mythical world or ancient seas and mysterious mermaids, one of them cried out, " 'Mermaids are beautiful enough, but law! / Think of becoming a poor naked squaw!' " Such a flight of fancy, begun on a leisurely afternoon in one of London's most beautiful precincts, could carry its own frisson of danger as well as darkness that competed with that of the great city itself.[2]

Thirty years later, Rudyard Kipling penned a similar bit of imaginary time travel. His 1895 poem "In the Neolithic Age" imagined a "dim, red Dawn of Man" across ancient Europe, in which the ancestors of the modern British worshiped strange "totems" and engaged in "savage warfare" using "tomahawks" to scalp their enemies. In 1911, he picked up again on these themes, describing in "The River's Tale" the primitive life of the "earliest Cockney" who with "paint on his face and club in his hand . . . was death to feather and fin and fur." Kipling continues by tracking the ecological depredations of this antediluvian hunter:

> He trapped my beavers at Westminster.
> He netted my salmon, he hunted my deer,
> He killed my heron off Lambeth Pier.

In his work, Kipling also saw the deep past as having connections to the urban present:

> Still a cultured Christian age sees us scuffle, squeak, and rage,
> Still we pinch and slap and jabber, scratch and dirk;

Still we let our business slide—as we dropped the half-dressed hide—
To show a fellow-savage how to work.

Deeply ironic, Kipling's verses illustrated the ways in which the British experience of empire—expressed in the use of the Powhatan term *tamahaac*
(tomahawk), the Ojibwe word *doodem* (totem), and the iconic imagery of
scalping—was also bound up in the experience of urban modernity. One
helped make sense out of the other; the seeming opposition of the urban and
the Indigenous was in fact a commingling and imbrication.[3] For both Kipling
and Thomson, the entanglement of London with faraway Indigenous territories shaped their sense of the city's distant past.

More than a century later, I walked into the Museum of London as part of
my first research foray for this book. After the chaos of the entry hall, flanked by
the café and gift shop, the first space the visitor enters is a gallery named "London
Before London," and it was here that I encountered a very different kind of history than the one with which this book is primarily concerned. Here, I came up
against a vision of the city's own indigenous past that could not have been more
different from those of Thomson and Kipling. Instead of a dehumanizing vision
inspired by the racisms of the past, it was a vision of indigenous humanity.

The first thing I noticed was the light. It almost seemed as though day-
light itself was streaming into the gallery, although that was of course impossible. And there was sound: I may be wrong, but I remember wind, water,
and even birdsong. The light and sound flooded a gallery rich with artifacts
of London's deep past. A massive aurochs skull greeted me at the entrance,
surrounded by other remains of long-extinct wildlife and dozens of skillfully
made stone spear points. An oaken idol stood mute and mysterious in a glass
case, while tools of stone and bone spoke to domestic pursuits.

But perhaps the most striking thing about "London Before London"
was the text on the walls. Here, writers-in-residence hired by the museum
had tried to give voice to the prehistoric people of London. Bernardine
Evaristo, for example, imagined her body floating "above a London of
birch / and pine forest of open grassland" where elephants and hippopotami
roamed the marshes of Trafalgar Square and Pall Mall, as she gazed long-
ingly "on sheets of marigold, meadowsweet, mint." She imagined the arrival
of the first people: "Welcome home. Welcome / first citizen" to a campfire

along the Thames, she wrote. Michael Rosen, meanwhile, interpolated his modern urban reality into an imagining of ancient river sacrifices:

> Oh Great River accept as a token of my power and strength this old envelope on which I write notes for poems which I hope that one day I will put in a book . . . [;] if that isn't good enough for you Oh River then take this frying pan and this eggy bread that so well pleases my children.

Other statements on the walls of the gallery similarly speak to the intellectual and spiritual lives—to the humanity—of those who peopled the distant landscapes of the prehistoric Thames Valley: "Then the great spirits came. They breathed on the ice and made camps across its surface." "People's lives were shaped by kinship, ancestry, and shared values." "We had ridden far to reach the shrine." "The land was rich in meanings and memories for those to whom it was home." Unlike the sardonic savagery of Thomson and Kipling, these evocations of distant time say, essentially, that "they" were not unlike "us."[4]

My first thought upon viewing "London Before London" was that it reminded me of the many museums that have been established by Indigenous communities and nations in the past half century, in which Indigenous people have taken charge of the public interpretation of their lived history and culture, presenting themselves not as static denizens of a distant past, but as active, dynamic participants in survivance. Out of this impression, I developed a theory. Beginning in the latter part of the twentieth century, Indigenous and other colonized peoples around the world have spoken back to museums and to the practitioners of anthropology and archaeology, demanding a different kind of story, one in which they appear as fully human. This demand has led to a revolution in everything from fieldwork protocols to exhibit design, from institutions like the National Museum of the American Indian in Washington, D.C., and the Te Papa Museum in Wellington, New Zealand, to the Bishop Museum in Honolulu and even, to some extent, the British Museum. In these places, Indigenous people have asserted their full humanity and insisted upon connections between the past and the present, between ancestors and descendants.

My theory, then, was that this new kind of Indigenous story had percolated its way back to the center of empire, transforming the way Londoners told stories about their own indigenous ancestors. And it turned out that I was correct. When I asked curator Jonathan Cotton about this very point, he admitted that one of the books that had influenced his thinking while developing the exhibit was Dee Brown's classic and game-changing work of revisionist Native American history, *Bury My Heart at Wounded Knee*. For this one Londoner, at least, the lessons of Indigenous history were applicable to London's own indigenous past. As he told me, "we wanted to show that these were people, not peoples."[5]

Nothing symbolizes this more than an object at the center of "London Before London." It is a human head, modeled in red clay and gazing straight into the eyes of all who come across it. This is Shepperton Woman, an ancestor found in a grave in far western London and dating back some five thousand years. Painstakingly based on her skeletal remains, her reconstructed face demands attention. Shepperton Woman, despite how little we can know of her life, is an opportunity to look history in the face, and perhaps for that history, in a way, to look back.

London's deep past had not always been told this way. Indeed, "London Before London" includes among its artifacts evidence of an older kind of story akin to those of Thomson and Kipling. Set into the wall at the far end of the exhibit space is a small diorama, dimly lit behind glass. It shows an ancient settlement that had been unearthed during the construction of a runway at Heathrow Airport. Unlike Shepperton Woman, the lone human figure in the diorama is faceless, and every few seconds, the entire scene fades and is replaced by a jumbo jet parked on the tarmac, ready for departure to who knows where. The urban, global future overwrites the ancient past, ghosting it into ephemerality. Formerly "squatting in a corridor," according to curator Cotton, the diorama remains evidence of an older, and subtly dehumanizing, way of interpreting London's early history.

Similarly, a nearby display of stone tools includes a copy of Worthington G. Smith's *Man the Primeval Savage* from 1894, a text that detailed discoveries of prehistoric artifacts across London and its surrounding countryside: a Paleolithic floor in Stoke Newington, for example, or quartzite implements pulled from the gravels of Edmonton. *Man the Primeval Savage* is as much a record of its own moment as it is of a distant prehistoric past. Smith's portrayal of ancient Londoners is replete with images of the subhuman: hairy women and children, bodies huddled around meals of putrid meat, no real

The reconstructed face of Shepperton Woman, from the "London Before London" exhibit. (© Museum of London)

language or even laughter, "scant sympathy for either pain or pleasure in their fellows," and couplings "which would now fill proper men and women with horror." All was refracted through Smith's claimed knowledge of the Indigenous societies that existed in his own time: "What modern savages are, alive and dead, is well known," he wrote. "Many of the surroundings, acts, and thoughts of these savages are known. By putting known facts together, and by assuming that our savage precursors of far-off times had ideas not very unlike those of savages of recent times, it is perhaps possible to galvanize the fragmentary bones of the primeval savage into temporary life."[6] Smith's transhistorical savage emerged out of Victorian scientific racism and encounters with living Indigenous peoples, turning ancient London into a howling wilderness peopled by the imagined subhuman. In this, his vision was not unlike that of Thomson and Kipling.

Encapsulated within a newer story of London's own indigenous heritage, the Heathrow diorama and Smith's book are counterpoints, symbols of an older story and an older way of making sense of London's place within a larger nineteenth-century world that still included Indigenous peoples. And this process of place-storying will not end, just as Indigenous peoples have not disappeared. Like his fellow psychogeographers, those authors and near-archaeologists who so diligently churn up the city's diverse and fugitive pasts, Will Self has drawn attention to London's ongoing dance with its own history. "Two thousand years of human interaction," he writes, "have worked over this tiny allotment of earth with savage intensity, digging into it, raising it up and covering over the very watercourses."[7] It is that working-over that keeps London's history from stagnating. In the form of Celtic skulls dredged from the riverbed, Roman eagles unearthed in the Minories, or coins, pottery, and other detritus recovered by modern-day mudlarks from the Thames foreshore, the city's past will never be past. Similarly, London will continue to excavate its relationship to its former empire. Thomson, Kipling, and Smith had written their evocations of London's prehistoric past at the height of that empire, and its language inflected theirs. In a parallel development, the writings of Evaristo and Rosen and the curation strategies of "London Before London" are a strange echo of the so-called "postcolonial moment" in which Indigenous peoples have demanded recognition of their histories and humanity, even here at the heart of empire.

London has an indigenous "British" past and, as this book has argued, it also has a rich, global Indigenous past. Neither is finished. If it is in the nature of the city to encompass everything, it is also in the dynamic, grasping nature of the city to unearth its own entanglements across both time and space, from a gravelly grave in Shepperton or the earth beneath Heathrow to places like Australia, New Zealand, the United States, Canada, and beyond. Like any good history, it is unfinished, open-ended, and indeterminate. And it is in that indeterminacy that space may be created for new kinds of histories, crafted in the moments when we ask ourselves a question with which empires and their storytellers must always be concerned: *When did we become real human beings?*

Appendix

Self-Guided Encounters with Indigenous London

Walking the land, history in hand, can be a usefully disorienting act. We see a landscape before us, and it is a layer cake of the lost and present, in which some things survive, others are long gone, and those that remain carry many conflicting, conflating, and conspiring meanings. The history of colonialism and empire only adds to the complexity of such landscapes and introduces a particular irony. In a place like Vancouver, for example—the traditional, ancestral, and unceded territory of three Coast Salish peoples—there is almost nothing to see of the deep Indigenous past, as so much has been destroyed. In contrast, in a place like London, the sites associated with Indigenous travelers remain, because they were (and still are) often sites of political, religious, or other forms of power.

At the same time, the London of the twenty-first century is not the London of previous centuries, and so accessing its Indigenous history requires exact imagining of the urban past as well. What follows are three tours through Indigenous London—two on foot, one on the river—plus a short list of additional off-tour sites of interest. Together, they ask the reader to imagine not only Indigenous presences within the urban landscape but the landscape's own pasts. Bring this book, a bottle of water, and your *London A-Z* or some other detailed street atlas.

TOUR ONE: WALKING FROM BLACKFRIARS TO OLD STREET

Two hours, plus optional time at St. Paul's Cathedral, the Museum of London, and Wesley's Chapel

Begin at the Blackfriars Tube station. Turn right coming out of the station and cross Queen Victoria Street into New Bridge Street. Follow New Bridge to Ludgate

Circus, then left into Fleet Street. Turn left into Bride Lane. Take the first stairs on the right into the narrow passage at St. Bride's Avenue; at its end, you'll find the entrance to St. Bride's Church.

Directly opposite the entrance to the church on the far wall is a small memorial to Virginia Dare, the first English child to be born in North America, whose parents were married in this church. A member of the Roanoke Colony, Dare was born in 1587, and would surely have been known by Manteo, Wanchese, and Towaye. She disappeared along with the rest of the colony sometime before 1590.

On the right side of the altar, you will find a very small memorial to church member Edward Winslow, a Puritan preacher and member of the Pilgrims who founded Plymouth Plantation in 1620. Winslow's writings include one of the few sources describing Tisquantum, whom Winslow would have known well during the last years of the Wampanoag man's life.

Leaving by the door you came in, go back to Fleet Street and turn left. Turn left into Salisbury Court and walk into Salisbury Square.

This was the site of the Church Missionary Society's motherhouse, and it was one of the places where the young Māori convert Maui spent time when he was not teaching young children near Edgware Road in 1816. In his day, Maui would have seen old houses and printing shops in addition to the society's offices; only no. 1 remains from that period. Such a seemingly small and out-of-the-way place, though, was also associated with many London luminaries, including Samuel Pepys, William Hogarth, Samuel Johnson, and John Boswell.

Return via Fleet Street to Ludgate Circus, cross the intersection, and proceed up Ludgate Hill.

Near what is now Limeburner Lane on the left (north) side of the street, a narrow passage just wide enough for a carriage once led back to the Bell Savage Inn. It was here that Rebecca Rolfe, known among her Powhatan people as Pocahontas, stayed while in London. Crowds often filled the passage and the inn's court, jostling to get a look at her and the rest of her delegation.

Continue up Ludgate Hill to St. Paul's Cathedral.

In front of the cathedral, notice the monument to Queen Anne. This is an 1886 replica of the original, which was erected here two years after the 1710 visit of the "Four Kings." The group includes a female figure with a bow, her foot on a severed head, representing the Americas. Should you decide to go into the cathedral (there is an admission fee), you will be able to imagine Indigenous history from bottom to top: from the crypt, where the Māori visitor Mahanga was particularly impressed by the tombs of Wellington and other British leaders in 1806, to the golden gallery on the very top of the cathedral, where Indigenous visitors like Atajuq and his Inuit family were often taken to look out over the city, which was supposed to impress them into submission.

Facing the front of St. Paul's, go to the left through the arch at Temple Bar into Paternoster Square.

In the sixteenth through eighteenth centuries, this square was one of the centers of London's print culture, with printing shops crowding all around it. From here, images like those of Eiakintomino and Matahan and the Four Kings' speech traveled around the city and beyond.

Cross the square diagonally, going between the buildings on the right. Find the St. Paul's Tube station and cross the street into St. Martin's Le Grand, following signs for the Museum of London in the Rotunda.

The Museum of London is must-see (and free) and will enrich the kind of historical imagining these tours require. Of particular interest: the "indigenous" gallery called "London Before London"; tobacco-related images of Indigenous Americans and a section on the Tahitian visitor Omai in the "Empire" display; and an immersive exhibit on pleasure gardens that will offer insight into the night Utsidihi and his Cherokee compatriots went to Vauxhall Gardens. (This is also a good place for a midtour rest stop.)

Outside the front door of the museum, take an immediate left and follow Bastion Highwalk until you find stairs leading down and to your left. Go down to street level and turn left.

Along the north, or left, side of the road known as London Wall, just outside the boundary of the old city, stood Bethlehem ("Bedlam"), the great and horrifying eighteenth-century hospital for the insane. Indigenous visitors were routinely brought here (and to its earlier incarnation in the city proper) to see the "enlightened" British approach to mental illness.

Continue along London Wall until you get to the intersection with Moorgate.

In the eighteenth century this area, known as Moorfields, was at the edge of the city. It was in a tabernacle here that Mohegan minister Samson Occom gave the first London sermon on his tour to raise funds for a Christian school for Indigenous boys. The tabernacle is long gone, but as you continue the tour, you'll be moving through a part of the city that was once populated by many dissenting churches; perhaps the best evidence of this is the cemetery you'll be seeing soon.

Turn left into Moorgate, and follow it to Finsbury Square.

Finsbury was still entirely rural at the end of the sixteenth century and the beginning of the seventeenth, and old maps from the city show this area being used for livestock, laundering, and archery. Two of the archery targets located here during this period were named the "Princes of America," possibly after Manteo and Wanchese or other visitors brought during the first years of English colonial expansion in the Americas.

Continue north just past Finsbury Square, keeping left into City Road. In about one block you will see Bunhill Fields cemetery on your left; facing it on your right is Wesley's Chapel.

John Wesley's Chapel, built in the eighteenth century, has been a landmark of dissenting Christianity in London ever since then; many of the city's dissident luminaries are buried across the street, while Methodist founders are buried in the cemetery behind the chapel. In 1863, one of Wesley's successors hosted several members of William Jenkins's Māori group, making a special point of showing them what they would have no doubt called an *urupa* (ancestral burying ground). The group also sat for a portrait in the Wesley House to the right of the chapel. That portrait appears in chapter 5; if the house is open, take the book in with you and see if you can determine in which room the portrait was made.

Meanwhile, at the entrance to the museum in the chapel crypt, notice the illustration of Wesley himself preaching to Indigenous North Americans. These "congregants" would have included Tomochichi, Senauki, and other Yamacraw people, whom Wesley visited in the 1730s.

Continue north on City Road to end this tour at the Old Street Tube station on the Northern Line.

TOUR TWO: WALKING FROM COVENT GARDEN TO WESTMINSTER ABBEY

Two hours, plus optional time at Westminster Abbey and Westminster Palace

Begin outside the Covent Garden Tube station on the Piccadilly Line. Find Long Acre on your left and turn right into it. Follow it until Bow Street, and turn right. Continue until you see the Royal Opera House on the right.

Here, we are in the heart of the old theater district; the Royal Opera House (also known as Covent Garden) has existed here since 1732. Many Indigenous visitors attended plays at places like the Royal; here, for example, Bennelong, the Eora man from Australia, came to see a performance of *Faust* in 1793. No doubt Bennelong was as much of a show as Dr. Faustus was.

Continue on Bow Street until you reach Russell Street, and notice the Theatre Royal off to your left.

The Theatre Royal in Drury Lane is one of the oldest theaters in London, and like many of the other major entertainment venues in this neighborhood, it saw Indigenous audience members. The Theatre Royal is where a near-riot broke out during the visit of the Four Kings in 1710.

Turn right into Russell Street and continue into Covent Garden.

Two years after the Four Kings left London, there was an outbreak of gang violence in the area around Covent Garden Market. Men were assaulted, women were raped, noses were cut off, and people were put into barrels and rolled down streets. The most feared of these gangs—even though there is some evidence they didn't exist—called themselves the Mohocks, illustrating eighteenth-century ideas about savagery.

Cross through Covent Garden Market and leave via King Street at the opposite end on the right. Midway down King Street on the right, above the shops, notice a small blue plaque.

Thomas Arne, the writer of the lyrics to "Rule Britannia!"—a virtual theme song for the Seven Years' War—lived here as an adult. As a very young child, he lived elsewhere with his upholsterer father, who hosted the Four Kings in their home. One wonders about the connection between Arne's childhood memories and his visions of empire.

Continue on as King Street becomes New Row, noticing the scale of the eighteenth-century street. At St. Martin's Lane, turn left and proceed down it to Trafalgar Square, where you will arrive at St. Martin-in-the-Fields.

After lying in state at the Adelphi, the coffins of Liholiho and Kamāmalu were placed in the Crypt here. The Crypt is now a café, and a good place for a midtour break (admission free).

Across from St. Martin-in-the-Fields, notice the National Gallery and look for the statue of a man on a horse.

The figure on the horse represents George IV. The massive columns at the front of the National Gallery were scavenged from his home, Carlton House, the palatial Pall Mall residence built for George when he was still the Prince of Wales. At Carlton House, the notorious royal entertained the Mohawk warrior and leader Thayendanagea, whom we might imagine walking between the columns.

Look for the building with the Canadian flags on the side of the square opposite St. Martin-in-the-Fields.

This is the Canadian High Commission, where representatives of the government of Canada have their offices. Throughout the nineteenth and twentieth centuries, such officials have consistently worked against the efforts of Indigenous Canadian activists who traveled to London in search of, for example, land rights. As such, the High Commission has been—and remains—a contested space. Look for interesting temporary exhibitions here, often having to do with Indigenous arts.

Go back to St. Martin-in-the-Fields and turn into Duncannon Street. Walk until you are across from Charing Cross Tube station.

Empire has everything to do with naming. Names like Boston, Salem, New York, Nova Scotia, and countless others are not without meaning; they are the transposition of British places onto territories that were imagined as deserving of colonial transformation. Charing Cross, where in the thirteenth century a memorial cross was erected for a dead queen, was one such place. In his maps of the far north of what is now Canada, sixteenth-century explorer Martin Frobisher named one headland Charing Cross, creating yet another entanglement between London and the broader world. The area around Charing Cross, meanwhile, was known in the early seventeenth century as the Bermudas, in part because of the prevalence of tobacco houses here—another exchange of places between the "old" and "new" worlds.

Carry on, crossing the Strand into Villiers Street, the (mostly) pedestrianized street going down the hill to the left of Charing Cross (train) Station. At John Adam Street, turn left and walk to the corner of Durham House Street on the left.

Sir Walter Raleigh's Durham House is long gone, but its name remains, along with those of other great houses that once stood along the Strand. This is where, in the late sixteenth century, Thomas Harriot and Manteo (and possibly Wanchese and Towaye) crafted the Ossomocomuck orthography, the key to a language spoken by the not-entirely-willing hosts of a failed colony.

Retrace your steps to Villiers Street and turn left. Partway down the hill, enter the Arches shopping arcade on the right and walk through the arcade until you emerge into Craven Street.

Craven Street is where the unnamed eleven-year-old Odawa boy attacked his captor and host upon discovering his kin's remains among a collection of human scalps.

Take Craven Street to the left to Northumberland Avenue. Cross the avenue and enter Whitehall Gardens, continuing on the length of the gardens until Horse Guards Avenue, where you should turn right.

Walking up this hill, it is impossible to miss the fact that you are passing through a landscape of raw power; for centuries, Whitehall has been the center of British sovereignty. No. 10 Downing Street is nearby, and the edifices around you now are simply the latest in a long series of buildings that housed the machinations of empire. From here until the end of the tour, you are at the true heart of English and British colonialism.

At the top of Horse Guards Avenue, cross the street and go through the gate between the guard stations, then under the archway into the parade ground.

To your right, you can see the masts and rigging of the Admiralty on top of the building. The Admiralty is the entity that oversaw the explorations of Captain James Cook (indeed, a monumental statue of him can be seen by going around the corner to the front of the building). From this place emanated scientific discovery, imperial competition, and doctrines such as *terra nullius*, which denied Indigenous presence on and title to the land. At the same time, Cook's experiences on his voyages were just as diverse as the people he encountered, ranging from diffidence to threat to peaceful trade to all-out violence, including Cook's death at Kealakekua Bay in 1779.

Continue across the Horse Guards Parade Ground to Horse Guards Road, and turn left. Turn left into Great George Street and carry on into Parliament Square. Westminster Abbey is to your right.

Westminster Abbey (admission fee) was a common destination for many Indigenous travelers, who each had their own distinct responses to the imposing space full of the dead. Liholiho and Kamāmalu chose not to enter it, for example, since the dead there were strangers. For S7aplek and his Salish counterparts in 1906, the abbey was of great interest—in particular the Stone of Scone and the shrine of Edward the Confessor. The Townshend monument, with its two atlantes modeled after the eleven-year-old Odawa captive, can be found in the south aisle.

On the other side of Abingdon Street, to the right of Big Ben, look for Westminster Palace.

Westminster Palace (admission fee) is one of the oldest structures in London. It is also the site of Indigenous London's beginning; it is where three men, likely Inuit, appeared in 1501 or 1502.

Go past Big Ben, on your right, and proceed to Westminster Bridge for a view of the Houses of Parliament.

The Houses of Parliament (admission fee), meanwhile, were a common destination for Indigenous visitors, especially in the nineteenth and twentieth centuries. One of the most notable visits included that of Hongi Hika and Waikato, which inspired something of a melee among the MPs straining to get a close look at them.

TOUR THREE: WESTMINSTER TO GREENWICH VIA THE THAMES

Forty-five minutes, plus optional time at Greenwich

From Embankment Pier near Westminster Tube station, take one of London's fast Thames ferries (not one of the slower guided tour boats) east toward Greenwich. Sit as close to the front of the boat as you can.

In this part of the river, in the spring of 1603, a group of "Virginians" was seen canoeing on the river. Although they were almost certainly from one of the eastern Algonquian nations, they were likely not from what is now Virginia, since Jamestown had yet to be founded. It is impossible to know how they got there or who they were. But we do know that thousands turned out to see them, both from the banks and from other watercraft. We also do not know what happened to them, although there was an outbreak of plague in London that summer that may have spelled their end. Their canoe, meanwhile, ended up in the collection of the newly knighted politician Sir Walter Cope.

On the right, watch for the landmark OXO Tower, formerly a power station. Just behind it is the Bargehouse, a repurposed industrial structure that now serves as a performance and exhibition space.

In 2013, the Bargehouse was the heart of a celebration of Indigenous culture in London, a series of events known as Indigeneity in the Contemporary World: Performance, Politics, Belonging. Hosted and organized by Royal Holloway College, University of London, Indigeneity in the Contemporary World featured artists from more than a score of Indigenous nations around the world and culminated in an exhibition at the Bargehouse titled "EcoCentrix: Indigenous Arts, Sustainable Acts," which included photos and videos of Tahltan artist Peter Morin's "cultural graffiti" interventions at sites of power in the London landscape. For information on the events, including videos and podcasts, visit www.indigeneity.net.

The next bridge you will come to is Blackfriars.

Atajuq and his family mistook Blackfriars Bridge as a natural formation until their host George Cartwright pointed out the chisel marks on it. Actually, that bridge is gone, replaced by the one you will see there. Very close to its south end, and also now gone, was the Leverian Museum, under whose rotunda Bennelong and Yemmerrawannie would have seen everything from camphor-wood and cinnamon coral to Hawaiian feather cloaks and spectacle snakes.

Coming up on the right, you'll see a replica of an Elizabethan theater.

This is Shakespeare's Globe, one of London's premier performance venues, and not just for Shakespeariana. Outside the legal and ecclesiastical control of the city of London, Southwark and the area around it were known as "the liberties," the red-light and entertainment district for the city as a whole. Here, bearbaiting, raucous fairs, and theaters catered to all classes— and to at least some Indigenous visitors, such as the Four Kings, who were brought here to experience the less-genteel sides of London life.

On the right, just before London Bridge, watch for a small black ship in a wet dock between buildings on the south bank. It is a replica of Sir Francis Drake's Golden Hinde.

Unlike many early English explorers, Francis Drake did not bring home Indigenous captives. His project was instead the circumnavigation of the planet and piracy against Spanish ships. But his journey helped make something called "empire" seem possible to the English. This tiny ship, then, is evidence of a century- and world-spanning history.

Just past the Golden Hinde, watch for a view of Southwark Cathedral between the high riverfront buildings. See "Other Sites to Visit" for a discussion of the site.

The Tower of London will be on your left. See "Other Sites to Visit" for a discussion of the Tower.

As the river curves to the left, watch for a small white pub called the Mayflower on the right side of the river. Further away from the river behind the pub, look for a church spire.

One of the oldest pubs on the river, the Mayflower is also a site of colonial history. It was from a dock here that the ship of the same name sailed for the place it would call Plymouth. Once there, its crew and passengers would encounter Tisquantum, a Wampanoag man who had already made four crossings of the Atlantic and two sojourns in London.

The church is St. Mary the Virgin, Rotherhithe, the spiritual center of an old seagoing neighborhood. It is here that a young Palauan man named Lebuu is buried. Sent to England in 1792 by his father, a traditional leader known as a *rupack*, Lebuu became a Christian and something of a cause célèbre before his untimely and highly sentimentalized death. There is a monument to him at St. Mary's and a small exhibit about him at the Museum of London Docklands, and near St. Mary's there is a small thoroughfare named Rupack Street.

On the left along the next curve of the river, you will see a sign for the Limehouse Basin Marina.

Limehouse was a maritime neighborhood, and its demographics reflected this. Sailors and others of African, East Asian, South Asian, and other descents were familiar sights on the streets here and formed nascent, if also transient, communities. The circumstances of their lives were not always good, however, and in the middle of the nineteenth century, reformers and missionaries sought to better foreign sailors' lives (and convert them to Christianity) by setting up "strangers' homes." One such home, here in Limehouse, was the residence for a time of the Christian Māori travelers who arrived in 1863 with Thomas Kendall. One of the men in the group also married a young Englishwoman at a church in Limehouse.

On the left, you'll soon see the skyscrapers of Canary Wharf on the Isle of Dogs.

Surrounded now by the high-tech and high-rise commerce of Canary Wharf, this area was once the center of an earlier kind of capitalism: just in from the river, the landscape is filled with huge artificial docks, through which sugar, rum, cotton, spices, and countless other commodities moved into Britain from the colonies and throughout the empire. It was in a West India Dock tavern that Nahiti, soon to depart as interpreter to his Māori people for the New Zealand Company, both gave and received toasts in 1839.

(The Museum of London Docklands, located in an old West India Company warehouse, deserves a visit. Aside from a wooden cigar-store Indian used to represent Pocahontas and a small exhibit dedicated to Lebuu, there is little of relevance to Indigenous London at the museum. But its exhibits on the city's maritime past, and in particular its stunning and challenging galleries dedicated to London's legacies of slavery, are absolutely worth a visit.)

On the right, watch for a small pier with a covered arcade. Nearby, you will see a small metal footbridge spanning the entrance to Greenland Dock.

In 1819, John Sackhouse, a young inuk, lived aboard a ship in the aptly named Greenland Dock, where whaling ships and their crews rested while in London. Onboard one of those ships, Sackhouse painted scenes of encounters between his people and the British, and on the waters of the dock and the Thames, and he gave kayak demonstrations for thousands of observers. He also died there.

On your right, just before coming to Greenwich, you will see the mouth of a small creek.

The 1730 Cherokee delegation waited aboard a ship here at Deptford Creek until they could be guaranteed an audience with the king, and the shipyards at Deptford were a common destination for other Indigenous visitors touring the city. Deptford Creek is also where a seventeenth-century Inuit barbed, ivory spear point was found on the bank of the river. How it got there, and when, is entirely a mystery. The spear point resides in the collections of the Museum of London.

Finally, you will arrive at Greenwich. Disembark here.

Greenwich was another common destination for Indigenous visitors to London, who were taken there—as well as to the Royal Arsenal in Woolwich farther downriver—to see for themselves British naval might. The architecture of Greenwich itself, meanwhile, made its own statement about British aspirations to greatness. While many visitors must have been impressed, in the case of Alexander Liholiho (Kamehameha IV) and Lot Kapuāiwa, they had a different take: seeing Johann Zoffany's *The Death of Captain James Cook*, they declared it the best piece of art they had seen anywhere in London. The original painting is on display at the National Maritime Museum. (For another Indigenous angle, notice the Pocahontas-like figure on the ceiling of the Painted Hall, representing the Americas.)

OTHER SITES TO VISIT

Indigenous London can be found all across the city; the sites above are simply ones that could easily be strung together into tours. There are several additional sites, however, which merit attention, particularly because they include visible, and in some cases tangible, remnants of London's Indigenous past and present.

THE BEAVER BUILDING AND HAT FACTORY, 105–109 OXFORD STREET. Here, the beaver gargoyles announce the ways in which Indigenous knowledge and labor created the capital that in turn made this particular building possible.

SOUTHWARK CATHEDRAL. This is where, in 1736, the Mohegan sachem Mahomet Weyonomon was laid to rest, having died of smallpox before he could present a petition to the king. The large stone monument to Mahomet, unveiled by the queen in 2006, can be found in the southeastern corner of the churchyard.

THE TOWER OF LONDON. By all accounts, most Indigenous visitors to London were taken to see the Tower and its menagerie. Of special interest to Indigenous London is the room reconstructed to look as it did when Sir Walter Raleigh was held captive in the Tower—and as it did when Pocahontas came to visit the doomed explorer (admission fee).

ST. OLAVE HART STREET. Just a short walk from the Tower—walk west on the busy Tower Hill and Byward Street, turn right up Seething Lane, and go to its end—Charles Dickens's "St Ghastly Grim" is a particularly powerful touchstone on the story of Indigenous London. This is where the unnamed inuk who was captured by Martin Frobisher in 1576 was buried and where, a year later, "Nutaaq" was laid to rest. In 2013, 436 years afterward, the verger here placed limits on what kind of Indigenous ceremony would be allowed in "his" church.

THE BRITISH MUSEUM. In addition to its vast holdings of Indigenous artifacts (and, it must be said, ancestral remains), the British Museum displays three things of particular interest to Indigenous London: the obsidian mirror of John Dee in the north chamber of room 1 (the "Enlightenment"), Māori taonga in room 24, and in room 26, a woven strap that belonged to one of the Four Kings.

Notes

CHAPTER I. THE UNHIDDEN CITY

Epigraphs: Richard Tames, *London: A Cultural History* (Oxford: Oxford University Press, 2006), xviii; Maya Mikdashi, "What Is Settler Colonialism?" *American Indian Culture and Research Journal* 37:2 (2013), 31.

1. Robert Cooke, *The Palace of Westminster: Houses of Parliament* (London: Burton Skira, 1987), 30–34.

2. *The Great Chronicle of London* (1580), ed. A. H. Thomas and I. D. Thornley (London, 1939), 288, discussed and quoted in James A. Williamson, *The Cabot Voyages and Bristol Discovery Under Henry VII* (Cambridge: Cambridge University Press, 1962), 128, 220. Translation follows.

3. See Williamson, *The Cabot Voyages and Bristol Discovery;* Peter E. Pope, *The Many Landfalls of John Cabot* (Toronto: University of Toronto Press, 1997), 167.

4. There is no singular definition of the term "indigenous." Even the United Nations Declaration on the Rights of Indigenous Peoples (UNDRIP) eschews a clear definition, offering instead the relatively blurry criteria of self-identification, community recognition, and shared history. For the purposes of this book, capital-I Indigenous mostly refers to peoples who have been on the receiving end of capitalist imperial expansion, primarily European in origin, over the course of the past five hundred years. Such a usage is necessarily imprecise but also signals my solidarity with the global movement for Indigenous rights, represented in part by UNDRIP itself (which Canada, the United States, Australia, and New Zealand alone initially refused to ratify).

5. In the interest of a workable book, I necessarily leave out important stories of other Indigenous people who came to London from other places.

They included several men from Trinidad, Guyana, and elsewhere around the Caribbean, brought to England by Sir Walter Raleigh and his crews and whose stories are less well known thanks to the fragmentary nature of the sixteenth-century archive. Other Indigenous travelers, however, are much better documented. They include Omai, a Raiatean man who came back with Captain James Cook's expedition in 1774, lived in London for two years, and became the celebrated living exemplar of the noble savage. In 1792, Lebuu, a young Palauan nobleman, thrilled London's Christians through published, highly sentimental accounts of his conversion and subsequent death from an unnamed disease. Sara Baartman, a Khoikhoi woman from South Africa, was turned into an object of ethnographic display in 1810, one of the starkest examples of prurient, racist colonial exploitation in the city's history. A group of Yamana people ("Fuegians") from Patagonia, carried to England by none other than Charles Darwin, received similar attention in the early 1830s. San people from southern Africa, including children, were meanwhile put on display by missionaries and others in the 1840s and 1850s. As one more example, Cetshwayo kaMpande, a deposed leader of the Zulu nation, spent part of his exile in London, where he became something of a celebrity. Each of these travelers offers important insights into the relationship between London and Indigenous territories and deserves more scholarly treatment than they have received to date. See Alden T. Vaughan, *Transatlantic Encounters: American Indians in Britain, 1500–1776* (Cambridge: Cambridge University Press, 2008), 21–41; Richard Connaughton, *Omai: The Prince Who Never Was* (London: Timewell, 2005); Daniel J. Peacock, *Lee Boo of Belau: A Prince in London* (Honolulu: University of Hawai'i Press, 1987); Clifton Crais and Pamela Scully, *Sara Baartman and the Hottentot Venus: A Ghost Story and a Biography* (Princeton: Princeton University Press, 2009); Anne Chapman, *European Encounters with the Yamana People of Cape Horn, Before and After Darwin* (Cambridge: Cambridge University Press, 2009); Sadiah Qureshi, *Peoples on Parade: Exhibitions, Empire, and Anthropology in Nineteenth-Century Britain* (Chicago: University of Chicago Press, 2011); and Neil Parsons, "No Longer 'Rare Birds' in London: Zulu, Ndebele, Gaza, and Swazi Envoys to England, 1882–1894," in *Black Victorians/Black Victoriana*, ed. Gretchen Gerzina (New Brunswick: Rutgers University Press, 2003), 110–41.

6. Thomas De Quincey, *Confessions of an English Opium-Eater* (London: Taylor and Hessey, 1822); Henry Mayhew, *London Labour and the London Poor* (London: George Woodfall and Son, 1851); the newspaper editor's

quotation can be found in Jennifer Westwood and Jacqueline Simpson, *The Lore of the Land: A Guide to England's Legends, from Spring-Heeled Jack to the Witches of Warboys* (London: Penguin, 2001), 470.

7. P. L. Travers, *Mary Poppins* (London: Reynal and Hitchcock, 1934); Jack London, *The People of the Abyss* (New York: Macmillan, 1903); Peter Ackroyd, *London: The Biography* (New York: Anchor, 2003). The quotation about Sinclair's "shamanic" histories comes from Will Self's *Psychogeography* (London: Bloomsbury, 2007), 13. For examples of Sinclair's own work, see *Lud Heat* (Cheltenham: Skylight, 1975) and his edited volume *London: City of Disappearances* (London: Penguin, 2006).

8. See J. K. Rowling's entire *Harry Potter* series; Neil Gaiman, *Neverwhere* (New York: Harper Perennial, 1997); and China Miéville, *Kraken* (New York: Del Rey, 2011).

9. Timothy Morton, *Hyperobjects: Philosophy and Ecology After the End of the World* (Minneapolis: University of Minnesota Press), 90–91.

10. Peter Ackroyd, *London Under* (London: Vintage, 2012); Paul Dobraszczyk, *London's Sewers* (Oxford: Shire, 2014); Steve Roud, *London Lore: The Legends and Traditions of the World's Most Vibrant City* (London: Arrow, 2010); and John Attwood Brooks, *Ghosts of London* (Stroud: Jarrold, 1993).

11. For three examples of guides promising hidden Londons, see Stephen Millar, *London's Hidden Walks* (London: Metro Publications, 2012); Andrew Duncan, *Secret London: Exploring the Hidden City* (London: New Holland, 2009); and John Rogers, *This Other London: Adventures in the Overlooked City* (London: U.K. General, 2014).

12. *Opinions of the English and United States Press on Catlin's North American Indian Museum; Exhibiting in the Egyptian Hall, Piccadilly* (London: C. Adlard, 1841), 7.

13. George Catlin, *Adventures of the Ojibbeway and Ioway Indians in England, France, and Belgium, Being Notes of Eight Years' Travel and Residence with His North American Indian Collection* (London: George Catlin, 1852), 144–48, 168.

14. In addition to those on stage in 1843, Catlin would sponsor other groups of Indigenous performers, including fourteen Ioway people in 1844 and another group of "Ojibbeway," led by Maungwaudas and discussed below, in 1845.

15. Catlin, *Adventures*, 110.

16. Ibid., 126–29.

17. *Opinions*, 1, 3, 12–13.

18. Kate Flint, *The Transatlantic Indian, 1776–1930* (Princeton: Princeton University Pres, 2009), 63–73.

19. Charles Dickens, "The Noble Savage," *Household Words*, 11 June 1853.

20. Catlin, *Adventures*, 127, 129–30, 152.

21. Ibid., 127–28, 137–38.

22. For Gakiiwegwanabi, see Peter Jones, *Life and Journals of Kah-Ke-Wa-Quo-Na-By (Rev. Peter Jones), Wesleyan Missionary* (Toronto: Anson Green, 1860); and Donald B. Smith, *Sacred Feathers: The Reverend Peter Jones (Kahkewaquonaby) and the Mississauga Indians* (Lincoln: University of Nebraska Press, 1987). For Gaagigegaabaw, see George Copway, *Running Sketches of Men and Places in England, France, Germany, Belgium, and Scotland* (New York: J. C. Riker, 1851). For Maungwdaus, see George Henry, *An account of the Chippewa Indians, who have been travelling in the United States, England, Ireland, Scotland, France, and Belgium* (Boston: George Henry, 1848). For Naaniibawikwe, see Celia Haig-Brown, "The 'Friends' of Nahnebahwequa," in *With Good Intentions: Euro-Canadian and Aboriginal Relations in Colonial Canada*, ed. Celia Haig-Brown and David A. Nock (Vancouver: UBC Press, 2006), 132–57.

23. Jones, *Life and Journals*, 300.

24. Henry, *An Account*, 198; Haig-Brown, "The 'Friends' of Nahnebahwequa."

25. Jones, *Life and Journals*, 338; Copway, *Running Sketches*, 89–90, 99–100, 276; Henry, *An Account*, 197–99.

26. Jones, *Life and Journals*, 405, 407–8; Haig-Brown, "The 'Friends' of Nahnebahwequa"; Smith, *Sacred Feathers*, 255; Henry, *An Account*, 201.

27. For survivance, see Gerald Vizenor, *Manifest Manners: Narratives on Postindian Survivance* (Lincoln: University of Nebraska Press, 1999). For examples of urban Indigenous experience and voices, see *American Indians and the Urban Experience*, ed. Susan Lobo and Kurt Peters (Walnut Creek: AltaMira, 2001); *Indigenous in the City: Contemporary Identities and Cultural Innovation*, ed. Evelyn Peters and Chris Andersen (Vancouver: UBC Press, 2013); Bonita Lawrence, *"Real" Indians and Others: Mixed-Blood Urban Native Peoples and Indigenous Nationhood* (Vancouver: UBC Press, 2004); Natacha Gagné, *Being Māori in the City: Indigenous Everyday Life in Auckland* (Toronto: University of Toronto Press, 2013); Penelope Edmonds, *Urbanizing Frontiers: Indigenous Peoples and Settlers in Nineteenth-Century Pacific Rim Cities* (Vancouver: UBC Press, 2010); and Coll Thrush, *Native Seattle: Histories from the Crossing-Over Place* (Seattle: University of Washington Press, 2007).

28. Julie Flavell, *When London Was Capital of America* (New Haven: Yale University Press, 2011), 169–75; Peter C. Mancall, "Tales Tobacco Told in Sixteenth-Century Europe," *Environmental History* 9:4 (2004), 648–78.

29. Jace Weaver, *The Red Atlantic: American Indigenes and the Making of the Modern World, 1000–1927* (Chapel Hill: University of North Carolina Press, 2014).

30. Miles Ogborn, *Spaces of Modernity: London's Geographies, 1680–1780* (New York: Guilford, 1998), 32–33.

31. Catherine Hall, *Civilizing Subjects: Metropole and Colony in the English Imagination, 1830–1867* (Chicago: University of Chicago Press, 2002). For further discussion, see Richard Price, "One Big Thing: Britain, Its Empire, and Their Imperial Culture," *Journal of British Studies* 45:3 (2006), 602–27.

32. Lorenzo Veracini, *Settler Colonialism: A Theoretical Overview* (Basingstoke, U.K.: Palgrave Macmillan, 2010), 33–52. For other key discussions and framings of settler colonialism, see Patrick Wolfe, *Settler Colonialism and the Transformation of Anthropology: The Politics and Poetics of an Ethnographic Event* (London: Bloomsbury, 1998); Walter L. Hixson, *American Settler Colonialism: A History* (Basingstoke, U.K.: Palgrave Macmillan, 2013); Alyosha Goldstein, ed., *Formations of United States Colonialism* (Durham, N.C.: Duke University Press, 2014); and James Belich, *Replenishing the Earth: The Settler Revolution and the Rise of the Anglo World, 1783–1939* (Oxford: Oxford University Press, 2009).

33. Philip J. Deloria, *Indians in Unexpected Places* (Lawrence: University Press of Kansas, 2004).

34. For treatments of Tekahionwake's life, see Carole Gerson and Veronica Strong-Boag, eds., *E. Pauline Johnson, Tekahionwake: Collected Poems and Selected Prose* (Toronto: University of Toronto Press, 2002); Mrs. W. Garland Foster, *The Mohawk Princess: Being Some Account of the Life of Tekahion-wake (E. Pauline Johnson)* (Vancouver: Lion's Gate, 1931); Charlotte Gray, *Flint and Feather: The Life and Times of E. Pauline Johnson, Tekahionwake* (Toronto: Harper Flamingo Canada, 2002); Betty Keller, *Pauline: A Biography of Pauline Johnson* (Vancouver: Douglas and McIntyre, 1981); and Veronica Strong-Boag and Carole Gerson, *Paddling Her Own Canoe: The Times and Texts of E. Pauline Johnson, Tekahionwake* (Toronto: University of Toronto Press, 2000).

35. Gray, *Flint and Feather*, 172–93; Keller, *Pauline*, 76–87.

36. Gray, *Flint and Feather*, 306–29; Keller, *Pauline*, 207–25.

37. Gerson and Strong-Boag, *E. Pauline Johnson*, 213, 216; Gray, *Flint and Feather*, 329; Foster, *The Mohawk Princess*, 112; Keller, *Pauline*, 221–23.

38. The "7" in S7aplek's name represents a glottal stop, which sounds like the little break in the middle of the phrase "uh-oh." His name is pronounced, roughly, "ss-aplek."

39. S7aplek and his colleagues were not the first Indigenous leaders from British Columbia to visit London. In 1904, a delegation led by Chilihitza, a chief of the Douglas Lake Band of the Upper Nicola people, and Louie, a chief of the Secwepmc at Kamloops, traveled to Europe under the supervision of a Catholic Oblate missionary, where among other things they met with Pope Pius X. Their return inspired further organizing throughout the First Nations of British Columbia. See Keith Thor Carlson, "Aboriginal Diplomacy: Queen Victoria Comes to Canada and Coyote Goes to London," in *Indigenous Diplomacies*, ed. J. Marshall Beier (London: Palgrave Macmillan, 2009).

40. "Redskins to See the King—Chiefs Go to Buckingham Palace Today," *Daily Express*, 13 August 1906.

41. Keith Thor Carlson, "Rethinking Dialogue and History: The King's Promise and the 1906 Aboriginal Delegation to London," *Native Studies Review* 16:2 (2005), 9–10. See also Keith Thor Carlson, "The Indians and the Crown: Aboriginal Memories of the Royal Promises in Pacific Canada," in Colin M. Coates, ed., *Majesty in Canada: Essays on the Role of Royalty* (Toronto: Dundurn, 2006), 68–95.

42. Carlson, "Rethinking," 19–20.

43. Ibid., 24.

44. "Redskins Depart Happy," *Daily Mirror*, 15 August 1906, p. 5.

45. This continued use remains controversial within the larger Squamish community.

46. Strong-Boag and Gerson, *Paddling Her Own Canoe*, 29–30; Gerson and Strong-Boag, *E. Pauline Johnson*, 230–34. E. Pauline Johnson, *The Legends of Vancouver* (Vancouver: David Spencer, 1911), 1–7.

47. Less than a generation after Tekahionwake's second visit to London, another Indigenous performer from Canada took the stages of London. Frances Nickawa, a young Cree woman, also made two trips to the city: one in 1921–22 and another in 1925. Although Nickawa did not perform her own original material, samples from Tekahionwake's corpus were a standard part of her repertoire. For an account of Nickawa's life, see Jennifer S. H. Brown, "Frances Nickawa: 'A Gifted Interpreter of the Poetry of Her Race,'" in *Recollecting: Lives of Aboriginal Women of the Canadian Northwest and Borderlands*, ed. Sarah Carter and Patricia McCormack (Edmonton, Alberta: Athabasca University Press, 2011), 263–85.

48. Carlson, "Rethinking," 20–22.

49. James Clifford, "Indigenous Articulations," *The Contemporary Pacific* 13:2 (2001), 470.

50. Antoinette Burton, "Traveling Criticism? The Dynamic History of Indigenous Modernities," *Journal of Cultural and Social History* 9:4 (2012).

51. Renato Rosaldo, *The Day of Shelly's Death: The Poetry and Ethnography of Grief* (Durham, N.C.: Duke University Press, 2014), 105.

52. China Miéville, "Oh, London, You Drama Queen," *New York Times*, 1 March 2012, www.nytimes.com/2012/03/04/magazine/china-mieville-london .html?_r=0, accessed 12 March 2013.

53. *The Prelude* (1850), in Mark Ford, *London: A History in Verse* (Cambridge: Harvard University Press, 2012), 336. Italics are mine.

INTERLUDE ONE: A DEVIL'S LOOKING GLASS

1. The most detailed account of the mirror's history is Hugh Tait, " 'The Devil's Looking Glass': The Magical Speculum of Dr John Dee," in *Horace Walpole: Writer, Politician, and Connoisseur: Essays on the 250th Anniversary of Walpole's Birth*, ed. Warren Hunting Smith (New Haven: Yale University Press, 1967), 195–212. For its cultural context, see Neil MacGregor, *Shakespeare's Restless World: A Portrait of an Era in Twenty Objects* (London: Penguin, 2013), 116–31.

For general biographies of John Dee, see Peter J. French, *John Dee: The World of an Elizabethan Mage* (London: Routledge and Kegan Paul, 1972); Benjamin Woolley, *The Queen's Conjurer: The Science and Magic of Dr. John Dee, Adviser to Queen Elizabeth I* (New York: Henry Holt, 2001). For more scholarly thematic studies, see William H. Sherman, *John Dee: The Politics of Reading and Writing in the English Renaissance* (Amherst: University of Massachusetts Press, 1995); Andrew Escobedo, *Nationalism and Historical Loss in Renaissance England: Foxe, Dee, Spenser, Milton* (Ithaca: Cornell University Press, 2004); Deborah E. Harkness, *John Dee's Conversations with Angels: Cabala, Alchemy, and the End of Nature* (Cambridge: Cambridge University Press, 1999); and *John Dee: Interdisciplinary Studies in English Renaissance Thought*, ed. Stephen Clucas (Dordrecht, Netherlands: Spring, 2006), especially William H. Sherman, "John Dee's Columbian Encounter," 131–40; and Robert Baldwin, "John Dee's Interest in the Application of Nautical Science, Mathematics, and Law to English Naval Affairs," 97–130. The quotations in this interlude come from *The Enochian Evocation of Dr. John Dee*, ed. and trans. Geoffrey James (San Francisco: Weiser, 2009); and Dee's *General and rare memorials pertayning to the Perfect Arte of Navigation* (1576). See also *John Dee: The Limits of the British Em-*

pire, ed. Ken MacMillan with Jennifer Abeles (Westport, Conn.: Praeger, 2004).

The most comprehensive discussion of Tezcatlipoca is Guilhem Olivier, *Mockeries and Metamorphoses of an Aztec God: Tezcatlipoca, "Lord of the Smoking Mirror,"* trans. Michel Besson (Boulder: University Press of Colorado, 2003).

For the fall of Tenochtitlan, important recent studies include James Lockhart, *We People Here: Nahuatl Accounts of the Conquest of Mexico* (Eugene, Ore.: Wipf and Stock, 2004); Camilla Townsend, "Burying the White Gods: New Perspectives on the Conquest of Mexico," *American Historical Review* 108:3 (June 2003), 659–87; Molly Harbour Basset, "Meeting the Gods: Apotheoses and Exchanges of the Early Encounter," *Material Religion* 8:4 (December 2012), 417–538; and Ross Hassig, *Mexico and the Spanish Conquest* (Norman: University of Oklahoma Press, 2006). For a powerful poetic evocation of the conquest of the Aztec Empire, also based on archival fragments, see Eduardo Galeano, *Genesis: Memory of Fire,* vol. 1 (New York: W. W. Norton, 1998).

CHAPTER 2. DAWNLAND TELESCOPES

Epigraph: Ruth Holmes Whitehead, *Stories from the Six Worlds: Micmac Legends* (Halifax: Nimbus, 2006), 209.

1. John W. Shirley's *Thomas Harriot: A Biography* (Oxford: Clarendon Press, 1983) remains the most comprehensive biography of Harriot. For the intellectual context of his life, especially in terms of his mathematical work and relationship with colonization, see Robert Fox, *Thomas Harriot and His World: Mathematics, Exploration, and Natural Philosophy in Early Modern England* (Farnham, U.K.: Ashgate, 2012). For discussions specifically of the orthography, see Shirley, *Thomas Harriot,* 108–12; Miriam Rukeyser, *Traces of Thomas Hariot* (New York: Random House, 1971), 164–67; and Vivian Salmon, "Thomas Harriot and the English Origins of Algonkian Linguists," Durham Thomas Harriot Seminar Occasional Paper No. 8 (Durham, U.K.: University of Durham, 1993). The only other known use of the orthography is on a seventeenth-century property map from Ireland; see Eric Klingelhoffer and James Lyttleton, "Molana Abbey and Its New World Master," *Archaeology Ireland* 24:4 (Winter 2010), 32–35. The meaning and use of Ossomocomuck is after Michael Leroy Oberg, *The Head in*

Edward Nugent's Hand: Roanoke's Forgotten Indians (Philadelphia: University of Pennsylvania Press, 2008).

2. The primary sources in question are Thomas Harriot, "A brief and true report of the new found land of Virginia," in *New American World: A Documentary History of North America to 1612,* ed. David B. Quinn (New York: Arno, 1979), 3:150–51; and "List of articles to be taken on Mace voyage of 1602," in *New American World,* ed. Quinn, 5:162–63. See also D. B. Quinn, "Thomas Harriot and the Virginia Voyages of 1602," *William and Mary Quarterly,* 3rd series, 27 (1970); and David Beers Quinn, ed., *The Roanoke Voyages, 1584–1590: Documents to Illustrate the English Voyages to North America Under the Patent Granted to Walter Raleigh in 1584* (London: Hakluyt Society, 1955). For a comprehensive account of the encounters at Roanoke, see Karen Ordahl Kupperman, *Roanoke: The Abandoned Colony* (Lanham, Md.: Rowman and Littlefield, 2008). For Harriot's work at Roanoke, see Stephen Clucas, "Thomas Harriot's *A briefe and true report*: Knowledge-Making and the Roanoke Voyage," in *European Visions: American Voices,* ed. Kim Sloan (London: British Museum, 2009), 17–23.

3. For more on this linguistic encounter in addition to the sources cited above, see Ed White, "Invisible Tagkanysough," *PMLA* 120:3 (May 2005), 751–67.

4. For syphilis on the Strand, see Deborah Harkness, *The Jewel House: Elizabethan London and the Scientific Revolution* (New Haven: Yale University Press, 2007), 11, 87–88. For the contemporary uses of sassafras, see Gillian Mirrlees, "Sassafras: A Cure-All of Harriot's Time," Durham Thomas Harriot Seminar Occasional Paper No. 12 (Durham, U.K., 1995).

5. The actual inscription is MATEOROIDN, literally "Manteo roi done," in keeping with the highly idiosyncratic and partial spelling and grammar seen, for example, in the Lord's Prayer at the top of the manuscript. The original is held in the archives of the Westminster School in London.

6. "Eastern Algonquian" is an anthropological term, not an Indigenous one. It refers to a contiguous zone of related languages that stretches from North Carolina to Québec and Labrador (and possibly Newfoundland), itself part of a vast grouping of languages as far-flung as the Cree and Anishnaabeg languages across much of Canada and the Great Lakes and the Blackfoot, Cheyenne, and Arapaho on the western Plains. I have adopted "Algonquian" in this chapter as a form of shorthand for a diverse set of Indigenous societies, distinct from one another yet sharing some important cultural practices, whose territories happen to be largely congruent with the first

attempts at English exploration and colonization in North America. For a
general history of the eastern Algonquian peoples' early encounters with
Europeans, see Karen Ordahl Kupperman, *Indians and English: Facing Off
in Early America* (Ithaca: Cornell University Press, 2000).

7. Jon E. Lewis, ed., *London: The Autobiography* (London: Constable and Robinson, 2008), 136; Peter C. Mancall, *Hakluyt's Promise: An Elizabethan's Obsession for an English America* (New Haven: Yale University Press, 2007), 104.

8. Stephen Inwood, *A History of London* (New York: Carroll and Graf, 1998), 161–62, 192–94; Lewis, *London: The Autobiography*, 130; Robert Gray, *A History of London* (New York: Dorset, 1978), 151. See also Lena Cowen Orlin, "Temporary Lives in London Lodgings," *Huntington Library Quarterly*, 71:1 (2008), 219–42.

9. Quinn, ed., *Roanoke Voyages*, 325, 337; John Donne, *A Sermon vpon the viii. verse of the 1. chapter of the Acts of the Apostles* (London, 1622), 21; Thomas Churchyard, *A Prayse and Report* (London, 1578), C4–C5; Christopher Carleill, "A Breef and Sommarie discourse upon the Entended Voyage to the Hethermoste Partes of America (April, 1583)," in *New American World*, ed. Quinn, 3:31; John Chamberlain, *The Chamberlain Letters: A Selection of the Letters of John Chamberlain Concerning Life in England from 1597 to 1626*, ed. Elizabeth McClure Thomson (New York: G. P. Putnam's Sons, 1965), 218; Susan Myra Kingsbury, ed., *The Records of the Virginia Company of London* (Washington: United States Government Printing Office, 1933), vol. 3, 259. See also Nicholas Canny, "The Permissive Frontier: The Problem of Social Control in English Settlements in Ireland and Virginia, 1550–1650," in *The Westward Enterprise: English Activities in Ireland, the Atlantic, and America, 1480–1650*, ed. K. R. Andrews, N. P. Canny, and P. E. H. Hair (Liverpool: Liverpool University Press, 1978), 25–26.

10. "Notes prepared by Richard Hakluyt the Elder for Sir Humphrey Gilbert (1578)," in *New American World*, ed. Quinn, 3:24, 26; Kingsbury, *The Records of the Virginia Company of London*, vol. 3, 99–100; "Martin Pring's voyage to North Virginia with the *Speedwell* and the *Discoverer*, April 10 to October 2, 1603," in *New American World*, ed. Quinn, 3:361; "John Brereton's narrative of Bartholomew Gosnold's voyage to North Virginia, March to July, 1602," in *New American World*, ed. Quinn, 3:350.

11. William Strachey, *A History of Travell* (London, 1612), 18–19; Canny, "The Permissive Frontier," 18; Harriot, "A briefe and true report"; see also Michael Leroy Oberg, *Dominion and Civility: English Imperialism and Native*

America, 1585–1685 (Ithaca: Cornell University Press, 1999), 12. For the place of Indigenous North Americans in the English historical imagination, see Sam Smiles, "John White and British Antiquity: Savage Origins in the Context of Tudor Historiography" in Sloan, *European Visions: American Voices*, 106–12.

12. "Instructions to Sir Thomas Gates for the government of Virginia, May 1609," in *New American World*, ed. Quinn, 5:214; "Lawes divine, morall, and martiall" promulgated for the colony of Virginia by Sir Thomas Dale, marshal and deputy governor of Virginia, June 22, 1611," in *New American World*, ed. Quinn, 5:225; Harriot, "A brief and true report," 3:141. For sanitary conditions in London, see Emily Cockayne, *Hubbub: Filth, Noise, and Stench in England, 1600–1770* (New Haven: Yale University Press, 2008).

13. This passage is a composite drawn from various sources in Quinn, ed., *New American World*.

14. "Instructions to Sir Thomas Gates," in *New American World*, ed. Quinn, 5:213; "Instructions to Thomas West, Lord De La Warr, governor of Virginia, 1610," in *New American World*, ed. Quinn, 5:220; James Rosier, "A true relation of the most prosperous voyage made in this present yeere 1605, by Captaine George Waymouth (London, 1605)," in *New American World*, ed. Quinn, 3:374. See also David C. Morey, *The Voyage of Archangell: James Rosier's Account of the Waymouth Voyage of 1605, a True Relation* (Gardiner, Maine: Tilbury House, 2005). For a discussion of Hunt's slaving, see Vaughan, *Transatlantic Encounters: American Indians in Britain, 1500–1776* (Cambridge: Cambridge University Press, 2007), 70, 75–76.

15. "Gabriel Archer's narrative of Gosnold's North Virginia voyage (1602)," in *New American World*, ed. Quinn, 3:355–56; Rosier, "A true relation," 3:370; Kingsbury, *The Records of the Virginia Company of London*, 3:71, 128–29. See also David G. Sweet and Gary B. Nash, eds., *Struggle and Survival in Colonial America* (Berkeley: University of California Press, 1981), 29–31.

16. "On the Sagadahoc expedition," in *New American World*, ed. Quinn, 3:427.

17. For Segipt and his family, see Vaughan, *Transatlantic Encounters*, 100–101.

18. Rosier, "A true relation," 3:378; Ferdinando Gorges, "A Brief Narration of the Original Undertakings of the Advancement of Plantations into the Parts of America," repr. in Maine Historical Society Collections, 1st series, 2 (1847), 3, quoted in Vaughan, *Transatlantic Encounters*, 57.

19. In addition to eastern Algonquian captives and travelers, there were a number of Inuit brought to Britain in the late sixteenth century, as well as a number of men from the Caribbean and northern coast of South America

in the late sixteenth and early seventeenth century. For the Inuit, see chapter 4 and Vaughan, *Transatlantic Encounters*, 1–12; for the others, see Vaughan, *Transatlantic Encounters*, 21–41.

20. For a discussion of the multivalent uses of Caliban, see Jodi Byrd, *The Transit of Empire: Indigenous Critiques of Colonialism* (Minneapolis: University of Minnesota Press, 2011). For the relationship between colonialism, theater, and pageants, including *The Memorable Mask*, see Bach, *Colonial Transformations*, 33–34, 115, 148–90.

21. George Percy, "A Discourse of the Plantation of the Southern Colonie in Virginia, 1606–1607," in *New American World*, ed. Quinn, 5:274; Sidney Lee, *Elizabethan and Other Essays*, ed. Frederick S. Boas (Freeport, N.Y.: Book for Libraries, 1968), 263–301; Vaughan, *Transatlantic Encounters*, 65–67; Ben Jonson, *Epicœne*, ed. Edward Partridge (New Haven: Yale University Press, 1971), 146–47; Ben Jonson, *The Staple of Newes* (London, 1626), act 2, scene 5, lines 118–24; *The London Encyclopaedia*, ed. Ben Weinreb and Christopher Hibbert (New York: Macmillan, 1983), 56.

22. Paula Gunn Allen, *Pocahontas: Medicine Woman, Spy, Entrepreneur, Diplomat* (New York: HarperOne, 2003), 233, 244; Robert Brenner, *Merchants and Revolution: Commercial Change, Political Conflict, and London's Overseas Traders, 1550–1653* (Cambridge: Cambridge University Press, 1993), 93–102; James Stuart, *Counterblaste to Tobacco* (1604), B2; Peter Mancall, "Tales Tobacco Told in Sixteenth-Century Europe," *Environmental History* 9:4 (2004), 648–78.

23. Gray, *A History of London*, 146; Shirley, *Thomas Harriot*, 71–80; Andrew Clark, ed., *"Brief Lives," Chiefly of Contemporaries, Set Down by John Aubrey, Between the Years 1669 and 1696* (Oxford: Clarendon Press, 1898), 2:183; Shirley, *Thomas Harriot*, 82–83; Bach, *Colonial Transformations*, 136; Paul Griffiths and Mark S. R. Jenner, eds., *Londinopolis: Essays in the Culture and Social History of Early Modern London* (Manchester, U.K.: Manchester University Press, 2000), 183.

24. "George Popham to James I, December 13, 1607," in *New American World*, ed. Quinn, 3:439; Brenner, *Merchants and Revolution*, 110; Samuel Purchas, *Hakluytus posthumus*, vol. 32, "The description of the Countrey of Mawooshen, discovered by the English in the yeere, 1602.3.5.6.7.8. and 9," 400–405; Vaughan, *Transatlantic Encounters*, 65–67.

25. Edward Wright, *Jamestown Narratives: Eyewitness Accounts of the Virginia Colony: The First Decade, 1607–1617* (Brighton: RoundHouse, 1998), 760–61; Brenner, *Merchants and Revolution*, 146; Lee, *Elizabethan and Other*

Essays, 287; Frederic W. Gleach, *Powhatan's World and Colonial Virginia: A Conflict of Cultures* (Lincoln: University of Nebraska Press, 1997), 144; Eric Gethyn-Jones, *George Thorpe and the Berkeley Company* (Stroud: Sutton, 1981), 55–58; Kingsbury, *Records of the Virginia Company*, 3:316.

26. There is a parallel for thinking about this kind of colonial knowledge production: the history of early modern science. Drawing on social history, material culture, history of the book, and postcolonial methodologies, scholars have transformed the history of science in the early modern period, moving from a linear progress of discoveries by isolated male elites to a much more complex, fluid process in which embodied practices, social relationships, and local, Indigenous, and other nonelite knowledges play significant parts. In the case of sixteenth-century London, for example, Deborah Harkness has described a metropolis of everyday experimentation "within . . . landmark buildings, on the streets around them, behind shopfronts, and upstairs in residences throughout the City [where] men and women were studying and manipulating nature." Harkness's scientific city was filled with "minor vernacular figures and their small successes, trial-and-error progress, and mundane aspirations," influenced by an urban sensibility that crossed class, ethnic, and even gender boundaries in the crowded urban landscape. "Networks of intellectual exchange and communities of inquiry," Harkness writes, "can be mapped onto the terrain of Elizabethan London in ways that illuminate the blind alleys and surprising twists and turns taken as science became the field of knowledge we recognize today." Harkness might just as easily be describing Algonquian London. See Harkness, *The Jewel House*.

27. Broadside 151 (1615), Lemon Collection, Society of Antiquaries of London.

28. Bach, *Colonial Transformations*, 125, 138; Vaughan, *Transatlantic Encounters*, 52–55; Helen C. Rountree, *The Powhatan Indians of Virginia: Their Traditional Culture* (Norman: University of Oklahoma Press, 1989), 102–3. For the most detailed discussion of the watercolor, see June Schlueter, *The Album Amicorum and the London of Shakespeare's Time* (London: British Library, 2011), 134–36.

29. Allen, *Pocahontas*, 60.

30. Gleach, *Powhatan's World*, 56–59; Rountree, *The Powhatan Indians*, 163 n. 142.

31. Ruth Holmes Whitehead, *Stories from the Six Worlds*, 6, 69–71, 72–74, 91; Ruth Holmes Whitehead, *The Old Man Told Us: Excerpts from Micmac History, 1500–1950* (Halifax, N.S.: Nimbus, 1991), 6; Frederick Matthew Wiseman, *The Voice of the Dawn: An Autohistory of the Abenaki Nation* (Hanover, N.H.: University Press of New England, 2001), 51; Rosier, "A true relation," 3:379–80.

32. Silas Rand, *Legends of the Micmacs* (1894), 232; James Freeman, *A Description of Duke's County, 1807*, Collections of the Massachusetts Historical Society 3, 2nd series (1815), 34–35; William S. Simmons, *Spirit of the New England Tribes: Indian History and Folklore, 1620–1984* (Hanover: University Press of New England, 1986), 70.

33. From J. D. Wilson, *Life in Shakespeare's London* (Harmondsworth: Pelican, 1944), 125–26.

34. Helen C. Rountree, *Pocahontas, Powhatan, Opechancanough: Three Indian Lives Changed by Jamestown* (Charlottesville: University of Virginia Press, 2005), 177–79; Allen, *Pocahontas*, 283–84.

35. John Chamberlain, *The Chamberlain Letters: A Selection of the Letters of John Chamberlain Concerning Life in England from 1597 to 1626*, ed. Elizabeth McClure Thomson (New York: G. P. Putnam's Sons, 1965), 215; "The Vision of Delight presented at covrt in Christmas, 1617," in *Ben Jonson*, ed. C. H. Herford (Oxford: Oxford University Press, 1952), 7:463–71.

36. Bach, *Colonial Transformations*, 191–219; Allen, *Pocahontas*, 264–66.

37. L. H. Roper, *The English Empire in America, 1602–1658: Beyond Jamestown* (London: Pickering and Chatto, 2009), 17, 73.

38. Rountree, *The Powhatan Indians*, 117, 131, 137; Rountree, *Pocahontas's People*, 62; Rountree, *Pocahontas et al.*, 179; Bruce Lenman, *England's Colonial Wars, 1550–1688: Conflicts, Empire, and National Identity* (Harlow, U.K.: Pearson Education, 2001), 232; Stephen R. Potter, "Early English Effects on Virginia Algonquian Exchange and Tribute in the Tidewater Potomac," in *Powhatan's Mantle: Indians in the Colonial Southeast*, ed. Gregory A. Waselkov, Peter H. Wood, and Tom Hatley (Lincoln: University of Nebraska Press, 2006), 222.

39. For summaries of the stories, including primary sources, see Vaughan, *Transatlantic Encounters*, 65–67. See also David J. Silverman, *Faith and Boundaries: Colonists, Christianity, and Community Among the Wampanoag Indians of Martha's Vineyard, 1600–1871* (Cambridge: Cambridge University Press, 2005), 13; and David G. Sweet and Gary B. Nash, eds., *Struggle and Survival in Colonial America* (Berkeley: University of California Press, 1981), 234, 236–37.

40. Mancall, "Native Americans and English Europeans," in *The Origins of Empire: British Overseas Enterprise to the Close of the Seventeenth Century*, ed. Nicholas Canny (Oxford: Oxford University Press, 1998), 339; Thomas Morton, *New England's Memorial* (1669), 25.

41. David B. Quinn, "'Virginians' on the Thames in 1603," *Terrae Incognitae* 2

(1970), 13; Charles G. Leland, *The Algonquin Legends of New England: Myths and Folk Lore of the Micmac, Passamaquoddy, and Penobscot Tribes* (Boston: Houghton, Mifflin, 1884), 127–29; Vaughan, *Transatlantic Encounters*, 97–99.

42. Rountree, *The Powhatan Indians*, 112; Strachey, *Historie of Travell*, 61; John White, *The Planter's Plea* (1630), 53–54; Haile, *Jamestown Narratives*, 760–61; Gleach, *Powhatan's World*, 144; Gethyn-Jones, *George Thorpe and the Berkeley Company*, 55–58.

43. Quinn, "'Virginians' on the Thames in 1603." For the river as a site of symbolic spectacle, from frost fairs to the appearances of strange fish, see Joseph P. Ward, "The Taming of the Thames: Reading the River in the Seventeenth Century," *Huntington Library Quarterly* 71:1 (2008), 55–76.

44. Kupperman, *Roanoke*, 175. For another Indigenous-centered account of the Roanoke colony's consequences, see Michael Leroy Oberg, "Lost Colonists, Lost Tribes," in Sloan, *European Visions: American Voices*, 101–5.

45. Alain Holt, "The Elizabethan Shooting Grounds," *Journal of the Society of Archer-Antiquaries* 28 (1985), 4. For Harriot's astronomical work and his later life, see Fox, *Thomas Harriot and His World*.

46. Rosier, "A true relation," 3:379–80; Roger Williams, *A Key into the Language of America and New England's Prospect* (1643), 156; John Smith, The *Generall Historie of Virgina, New-England, and the Summer Isles (1624)* (Chapel Hill: University of North Carolina Press, 1986), 149–52.

INTERLUDE TWO: A DEBTOR'S PETITION

1. The two ballads included here are "Good News for England or, The Worst Is Past" (1663–85?), Magdalene College Pepys Library, 4.296, and "The Siluer Age, or the VVorld turned backward" (1623?), Magdalene College Pepys Library 1.154, 1.155. Also available in the University of California, Santa Barbara, English Broadside Ballad Archive, ebba.english.ucsb.edu.

For the life of John Wampas and his time in England, see Jenny Pulsipher, "'Subjects unto the Same King': New England Indians and Royal Authority," *Massachusetts Historical Review* 5 (2003), 29–57; and Vaughan, *Transatlantic Encounters*, 104–6. Wampas's petition is "The Humble Peticion of John Wampas alias White," PRO CO 1/37 fol. 175, and the response is "Response to petition of John Wampas alias White," CO 389/4, 150, both in the National Archives of the United Kingdom. See also Charles II to John Leverett, 22 August 1676, in Robert Earle Moody, ed., *Saltonstall Papers 1607–1815* (Boston: Massachusetts Historical Society, 1972), 1:164–65.

Additional petitions from the debtor's prisons of London used here are "The humble Petition of the poor distressed Prisoners in the Compter at Bishopsgate" (London: J. F., 1666); "The Humble Petition of the Poor Prisoners in Ludgate" (n.p., n.d., 1700?); "Imprisonment of Mens Bodys for Debt, as the practice of England now stands" (London, 1641); and "The petition and Case of the Poor Prisoners for Debt" (n.p., n.d., 1700?).

For the history of King Philip's War, see Jill Lepore, *The Name of War: King Philip's War and the Origins of American Identity* (New York: Vintage, 1999).

Algonquian words and place names come from James Hammond Trumbull, *Natick Dictionary: A New England Indian Lexicon* (Lincoln: University of Nebraska Press, 2009).

CHAPTER 3. ALIVE FROM AMERICA

Epigraphs: *London: A History in Verse*, ed. Mark Ford (Cambridge: Harvard University Press, 2012), 280; James Thomas Stevens, *Bulle/Chimère* (Lawrence: First Intensity, 2006), n.p.

1. For secondary treatments of the incident at Vauxhall, see Alden Vaughan, *Transatlantic Encounters: American Indians in Britain, 1500–1776* (Cambridge: Cambridge University Press, 2007), 172–73; and John Oliphant, "The Cherokee Embassy to London, 1762," *Journal of Imperial and Commonwealth History* 27:1 (1999), 1–26. For two studies produced by the Museum of the Cherokee Indian, see the anthology *Culture, Crisis, and Conflict: Cherokee British Relations 1756–1765*, eds. Anne F. Rogers and Barbara R. Duncan (Cherokee, N.C.: Museum of the Cherokee Indian, 2009); and the museum catalog *Emissaries of Peace: The 1762 Cherokee and British Delegations* (Cherokee, N.C.: Museum of the Cherokee Indian, 2006).

2. See Joseph Burke and Colin Caldwell, *Hogarth: The Complete Engravings* (London: Thames and Hudson, 1968); and David Coke and Alan Borg, *Vauxhall Gardens: A History* (New Haven: Yale University Press, 2011). For Vauxhall's imperial implications, see Miles Ogborn, *Spaces of Modernity: London's Geographies, 1680–1780* (New York: Guilford, 1998), 142–57.

3. Coke and Borg, *Vauxhall Gardens*, 157.

4. For overviews of the four groups, see Vaughan, *Transatlantic Encounters*, 113–64. In addition to the groups that are the focus of this chapter, a young Yamasee man was brought to London in 1713 by the Society for the Propagation of the Gospel. Baptized as "George" by the Bishop of London, the

otherwise unnamed "prince" spent up to three years in Britain undergoing training in English and Christianity. His ultimate fate is unknown. In 1719, three poorly documented "Indian Kings"—Oakecharinga and Tuskeetanagee, plus a third unnamed man—spent time on display in the city. None of these men left significant archival footprints. See Vaughan, *Transatlantic Encounters,* 133–36.

5. For the shop sign exhibition, see Mark Bills, *The Art of Satire: London in Caricature* (London: Philip Wilson, 2006), 50.

6. Adrian Johns, *The Nature of the Book: Print and Knowledge in the Making* (Chicago: University of Chicago Press, 2000), 62–74. See also John Brewer, *The Pleasures of the Imagination: British Culture in the Eighteenth Century* (London: Routledge, 1997), 131–44; and Robert O. Bucholz and Joseph P. Ward, *London: A Social and Cultural History, 1550–1750* (Cambridge: Cambridge University Press, 2012), 171–86.

7. *The Four Indian Kings Speech* (London, 1710), Huntington Library.

8. For the most comprehensive accounts of the journey, see Richmond P. Bond, *Queen Anne's American Kings* (Oxford: Oxford University Press, 1952); and Eric Hinderaker, "The 'Four Indian Kings' and the Imaginative Construction of the British Empire," *William and Mary Quarterly* 53:3 (July 1996), 487–526. For the political context of their voyage, see Matthew Dennis, *Cultivating a Landscape of Peace: Iroquois-European Encounters in Seventeenth-Century America* (Ithaca: Cornell University Press, 1993).

9. For the Mahican, see Patrick Frazier, *The Mohicans of Stockbridge* (Lincoln: University of Nebraska Press, 1992). For general discussion of the Covenant Chain in the colonial period, see Daniel K. Richter, *The Ordeal of the Longhouse: The Peoples of the Iroquois League in the Era of European Colonization* (Chapel Hill: University of North Carolina Press, 1992).

10. For their itinerary, see Bond, *Queen Anne's American Kings.*

11. *The Four Kings of Canada* (London: J. Baker, 1710), 6–8; *The Spectator,* 27 April 1711.

12. Brewer, *The Pleasures of the Imagination,* xvii, xxx, 28–29, and 50–51. For forms of knowledge production and dissemination beyond formal print sources—and beyond London—see Kathleen Wilson, *The Sense of the People: Politics, Culture, and Imperialism in England, 1715–1785* (Cambridge: Cambridge University Press, 1998).

13. *The Four Kings of Canada,* 3–4; *History and Progress of the Four Indian Kings* (London: A. Hinde, 1710), 3; Elkanah Settle, *A Pindaric Poem* (1711), 3.

14. Charles Harding Firth, *An American Garland* (Oxford: B. H. Blackwell,

1915), 60–68. As Paula McDowell has shown in *The Women of Grub Street: Press, Politics, and Power in the London Literary Marketplace, 1678–1730* (Oxford: Clarendon Press, 1998), women played a small but significant role in the print culture of the late seventeenth and early eighteenth centuries. However, none of the authors of accounts of Indigenous visitors during this period are identifiably female, suggesting the connection between portrayals of Indigenous people and women, discussions of transatlantic politics, and male prerogatives.

15. *History and Progress*, 5–6.

16. For primary sources and discussion of representations of the Four Kings, see Bond, *Queen Anne's American Kings*, 10, 66–68, 70. Lower-class cultural expressions of interest in the visitors have tended to draw scorn from scholars. Bond, for example, described these sorts of sources using phrases such as "a collaboration of inadequacy," "thin gruel warmed over," "inexcusable couplets," "dim, dull words signifying next to nothing," and the work of "a busy scissors-and-paster."

17. *The Spectator*, 27 April 1711; and *The Four Kings of Canada*, 6–8.

18. The most well documented wampum—and perhaps the most powerful— is the Two-Row Wampum (Kasentha, in the Mohawk language), used in negotiations to represent the parallel but separate realms of European and Indigenous societies. As Taiaiake Alfred writes in *Peace, Power, and Righteousness: An Indigenous Manifesto* (Oxford: Oxford University Press, 2008), the Kasentha represents "two vessels, each possessing its own integrity, travelling the river of time together" (52). For the implications of wampum and the ideas it represents for modern Indigenous-settler relations, see John Borrows, "Wampum at Niagara: The Royal Proclamation, Canadian Legal History, and Self-Government," in *Aboriginal and Treaty Rights in Canada*, ed. Michael Asch (Vancouver: UBC Press, 1997), 155–72.

19. For a discussion of the event, see James Roach, *Cities of the Dead: Circum-Atlantic Performance* (New York: Columbia University Press, 1996), 8, 161–73. See also Hinderaker, "The 'Four Indian Kings,'" 498.

20. Bond, *Queen Anne's American Kings*, 10–12, 23; Abel Boyer, *History of the Reign of Queen Anne Digested into Annals* (London, 1703–13), 9:197–99, 201; Thomas Hearne, *Remarks and Collections of Thomas Hearne*, ed. David Watson Rannie (Oxford: Clarendon Press, 1901), 2:385. For the general context of the Sacherevell Riots, see John Stevenson, *Popular Disturbances in England, 1700–1832* (London: Longman Group, 1992), 73–76; Mark Knights, *The Devil in Disguise: Deception, Delusion, and Fanaticism in the*

Early English Enlightenment (Oxford: Oxford University Press, 2011), 142–92; and Bucholz and Ward, *London: A Social and Cultural History,* 304–5. A German visitor, Zacharias von Uffenbach, witnessed much of the Sacherevell trial and made no mention of the Four Kings at all, suggesting that the story of their intervention is spurious. See Uffenbach, *London in 1710, from the Travels of Zacharias Conrad von Uffenbach* (London: Faber and Faber, 1934), 126.

21. Lady Strafford, "The Mohock Club," *The Wentworth Papers 1705–1739,* ed. Thomas Wentworth (1883), quoted in Jon E. Lewis, *London: The Autobiography,* 199–200; and John Fuller, ed., *John Gay: Dramatic Works,* vol. 1 (Oxford: Clarendon Press, 1983), 3–5, 81, 98–99. For comprehensive discussions of the Mohocks, see Daniel Statt, "The Case of the Mohocks: Rake Violence in Augustan London," *Social History* 20:2 (May 1995), 179–99; and John Timbs, *Clubs and Club Life in London* (London: Chatto and Windus, 1872), 33–37.

22. R. A. Roberts, ed., *Manuscripts of the Earl of Egmont: Diary, 1730–1747* (London: Historical Manuscripts Commission, 1920–23), 2:124; Bill Grantham, *Creation Myths and Legends of the Creek Indians* (Gainesville: University Press of Florida, 2002), 58; Stephen C. Hahn, *The Invention of the Creek Nation, 1670–1763* (Lincoln: University of Nebraska Press, 2004), 154–55; and Julie Anne Sweet, *Negotiating for Georgia: British-Creek Relations in the Trustee Era, 1733–1752* (Athens: University of Georgia Press, 2005), 24–27.

23. Sweet, *Negotiating for Georgia,* 48.

24. Sir Alexander Cuming, "Journal of Sir Alexander Cuming (1730)," in *Early Travels in the Tennessee Country, 1540–1800,* ed. Samuel Cole Williams (Johnson City, Tenn.: Watauga, 1928), 126, 138–39, 143; Alexander Pope, "Windsor-Forest," in *The Poems of Alexander Pope,* ed. John Butt (New Haven: Yale University Press, 1963), 210.

25. Roberts, *Manuscripts of the Earl of Egmont: Diary,* 2:113–14. For discussion of the political context of the Yamacraw, see Matthew Jennings, *New Worlds of Violence: Cultures and Conquests in the Early American Southeast* (Knoxville: University of Tennessee Press, 2011), 169–74.

26. "Conversation Between Governor Glen and Little Carpenter," December 1755, *Early American Indian Documents,* vol. 13: *North and South Carolina Treaties, 1654–1756,* ed. W. Stitt Robinson (Frederick, Md.: University Publications of America, 2001), 300; Cuming, "Journal," 127; and Nancy Shoemaker, *A Strange Likeness: Becoming Red and White in Eighteenth-Century North America* (Oxford: Oxford University Press, 2004), 41.

278 NOTES TO PAGES 86–88

27. *Emissaries of Peace*, 36. For political genealogies of the Cherokee, see Stan Hoig, *The Cherokees and Their Chiefs: In the Wake of Empire* (Little Rock: University of Arkansas Press, 1999).

28. Vaughan, *Transatlantic Encounters*, 139–50. Roberts, *Manuscripts of the Earl of Egmont: Diary*, 2:122–23. Hahn, *The Invention of the Creek Nation*, 150. Henry Timberlake, *Memoirs of Lieut. Henry Timberlake* (London, 1765), 124. "Conference of Governor Boone and the Council with Osteneco (Judd's Friend) about his Visit to England," 3 November 1762, *Early American Indian Documents*, vol. 14: *North and South Carolina Treaties, 1757–1775*, ed. W. Stitt Robinson (Frederick, Md.: University Publications of America, 2003), 201; "The Earl of Egmont's Report on the Royal Audience," 1 August 1734, *Early American Indian Documents*, vol. 11: *Georgia Treaties, 1733–1763*, ed. John T. Juricek (Frederick, Md.: University Publications of America, 1989), 23; John Perceval, *Journal of the Earl of Egmont: Abstract of the Trustees Proceedings for Establish the Colony of Georgia, 1732–1738*, ed. Robert C. McPherson (Athens: University of Georgia Press, 1962), 60–62; and "Talks with the Trustees on Trade Regulation," 11 September 1734, *Early American Indian Documents*, vol. 11, 24.

29. Richard D. Altick, *The Shows of London* (London: Belknap Press, 1978), 47; *Gazette and London Daily Advertiser*, 5 August 1762. For accounts of the very real lives behind the categories of "mob" and "European savage," see Lucy Moore, *Con Men and Cutpurses: Scenes from the Hogarthian Underworld* (New York: Penguin, 2004).

30. Cuming, *Journal*, 119; *Dublin Intelligence*, 27 June 1730 and 4 July 1730; Roberts, *Manuscripts of the Earl of Egmont: Diary*, 2:122–23; Oliphant, "The Cherokee Embassy," 19–20.

31. For general studies of gender dynamics in the period, see Susan Kingsley Kent, *Gender and Power in Britain, 1640–1990* (London: Routledge, 1999); G. J. Barker-Benfield, *The Culture of Sensibility: Sex and Society in Eighteenth-Century Britain* (Chicago: University of Chicago Press, 1992); Vivien Jones, ed., *Women in the Eighteenth Century: Constructions of Femininity* (London: Routledge, 1990); Kathleen Wilson, *The Sense of the People: Politics, Culture, and Imperialism in England, 1715–1785* (Cambridge: Cambridge University Press, 1995); Felicity Nussbaum, *Torrid Zones: Maternity, Sexuality, and Empire in Eighteenth-Century English Narratives* (Baltimore: Johns Hopkins University Press, 1995); Anthony Fletcher, *Gender, Sex, and Subordination in England, 1500–1800* (New Haven: Yale University Press, 1995).

32. "New Humourous Song on the Cherokee Chiefs, Inscribed to the Ladies of Great Britain" (London: H. Howard, 1762).

33. See M. Dorothy George, *London Life in the Eighteenth Century* (New York: Penguin, 1966), 41–55; Patrick Dillon, *Gin: The Much Lamented Death of Madame Geneva: The Eighteenth Century Gin Craze* (Boston: Justin, Charles, 2004); Jessica Warner, *Craze: Gin and Debauchery in an Age of Reason* (New York: Random House, 2003); and Lee Davison, "Experiments in the Social Regulation of Industry: Gin Legislation, 1729–1751," in *Stilling the Grumbling Hive: The Response to Social and Economic Problems in England, 1689–1750,* ed. Robert B. Shoemaker (New York: Macmillan, 1992), 25–48.

34. Roberts, *Manuscripts of the Earl of Egmont: Diary,* 2:122, 129; Timberlake, *Memoirs,* 57–58.

35. Roy Porter, *English Society in the Eighteenth Century* (London: Allen Lane/Pelican, 1982), 118; Bond, *Queen Anne's American Kings,* 88–89.

36. Philip Otterness, *Becoming German: The 1709 Palatine Migration to New York* (Ithaca: Cornell University Press, 2004), 53, 63–64; David L. Preston, *The Texture of Contact: European and Indian Settler Communities on the Frontier of Iroquoia, 1667–1783* (Lincoln: University of Nebraska Press), 71–85; Sweet, *Negotiating for Georgia,* 40; Francis Moore, *A Voyage to Georgia: Begun in the Year 1735* (London: Jacob Robinson, 1744), 34–35, 98; "Conference of the Cherokees with Governor Glen, April 29, 1745," *Early American Indian Documents,* vol. 13, 185; and Timberlake, *Memoirs,* 53.

37. "Governor Robert Hunter's Conference with the Five Nations, Schaghticoke, and River Nations at Albany," August 1710, *Early American Indian Documents,* vol. 8: *New York and New Jersey Treaties, 1683–1713,* ed. Barbara Graymont (Frederick, Md.: University Publications of America, 1995), 613; Patrick Frazier, *The Mohicans of Stockbridge* (Lincoln: University of Nebraska Press, 1994), 7; Richter, *The Ordeal of the Longhouse,* 266; and Izumi Ishii, *Bad Fruits of the Civilized Tree: Alcohol and the Sovereignty of the Cherokee Nation* (Lincoln: University of Nebraska Press, 2008),13–37.

38. Richter, *The Ordeal of the Longhouse;* Alan Taylor, *The Divided Ground: Indians, Settlers, and the Northern Borderland of the American Revolution* (New York: Vintage, 2007); Cameron B. Wesson, *Households and Hegemony: Early Creek Prestige Goods, Symbolic Capital, and Social Power* (Lincoln: University of Nebraska Press, 2008), 23; Moore, *A Voyage to Georgia,* 36, 106–7; Ishii, *Bad Fruits of the Civilized Tree,* 13–37; and Theda Perdue, *Cherokee Women: Gender and Culture Change, 1700–1835* (Winnipeg: Bison, 1999), 84, 86–108.

39. Roach, *Cities of the Dead*, 30, and James Oglethorpe, "A Curious Account of the Indians," in *Early American Indian Documents*, vol. 11, 9–10.

40. For discussion of the waxworks, see Troy Bickham, " 'A Conviction of the Reality of Things': Material Culture, North American Indians, and Empire in Eighteenth-Century Britain," *Eighteenth-Century Studies* 39:1 (2005), 29–47. For the case of the Mohawks, see Altick, *The Shows of London*, 47; and Vaughan, *Transatlantic Encounters*, 182–86.

41. For the 1790s delegation, see Stephanie Pratt, "Representatives and Representation: Southern Indians in Eighteenth-Century Britain," in *Native Americans and Anglo-American Culture, 1750–1850*, ed. Tim Fulford and Kevin Hutchings (Cambridge: Cambridge University Press, 2013), 112–35.

42. Bond, *Queen Anne's American Kings*, 51–52; 64; Barbara J. Sivertsen, *Turtles, Wolves, and Bears: A Mohawk Family History* (Berwyn Heights, Md.: Heritage, 2009), 58–71; and Hinderaker, "The 'Four Indian Kings.' "

43. Roberts, *Manuscripts of the Earl of Egmont: Diary*, 2:125–26; Thomas Christie to the Trustees, 19 March 1734/1735, *Colonial Records of the State of Georgia* (Atlanta: Franklin Printing, 1904–16), 20:269–73; and Hahn, *The Invention of the Creek Nation*, 169–70, 186; Jennings, *New Worlds of Violence*, 173.

44. See Hoig, *The Cherokees and Their Chiefs*, 127–28 n. 39.

45. All correspondence comes from Derek Jarrett, ed., *Memoirs of the Reign of King George III*, The Yale Edition of Horace Walpole's Correspondence (1937–83) (New Haven: Yale University Press, 2000), as follows: Walpole to Laddy Ossory, 9 October 1789, 34:73; Walpole to Horace Mann, 2 February 1785, 25:557; Walpole to Mann, 21 August 1755, 20:492; Walpole to Lord Strafford, 12 June 1780, 35:354; Walpole to Mann, 30 March 1784, 25:490; Walpole to C. H. Williams, 7 September 1745, 30:94; and Walpole to Montagu, 28 July 1762, 10:36.

46. Stephen Storace, *The Cherokee: An Opera in Three Acts* (London, 1795), British Library.

47. Eric Hinderaker, *The Two Hendricks: Unraveling a Mohawk Mystery* (Cambridge: Harvard University Press, 2010), 87.

INTERLUDE THREE: ATLANTES

1. For references to the boy, discussion of Townshend's relationship with the Odawa, and the history of the Townshend monument in Westminster Abbey, see John Fleming, "Robert Adam, Luc-François Breton, and the

Townshend Monument in Westminster Abbey," *Connoisseur* 150:165 (July 1962), 162–71; Thomas Gray, *Correspondence of Thomas Gray*, ed. Paget Toynbee and Leonard Whibley, vol. 2, letter 308, to Thomas Wharton, 23 January 1760 (Oxford: Oxford University Press, 1935), 367; Hugh Honour, *The New Golden Land: European Images of America from the Discoveries to the Present Time* (London: Allen Lane, 1975), 128; Alan McNairn, *Behold the Hero: General Wolfe at the Arts in the Eighteenth Century* (Liverpool: Liverpool University Press, 1997), 168; Stephanie Pratt, *American Indians in British Art, 1700–1840* (Norman: University of Oklahoma Press, 2005), 45–48; and the Townshend manuscript at the British Library: Add MSS 50006.

CHAPTER 4. "SUCH CONFUSION AS I NEVER DREAMT"

Epigraphs: Jean-Jacques Rousseau, *The Major Political Writings of Jean-Jacques Rousseau: The Two Discourses and the Social Contract*, ed. and trans. John C. Scott (Chicago: University of Chicago Press, 2012), 148; and John Bennett and Susan Rowley, comps. and eds., *Uqalurait: An Oral History of Nunavut* (Montreal: McGill-Queen's University Press, 2004), 120.

1. Moritz is quoted in Jerry White, *London in the Eighteenth Century: A Great and Monstrous Thing* (New York: Vintage), 77.

2. Jeremy Black, *London: A History* (New York: International Publishers Marketing, 2013), 177; John Summerson, *Georgian London* (London: Paul Mellon Centre, 2003), 15; Lawrence Klein, *Shaftesbury and the Culture of Politeness: Moral Discourse and Cultural Politics in Early Eighteenth-Century England* (Cambridge: Cambridge University Press, 1994); James Stuart, *Critical Observations on the Buildings and Improvements of London* (London: J. Dodsley, 1771), 4; Todd Longstaffe-Gowan, *The London Square: Gardens in the Midst of Town* (London: Paul Mellon Centre, 2012); Miles Ogborn, *Spaces of Modernity: London's Geographies, 1680–1780* (New York: Guilford, 1998); Paul A. Elliott, *Enlightenment, Modernity, and Science: Geographies of Scientific Culture and Improvement in Georgian England* (London: I. B. Tauris, 2010), 220.

3. Quoted in White, *London in the Eighteenth Century*, 66; Stuart, *Critical Observations*, 49–50.

4. John Gwynn, *London and Westminster Improved* (London, 1766), n.p.

5. John Bruce, *The Poetical Works of William Cowper, with Notes and a Memoir* (London, 1865), 2:31.

6. For images of Indigenous North Americans in the eighteenth century, see

Troy Bickham, *Savages Within the Empire: Representations of American Indians in Eighteenth-Century Britain* (Oxford: Oxford University Press, 2005); and Tim Fulford and Kevin Hutchings, eds., *Native Americans and Anglo-American Culture, 1750–1850: The Indian Atlantic* (Cambridge: Cambridge University Press, 2009); and Robert F. Berkhofer Jr., *The White Man's Indian: Images of the American Indian from Columbus to the Present* (New York: Vintage, 1978), 76–77. Boswell is quoted in P. J. Marshall and Glyndwr Williams, *The Great Map of Mankind: Perceptions of New Worlds in the Age of Enlightenment* (Cambridge: Harvard University Press, 1982), 196.

7. Robertson is quoted in Marshall and Williams, *The Great Map of Mankind*, 219–20. For discussions of Johnson and Ashley-Cooper's attitudes and their relationship to broader ideas, see Kate Fullagar, *The Savage Visit: New World People and Imperial Popular Culture in Britain, 1710–1795* (Berkeley: University of California Press, 2012), 4–8.

8. Roy Porter, *Enlightenment* (London: Penguin U.K., 2001), 18.

9. Samson Occom, "Saying What Think Ye of Christ (II)," in *The Collected Writings of Samson Occom, Mohegan: Leadership and Literature in Eighteenth-Century Native America*, ed. Joanna Brooks (Oxford: Oxford University Press, 2006), 174–76. The biblical passage comes from the New Revised Standard Version.

10. Lisa Brooks, *The Common Pot: The Recovery of Native Space in the Northeast* (St. Paul: University of Minnesota Press, 2008). The Mohegan, though also an Algonquian people, are distinct from the similarly named Mahican.

11. For these religious developments in North America, see Thomas S. Kidd, *The Great Awakening: The Roots of Evangelical Christianity in Colonial America* (New Haven: Yale University Press, 2009).

12. For Occom's early engagements with the Great Awakening and his work on Indigenous rights, see his biographical profile in *The Collected Writings*. For the Great Awakening among Indigenous people more generally, see Linford Fisher, *The Indian Great Awakening: Religion and the Shaping of Indian Cultures in Early America* (Oxford: Oxford University Press, 2012).

13. Nancy L. Rhoden, *English Atlantics Revisited: Essays Honoring Ian K. Steele* (Montreal: McGill-Queens University Press, 2007); for discussions of George Whitefield, see Frank Lambert, *"Pedlar in Divinity": George Whitefield and the Transatlantic Revivals* (Princeton: Princeton University Press, 1994).

14. Leon Burr Richardson, *An Indian Preacher in England: Being Letters and*

Diaries Relating to the Mission of the Reverend Samson Occom and the Reverend Nathaniel Whitaker (Hanover, N.H.: Dartmouth College Publications, 1933), 82–83.

15. Jacques Casanova, *The Memoirs of Jacques Casanova,* ed. Joseph Monét (New York: Wiley, 1946), 68; Tobias Smollett, *The Expedition of Humphry Clinker* (San Francisco: Reinhart, 1950), 97; James Boswell, *A London Journal, 1762–1763* (New Haven: Yale University Press, 2004), 44.

16. Richardson, *An Indian Preacher,* 83–85.

17. Samson Occom to Benjamin Forfitt, March 1771, *The Collected Writings,* 95.

18. Richardson, *An Indian Preacher,* 84.

19. Ibid., 83–85.

20. Alden Vaughan, *Transatlantic Encounters: American Indians in Great Britain, 1500–1776* (Cambridge: Cambridge University Press, 2007), 203–4.

21. The spelling of the party's names is drawn from Louis Jacques Dorais, *The Inuit Language in Southern Labrador, 1694–1785* (Ottawa: National Museum of Canada, 1980), 12, 13, 18, 19, 22, 26. For the accounts of London, see George Cartwright, *A Journal of Transactions and Events During a Residence of Nearly Sixteen Years on the Coast of Labrador* (Newark, U.K.: Allin and Ridge, 1792), 1:266–67.

22. Cartwright, *A Journal,* 1:266–67, 269.

23. Richard H. Jordan, "Inuit Occupation of the Central Labrador Coast Since 1600 AD," in *Our Footprints Are Everywhere: Inuit Land Use and Occupancy in Labrador,* ed. Carol Brice-Bennett (Nain, N.L.: Labrador Inuit Association, 1977), 43–48; Dorais, *The Inuit Language,* 1–3; Cartwright, *A Journal,* 1:B2. For a detailed discussion of Mikkuq and her child, see Kevin Major, *As Near to Heaven by Sea: A History of Newfoundland and Labrador* (Toronto: Penguin, 2001), 136–43.

24. George Cartwright, *The New Labrador Papers of Captain George Cartwright,* ed. Marianne Stopp (Montreal: McGill-Queen's University Press, 2008), 26, 30–31, 178.

25. Cartwright, *A Journal,* 1:267–68.

26. Ibid., 1:268, 270–71.

27. Ibid., 1:266–67, 270.

28. John R. Bennett and Susan Rowley, *Uqalurait: An Oral History of Nunavut* (Montreal: McGill-Queen's University Press, 2008), 157–59.

29. Hugh Brody, *The Other Side of Eden: Hunters, Farmers, and the Shaping of the World* (Vancouver: Douglas and McIntyre, 2001), 46–47; Jean L. Briggs, *Never in Anger: Portrait of an Eskimo Family* (Cambridge: Harvard Univer-

sity Press, 1970); Keavy Martin, "The Sovereign Obscurity of Inuit Literature," *The Oxford Handbook of Indigenous American Literature,* eds. Daniel Heath Justice and James H. Cox (Oxford: Oxford University Press, 2014).

30. Charles P. Moritz, *Travels, Chiefly on Foot, Through Several Parts of England in 1782. Described in Letters to a Friend by Charles P. Moritz, Translated from the German by a Lady* (London, 1795), 11, 44; Cartwright, *A Journal,* 1:266.

31. Cartwright, *A Journal,* 1:265–66 (second pagination); Black, *London: A History,* 201; Smollett, *The Expedition of Humphry Clinker,* 97; Gwynn, *London and Westminster Improved,* n.p.

32. Daniel Defoe, *A Tour thro' the Whole Island of Great Britain Divided into Circuits or Journies by Daniel Defoe, Gent, 1724–1726,* ed. Pat Rogers (Harmondsworth, U.K., 1971), 287; White, *London in the Eighteenth Century,* 70; Cartwright, *A Journal,* 1:268–69.

33. J. K. Laughton, "Dance, Sir Nathaniel (1748–1827)," *Oxford Dictionary of National Biography* (ODNB), and Sally Jeffery, "Dance, George, the Elder," *Oxford Dictionary of National Biography,* www.oxforddnb.com. The drawing is in the collection of the Knatchbull family and can be seen in Marianne P. Stopp, "Eighteenth Century Labrador Inuit in England," *Arctic* 62:1 (2009), 58.

34. *London Magazine,* July 1776; James Boswell, *The Ominous Years: 1774–1776* (New York: McGraw-Hill, 1963), 341–42.

35. Isabel Thompson Kelsay, *Joseph Brant, 1743–1807: Man of Two Worlds* (Syracuse: Syracuse University Press, 1986), 161–62; *Daily Advertiser,* 1 March 1776.

36. Kelsay, *Joseph Brant,* 166.

37. *Gazetteer and New Daily Advertiser,* 1 March 1776; Germaine to General John Burgoyne, 28 March 1776 and 23 August 1776, in Kelsay, *Joseph Brant,* 165.

38. *Gazetteer and New Daily Advertiser,* 20 March 1776.

39. Daniel Claus, *Captain Brant and the Old King: The Tragedy of Wyoming* (Buffalo, N.Y.: Buffalo Historical Society, 1889), 14; Kelsay, *Joseph Brant,* 167–69; James W. Paxton, *Joseph Brant and His World: Eighteenth-Century Mohawk Warrior and Statesman* (Toronto: James Lorimer, 2008), 39–40.

40. Kelsay, *Joseph Brant,* 172. For the Freemasons in the context of improvement, see Elliott, *Enlightenment, Modernity, and Science.*

41. See Elizabeth Elbourne, "Family Politics and Anglo-Mohawk Diplomacy: The Brant Family in Imperial Context," *Journal of Colonialism and Colonial History* 6:3 (2005).

42. Helen Caister Robinson, *Joseph Brant: A Man for His People* (New York: Longman, 1972), 117–22; Paxton, *Joseph Brant and His World*, 57–58.

43. Horace Walpole, *The Last Journals of Horace Walpole During the Reign of George III*, ed. A. Francis Steuart (London: J. Lane, 1910), 2:404–5; Mary Hamilton, *Mary Hamilton: At Court and at Home from Letters and Diaries 1756 to 1816*, ed. Elizabeth and Florence Anson (London: John Murray, 1925), 170–71; Harvey Chalmers, *Joseph Brant: Mohawk* (East Lansing: Michigan State University Press, 1955), 80–81; Steven Parissien, *George IV: The Grand Entertainment* (London: John Murray, 2001); Christopher Hibbert, *George IV* (London: Penguin, 1972), esp. 50–67. For scathing popular representations of George both before and during his reign, see Kenneth Baker, *George IV: A Life in Caricature* (London: Thames and Hudson, 2005).

44. Elliott, *Enlightenment, Modernity, and Science*, 219–46; Kelsay, *Joseph Brant*, 387.

45. Samson Occom to Robert Keen, September 1768, *The Collected Writings*, 82; To Eleazar Wheelock, 24 July 1771, *The Collected Writings*, 98; Occom to Eleazar Wheelock, July 24, 1771, *The Collected Writings*, 98; Occom to John Bailey, June or July 1783, *The Collected Writings*, 115.

46. Samson Occom, "They Don't Want Indians to Go to Heaven with Them" (1768), *The Collected Writings*, 86; To the Oneida Tribe, 1775, *The Collected Writings*, 111–12; "The Most Remarkable and Strange State Situation and Appearence of Indian Tribes in this Great Continent" (1783), *The Collected Writings*, 58; To John Thornton, January 1, 1777, *The Collected Writings*, 114. For an extensive and comprehensive account of the Mohegan land case, see Paul Grant-Costa, "The Last Indian War in New England: The Mohegan Indians v. the Governour and Company of the Colony of Connecticut, 1703–1774" (Ph.D. diss., Yale University, 2008).

47. See Thomas Campbell, *Gertrude of Wyoming; A Pennsylvanian Tale* (London: Bolt Court, 1809). For discussion of Campbell's work, see Tim Fulford, *Romantic Indians: Native Americans, British Literature, and Transatlantic Culture, 1756–1830* (Oxford: Oxford University Press, 2006). For discussion of Thayendanegea's activism in the context of Mohawk sovereignty more generally, see Rick Monture, *We Share Our Matters: Two Centuries of Writing and Resistance at Six Nations of the Grand River* (Winnipeg: University of Manitoba Press, 2014).

48. M. P. Stopp and Greg Mitchell, "'Our Amazing Visitors': Catherine Cartwright's Account of Labrador Inuit in England," *Arctic* 63:4 (2010), 399–

413; Cartwright, *A Journal*, 1:271–73 (second pagination); Cartwright, *The New Labrador Papers*, 177.

INTERLUDE FOUR: A LOST MUSEUM

1. For the founding of Sydney and its relations with the local Eora people, see Grace Karskens, *Colony: A History of Early Sydney* (Crows Nest, N.S.W.: Allen and Unwin, 2011).

Accounts of Bennelong and Yemmerrawannie's time in England can be found in Jack Brook, "The Forlorn Hope: Bennelong and Yemmerrawannie Go to England," *Australian Aboriginal Studies* 1 (2001), 36–47; Kate Fullagar, "Bennelong in Britain," *Aboriginal History* 33 (2009), 31–51; and John Turnbull, *A voyage around the world, in the years 1800, 1801, 1802, 1803, and 1804; in which the author visited the principal islands in the Pacific Ocean, and the English settlements of Port Jackson and Norfolk* (Philadelphia: Benjamin and Thomas Kite, 1810), 42–44. See also the Web site findingbennelong.com.

For the history of the Leverian Museum, see Adrienne L. Kaeppler, *Holophusicon: The Leverian Museum: An Eighteenth-Century Institution of Science, Curiosity, and Art* (Munich: Zkf, 2011). Original accounts of the museum include *A Companion to the museum (late Sir Ashton Lever's), removed to Albion Street, the Surry end of Black Friars Bridge* (London, 1790) and Anthony Ella, *Visits to the Leverian Museum; containing an account of several of its principal curiosities, both of nature and art: intended for the instruction of young persons in the first principles of natural history* (London: Tabart, n.d.); and *Catalog of the Leverian Museum* (London, 1806).

The song is recorded in Edward Jones, *Musical Curiosities; of a selection of the most characteristic national songs and airs, many of which were never before published: consisting of Spanish, Portuguese, Russian Danish, Lapland, Malabar, New South Wales, French, Italian, Swiss, and particularly some English and Scotch National Melodies, to which are added Variations for the Harp or the Piano Forte; and most Humbly Inscribed by Permission, to Her Royal Highness the Princess Charlotte of Wales* (London, 1811), 15.

CHAPTER 5. THAT KIND URBANITY OF MANNER

1. *Journal of Archibald Menzies, 1791–94*, British Library, Add. MS. 32641.
2. *Edward Bell's Journal of the voyage of HMS Chatham to the Pacific Ocean*, 95–97, Alexander Turnbull Library, Wellington, N.Z.; David A. Chappell,

Double Ghosts: Oceanian Voyagers on Euroamerican Ships (Armonk, N.Y.: M. E. Sharpe, 1997), 128; and Nicholas Thomas, *Islanders: The Pacific in the Age of Empire* (New Haven: Yale University Press, 2012), 1–2.

3. Maurice J. Quinlan, *Victorian Prelude: A History of English Manners, 1700–1830* (London: Frank Cass, 1965), esp. 179–201. See also Andrew St. George, *The Descent of Manners: Etiquette, Rules, and the Victorians* (London: Chatto and Windus, 1993).

4. Charles William Day, *Hints on Etiquette* (1836), 12.

5. Quoted in Michael Curtin, *Propriety and Position: A Study of Victorian Manners* (New York: Garland, 1987).

6. *The Book of Fashionable Life: comprising the etiquette of the drawing room, dining room and ball room. By a member of the Royal Household* (London: Hugh Cunningham, 1845), 10–11. In the eyes of the author, Indigenous North Americans fared better than their white American counterparts: in terms of manners, he or she wrote, "there is much more . . . among the Indians of the Forest, than among the *soi-disant* 'citizens' " (61).

7. *Brief Remarks on English Manners, and an Attempt to Account for Some of Our Most Striking Peculiarities* (London: Printed for John Booth, 1816), 107–8.

8. John Savage, *Some Account of New Zealand* (London: J. Murray, 1807), 102–5. Translations into te reo Māori come from Anne Salmond, *Between Worlds: Early Exchanges Between Māori and Europeans, 1773–1812* (Honolulu: University of Hawai'i Press, 1998), 344–45.

9. Savage, *Some Account of New Zealand*, 108.

10. Ibid., 106–9.

11. Peter Dillon, *Narrative and Successful Result of a Voyage in the South Seas* (London: Hurst, Chance, 1829), 201. Mahanga's time in London was not spent solely among elites like Fitzwilliam and the royals; with money gifted to him by Queen Charlotte, Mahanga engaged a prostitute named Nancy, who became pregnant from the encounter.

12. James Belich, *Making Peoples: A History of the New Zealanders to 1900* (New York: Penguin, 2012), 140–41; Chappell, *Double Ghosts*, 124–25; John Liddiard Nicholas, *Narrative of a Voyage to New Zealand* (Auckland: Wilson and Horton, 1971), 428–31; R. C. Barstow, *Transactions and Proceedings of the Royal Society of New Zealand 1868—1961*, vol. 15 (1882), 423; Ormond Wilson, *From Hongi Hika to Hone Heke: a Quarter Century of Upheaval* (Dunedin, N.Z.: J. McIndoe, 1985), 15–16; and Salmond, *Between Worlds*, 347.

13. Samuel Marsden, "Some Account of New Zealand, Obtained by the Rev. S. Marsden, from Duaterra, a Young Man of that Country, and Communicated to a Friend in London" (1809), Hocken Archives, University of Otago, n.p.; Belich, *Making Peoples*, 141–42; Chappell, *Double Ghosts*, 125; Samuel Marsden, *Letters and Journals of Samuel Marsden, 1764–1838*, ed. James Rawson Elder (Dunedin, N.Z.: Coulls, Somerville, Wilkie and A. H. Reed, 1932), 64–65; Salmond, *Between Worlds*, 410–11.

14. Belich, *Making Peoples*, 144; Robert McNab, *Historical Records of New Zealand* (Wellington, N.Z.: John McKay, 1908), 347; Nicholas, *Narrative of a Voyage*, 284; Chappell, *Double Ghosts*, 125–26; Marsden, *Letters and Journals*, 70–71; and "Memoir of Mowhee, a young New Zealander, who died at Paddington, Dec. 28, 1816," *Missionary Papers for the Use of the Weekly and Monthly Contributors to the Church Missionary Society* 10 (1818), n.p.

15. Chappell, *Double Ghosts*, 125; *Transactions and Proceedings of the Royal Society of New Zealand 1868–1961*, vol. 1 (1868), 423; Robert McNab, *From Tasman to Marsden: A History of Northern New Zealand from 1642 to 1818* (Dunedin, N.Z.: J. Wilkie, 1914), 120.

16. Chappell, *Double Ghosts*, 126; and Ormond Wilson, *Kororareka and Other Essays* (Dunedin, N.Z.: John McIndoe), 40–41; *The Times*, 8 July 1823, p. 2; and Brian Mackrell, *Hariru Wikitoria: Illustrated History of the Maori Tour of England, 1863* (Oxford: Oxford University Press, 1985), 11. Kiatara died a few weeks later, while the pair was performing at Leamington Spa in Warwickshire; he was buried there. See *The Times*, 20 August 1823, p. 2. Amahau died at Leeds and his body was preserved for display, likely ending up in a collection in Vienna. See Christian F. Feest, *Indians and Europe: An Interdisciplinary Collection of Essays* (Lincoln: University of Nebraska Press, 1999), 225.

17. John Rawson Elder, ed., *Marsden's Lieutenants* (Dunedin, N.Z.: Coulls, Somerville, Wilkie, and Reed, 1934), 163–66; Dorothy Cloher, *Hongi Hika: Warrior Chief* (Auckland: Penguin, 2003), 125–45; Judith Binney, *Legacy of Guilt: A Life of Thomas Kendall* (Wellington, N.Z.: Bridget Williams, 2005), 62–65; Wilson, *From Hongi Hika to Hone Heke*, 17–19; and Belich, *Making Peoples*, esp. 156–64.

18. For various explanations of the breaking of the 'Aikapu, see Noenoe Silva, *Aloha Betrayed: Native Hawaiian Resistance to American Colonialism* (Durham: University of North Carolina Press, 2004), 28–30. For the specific role that gender, and relationships between Hawaiian women and American missionaries, played in the process, see Jennifer Thigpen, *Island Queens*

and Mission Wives: How Gender and Empire Remade Hawai'i's Pacific World (Durham: University of North Carolina Press, 2014).

19. Lord Byron, *Voyage of the H.M.S. Blonde to the Sandwich Islands, in the years 1824–1925: Captain the Right Hon. Lord Byron, commander* (London: John Murray, 1826), iv–v, 52–53.

20. Mary Kawena Pukui, *'Olelo No'eau: Hawaiian Proverbs and Poetical Sayings* (Honolulu: Bishop Museum, 1997), 251. See also Kamanamaikalani Beamer, *Na Mākou Ka Mana: Liberating the Nation* (Honolulu: Kamehameha, 2014), 95.

21. For the identities of the party members, see Beamer, *Na Mākou Ka Mana*, 94–95.

22. For discussion of *'ahu'ula*, see Patrick Vinton Kirch, *A Shark Going Inland Is My Chief: The Island Civilization of Ancient Hawai'i* (Berkeley: University of California Press, 2012), 218–19.

23. Frank Lester Pleadwell, "The Voyage to England of King Liholiho and Queen Kamamalu," presented at the Social Science Association Annual Meeting, 1952, Hawai'i Historical Society, MS B K122p, n.p.; Adrienne L. Kaeppler, "'L'Aigle' and HMS 'Blonde': The Use of History in the Study of Ethnography," *Hawaiian Journal of History* 12 (1978), 29.

24. *The English Chronicle and Whitehall Evening Post*, 27 May 1824, 2; Pleadwell, "The Voyage to England," n.p.; Byron, *Voyage of the H.M.S. Blonde*, 63–64.

25. *The Times*, 20 May 1824, p. 2; *The Examiner*, 23 May 1824, 331; *Journal and Correspondences of Miss Berry from the Year 1783 to 1852*, ed. Lady Mary Theresa Lewis (London, 1865), 3:352–54; *The Journal of Mrs. Arbuthnot*, ed. Francis Bamford (London: Macmillan, 1950), 1:315–19.

26. Byron, *Voyage of the H.M.S. Blonde*, 59–60, 61, 63; *The Times*, 1 June 1824, p. 3.

27. *Journal of Mrs. Arbuthnot*, 1:319; *The Times*, 1 June 1824, p. 3. For discussion of *alaka'ina*, see Malcolm Nāea Chun, *No Nā Mamo, Traditional and Contemporary Hawaiian Beliefs and Practices* (Honolulu: University of Hawai'i Press, 2011).

28. Beamer, *Na Mākou Ka Mana*, 91.

29. Byron, *Voyage of the H.M.S. Blonde*, 62.

30. Pukui, *'ōlelo No'eau*, 225.

31. Beamer, *Na Mākou Ka Mana*, 91; Byron, *Voyage of the H.M.S. Blonde*, 101; *The Times*, 15 July 1824, p. 2.

32. Donald Angus, compiler, "London visit and death of King Liholiho and

Queen Kamamalu, official correspondence," Hawai'i Historical Society, MS B K122a, 2–3; *The Times*, 13 July 1824, p. 3; *Derby Mercury*, 14 July 1824; Chun, *No Nā Mamo*, 8.

33. Angus, "London visit and death," 6.

34. *The Times*, 13 July 1824, p. 3; *The Times*, 15 July 1824, p. 3; Byron, *Voyage of the H.M.S. Blonde*, 71; *The Times*, 16 July 1824, p. 2; Pleadwell, "The Voyage to England," n.p.; *The Times*, 13 July 1824, p. 3; *The Times*, 15 July 1824, p. 2.

35. Byron, *Voyage of the H.M.S. Blonde*, 70, 73; Angus, "London visit and death," 18, 29.

36. Pukui, *'Ōlelo No'eau*, 109.

37. *The Hermit in London; or, sketches of English Manners* (1819), 3:248; *The Times*, 31 May 1838, p. 3; *Ipswich Journal*, 9 June 1838; *Trewman's Exeter Flying Post and Cornish Advertiser*, 7 June 1838; *Morning Chronicle*, 17 May 1838.

38. *Trewman's Exeter Flying Post and Cornish Advertiser*, 7 June 1838; *The Times*, 31 May 1838, p. 3; John Ward, *Information Relative to New Zealand: Compiled for the Use of Colonists* (London: John W. Parker, 1840), 71–72.

39. *The Times*, 31 May 1838, p. 3. For a history of the company, see Patricia Burns, *Fatal Success: A History of the New Zealand Company*, ed. Henry Richardson (Auckland: Heinemann Reed, 1989).

40. *Morning Chronicle*, 29 April 1839.

41. Poia Rewi, *Whaikōrero: The World of Māori Oratory* (Auckland: Auckland University Press, 2010), 37–55.

42. Ward, *Information Relative to New Zealand*, 71–72.

43. Amiria J. M. Henare, *Museums, Anthropology, and Imperial Exchange* (Cambridge: Cambridge University Press, 2005), 133–34.

44. Ward, *Information Relative to New Zealand*, 72–73.

45. Alexander Liholiho, *The Journal of Prince Alexander Liholiho*, ed. Jacob Adler (Honolulu: University of Hawai'i Press, 1967), 36.

46. Jonathan K. K. Osorio, *Dismembering Lāhui: A History of the Hawaiian Nation to 1887* (Honolulu: University of Hawai'i Press, 2003), 44–50. For further discussion, see Silva, *Aloha Betrayed*, 41–43; and Haunani-Kay Trask, *From a Native Daughter: Colonialism and Sovereignty in Hawai'i* (Honolulu: University of Hawai'i Press, 1993), 8–9.

47. *The Times*, 27 December 1849, p. 6.

48. *The Times*, 20 April 1850, p. 8; *The Times*, 29 April 1850, pp. 4–5; Liholiho, *The Journal*, 88.

49. Liholiho, *The Journal*, 31, 35, 88, 90–91, 96.

50. Ibid., 32, 88, 96; Lot Kamehameha, *Journal of Voyages to the United States, Great Britain, and France Written on Board the Schooner* Honolulu (original ms. in the Bishop Museum, typescript by Margo Morgan), 44, 48–49.

51. Kamehameha, *Journal*, 41.

52. Ibid., 51. The brothers' resistance to outside authority over Hawai'i can also be seen in the fact that in 1854 Alexander, as Kamehameha IV, canceled all negotiations over possible annexation to the United States, claiming instead what he and his government called "sovereignty with reciprocity" with foreign powers. For these events in the broader context of the Hawaiian sovereignty movement, see Trask, *From a Native Daughter*, 7.

53. For Tamihana's account of his father's exploits, see *Life and Times of Te Rauparaha by His Son Tamihana Te Rauparaha*, ed. Peter Butler (Martinborough, N.Z.: Alister Taylor, 1980); Belich, *Making Peoples*, 204–6; Mackrell, *Hariru Wikitoria*, 11–13; and H. W. Hipango, "The Haerenga ki Rawahi: From the Writings of H. W. Hipango," *Te Wharekura* 16 (1969), 17–31.

54. Belich, *Making Peoples*, 230–45.

55. The full roster of the touring group, with their *iwi*, was as follows: Kihirini Te Tuahu, of Tuhourangi; Huria Ngahuia, of Ngāti Whanaunga; Takerei Ngawaka, of Ngāti Tuwharetoa; Hapimana Ngapiko, of Te Āti Awa; and from the Ngāpuhi, in addition to the Pomare couple, Horomona Te Atua, Reihana Te Taukawau, Kamariera Te Hautakiri Wharepapa, Hariata Haumu, Paratene Te Manu, Tere Hariata Te Iringa, Wiremu Pou (also known as Wiremu Te Wana or Te Whai), and Hirini Pakia.

56. "Statements of Reihana Taukawau," 8 March 1864, *Church of England in New Zealand: Letters from and Concerning Māori Chiefs Who Visited England in 1864*, quoted in Mackrell, *Hariru Wikitoria*, 25.

57. For the identities of the members of the group, see Mackrell, *Hariru Wikitoria*, 21–23; see also Paula Morris, *Rangatira: A Novel* (Auckland: Penguin, 2011), xii.

58. Mackrell, *Hariru Wikitoria*, 34.

59. *Morning Herald*, 15 June 1863; Mackrell, *Hariru Wikitoria*, 34–36, 79–83; "The Queen and the Maori Chiefs," *Aborigines' Friend and Colonial Intelligencer*, January 1863–December 1864, 378–79.

60. Mackrell, *Hariru Wikitoria*, 36–37, 39–40, 45.

61. Ibid., 22, 35, 47–50; James Cowan, *Pictures of Old New Zealand: The Partridge Collection of Maori Paintings by Gottfried Lindauer* (Auckland: Whitcombe and Tombs, 1930), 81.

62. Mackrell, *Hariru Wikitoria*, 65–66; *Caledonian Mercury*, 30 September 1863, p. 1; *Daily News*, 22 March 1864, p. 2.

63. *Hampshire Telegraph and Sussex Chronicle*, 27 September 1865, pp. 4–5; *The Times*, 5 July 1865, p. 6; *Jackson's Oxford Journal*, 22 July 1865, p. 3; and *The Times*, 28 October 1865, p. 7.

64. 1865 Journal of Queen Emma, Bishop Museum Archives, MSMC K4, box 2.2, unproofed/unedited typescript, 19 July, 28 July, and 7 August.

65. 1866 Journal of Queen Emma, Bishop Museum Archives, MSMC K4, box 2.5, unproofed/edited typescript, 2 July, 16 July, 23 July, and 30 July.

66. 1865 Journal of Queen Emma, 18 July, 22 July, and 24 July.

67. For discussion of later-nineteenth-century developments in New Zealand, see Belich, *Making Peoples*. For one of the most comprehensive and critical treatments of Hawaiian-American relations in the late nineteenth century, see Silva, *Aloha Betrayed*.

INTERLUDE FIVE: A HAT FACTORY

1. For a general overview of the trade in beaver pelts in the late nineteenth century, see Arthur J. Ray, *The Canadian Fur Trade in the Industrial Age* (Toronto: University of Toronto Press, 1990).

   The primary sources quoted here are the pamphlet "Ye Felt Hatterie in the Exhibition of 1884," number 5874 in the British Library's Evanion Collection; the back page of Charles Dickens's *London, 1879: An Unconventional Handbook* (London: Charles Dickens, 1879); and transcripts of Cree elders' statements about hunting, from Lynn Whidden, *Essential Song: Three Decades of Northern Cree Music* (Waterloo, Ont.: Wilfrid Laurier University Press, 2007).

   Words for "beaver house" in Cree, Ojibwe, and Dene come respectively from the Online Cree Dictionary (www.creedictionary.com), Ojibwe People's Dictionary (ojibwe.lib.umn.edu/), and the South Slavey Topical Dictionary (www.ssdec.nt.ca/Dictionary/dict_home2.html).

CHAPTER 6. CIVILIZATION ITSELF CONSENTS

Epigraph: "If It Wasn't for the 'Ouses in Between," lyrics by Edgar Bateman, in Paul Bailey, *The Oxford Book of London* (Oxford: Oxford University Press, 1996), 199–200.

1. *The Era*, 29 October 1876; see also Jerry Wasserman, "Aboriginal Dance,

Military Drill: Captain MacDonald's Trained Indians and 19th-Century Variety Entertainment," in *A World of Popular Entertainments: An Edited Volume of Critical Essays*, ed. Gillian Arrighi and Victor Emeljanow (Cambridge: Cambridge Scholars, 2012), 3–16.

2. Arthur W. Symons, *London: A Book of Aspects* (London: Chiswick, 1909), 13–17.

3. See Lara Baker Phelan, *Class, Culture, and Suburban Anxieties in the Victorian Era* (London: Routledge, 2010); Stephen Inwood, *A History of London* (London: Macmillan, 2000), 541–89.

4. James Cantlie, *Degeneration Among Londoners* (London: Leadenhall, 1885), 24–25.

5. Gail Cunningham, "Navigating Suburbia in Late Victorian Writing," *Victorian Literature and Culture* 32:2 (2004), 423; Patrick Brantlinger, *Taming Cannibals: Race and the Victorians* (Syracuse: Cornell University Press, 2011), 20.

6. Thomas Crosland, *The Suburbans* (London: John Long, 1905), 20.

7. Cantlie, *Degeneration*, 52; John Tosh, "Masculinities in an Industrializing Society: Britain, 1800–1914," *Journal of British Studies* 44:2 (2005), 330–42; and Todd Kuchta, *Semi-Detached Empire: Suburbia and the Colonization of Britain, 1880 to the Present* (Charlottesville: University of Virginia Press, 2010), 15.

8. Richard Holt, *Sport and the British: A Modern History* (Oxford: Clarendon Press, 1990), 88; Derek Birley, *Sport and the Making of Britain* (Manchester, U.K.: Manchester University Press, 1993); *The Times* quoted in Greg Ryan, *Forerunners of the All Blacks: The 1888–89 New Zealand Native Football Team in Britain, Australia, and New Zealand* (Canterbury, N.Z.: Canterbury University Press, 1993), 50.

9. Symons, *London: A Book of Aspects*, 13.

10. *Liverpool Mercury*, 11 September 1861.

11. For the life of Hutgohsodoneh, see Rob Hadgraft, *Deerfoot, Athletics' Noble Savage: From Indian Reservation to Champion of the World* (Southend-on-Sea, U.K.: Desert Island, 2007).

12. Holt, *Sport and the British*, 194.

13. Birley, *Sport and the Making of Britain*, 239–42.

14. Hadgraft, *Deerfoot*, 34–35.

15. For Hutgohsodoneh's early life, see Hadgraft, *Deerfoot*, 13–32. For the broader political and cultural contexts of his upbringing, see Laurence M. Hauptman, *Conspiracy of Interests: Iroquois Dispossession and the Rise of New York State* (Syracuse: Syracuse University Press, 1999).

16. *Caledonian Mercury,* 11 December 1861; *Belfast News-letter,* 12 December 1861.

17. *The Era,* 15 September 1861.

18. Ibid., 29 September 1861.

19. *Glasgow Herald,* 12 September 1861; *Morning Chronicle,* 26 November 1861; *The Era,* 29 September 1861; *Liverpool Mercury,* 11 September 1861; and *The Era,* 15 September 1861.

20. *The Era,* 29 September 1861; *Derby Mercury,* 16 October 1861; *The Times,* 26 November 1861; *Morning Chronicle,* 24 October 1861; and *The Times,* 17 December 1861.

21. *Daily News,* 10 January 1863; Hadgraft, *Deerfoot,* 95–106.

22. Hadgraft, *Deerfoot,* 9–12, 185–205; Birley, *Sport and the Making of Britain,* 242, 279.

23. Jungunjinanuke also appears as "Kickakick" in James Joyce's *Ulysses;* see Anthony Bateman, *Cricket, Literature, and Culture: Symbolising the Nation, Destabilising Empire* (Farnham, U.K.: Ashgate, 2009), 86–87.

24. Charles Box, *The English Game of Cricket: Comprising a Digest of Its Origins, Character, History, and Progress* (London: Field Office, 1877), 328.

25. Frank Gerald, *A Millionaire in Memories* (London: George Routledge and Sons, 1936), 213; Ashley Mallett, *The Black Lords of Summer: The Story of the Aboriginal Tour of England and Beyond* (St. Lucia, Australia: University of Queensland Press, 2002), 107–10.

26. *Bell's Life in London,* 23 May 1868, quoted in Mallett, *The Black Lords,* 90–91.

27. Holt, *Sport and the British,* 178.

28. *Reynold's Newspaper,* 31 May 1868, p. 8.

29. Mallett, *The Black Lords,* 95–96; Box, *The English Game of Cricket,* 328–29.

30. Box, *The English Game of Cricket,* 327.

31. Mallett, *The Black Lords,* 105, 111; Frank Gerald, *A Millionaire in Memories,* 211; Bateman, *Cricket, Literature, and Culture,* 140–41.

32. *American Cricketer,* 24 May 1885, quoted in Mallett, *The Black Lords,* 111; Box, *The English Game of Cricket,* 324.

33. Keith A. P. Sandiford, "Cricket and the Victorian Society," *Journal of Social History* 17:2 (1983), 304–5.

34. Anthony Bateman, *Cricket, Literature, and Culture,* 121; and Mike Marqusee, *Anyone But England: An Outsider Looks at English Cricket* (London: Aurum, 2005), 73. See also Manthia Diawara, "Englishness and Blackness: Cricket as Discourse on Colonialism," *Callaloo* 13:4 (Autumn 1990), 830–44; Rowland Bowen, *Cricket: A History of Its Growth and Development Throughout*

the World (London: Eyre and Spottiswoode, 1970); and J. A. Mangan, *The Games Ethic and Imperialism: Aspects of the Diffusion of an Ideal* (New York: Viking, 1985).

35. M. F. Christie, *Aborigines in Colonial Victoria, 1835–86* (Sydney: Sydney University Press, 1979), 29–31, 41; Robert Kenny, *The Lamb Enters the Dreaming: Nathanael Pepper and the Ruptured World* (Melbourne: Scribe, 2007), 218–22; Giordano Nanni, *The Colonisation of Time: Ritual, Routine, and Resistance in the British Empire* (Manchester, U.K.: Manchester University Press, 2012).

36. *Bell's Life in London*, 28 May 1868, quoted in Mallett, *The Black Lords*, 90–91.

37. Ibid.; *Reynold's Newspaper*, 28 June 1868, p. 5; Mallett, *The Black Lords*, 140.

38. Holt, *Sport and the British*, 222; Mallett, *The Black Lords*, 102–3, 152–69, 193; Kenny, *The Lamb Enters the Dreaming*, 306–7.

39. Ryan, *Forerunners of the All Blacks*, 52–54.

40. Ibid., 16; Scott A. G. M. Crawford, "A Sporting Image: The Emergence of a National Identity in a Colonial Setting, 1862–1906," *Victorian Periodicals Review* 21:2 (1988), 56–63; Timothy J. L. Chandler and John Nauright, eds., *Making Men: Rugby and Masculine Identity* (London: Frank Cass, 1996), 70–80.

41. Michelle Erai, "A Queer Caste: Mixing Race and Sexuality in Colonial New Zealand," in *Queer Indigenous Studies*, ed. Qwo-Li Driskill, Chris Finley, Brian Joseph Gilley, and Scott Lauria Morgensen (Tucson: University of Arizona Press, 2011); and Angela Wanhalla, *Matters of the Heart: A History of Interracial Marriage in New Zealand* (Auckland: Auckland University Press, 2013).

42. Margaret Jolly, "Moving Masculinities: Memories and Bodies Across Oceania," *The Contemporary Pacific* 20:1 (2008), 1–24; Malcolm MacLean, "Of Warriors and Blokes: The Problem of Maori Rugby for Pakeha Masculinity in New Zealand," in *Making the Rugby World: Race, Gender, Commerce*, ed. Timothy J. L. Chandler and John Nauright (London: Frank Cass, 1999), 9; Brendan Hokowhitu, "Māori Rugby and Subversion: Creativity, Domestication, Suppression, and Decolonization," *International Journal of the History of Sport* 26:16 (2009), 2314–44; Lachy Paterson, "Hawekaihe: Maori Voices on the Position of 'Half-Castes' Within Maori Society," *Journal of New Zealand Studies*, 135–55.

43. Ryan, *Forerunners of the All Blacks*, 12–15, 133–40 (for biographies of all the players); Eric Dunning and Keith Sheard, *Barbarians, Gentlemen, and Players: A Sociological Study of the Development of Rugby Football* (Oxford:

Martin Robertson, 1979), 101; Tony Collins, *Rugby's Great Split: Class, Culture, and the Origins of Rugby League Football* (London: Frank Cass, 1998).

44. Quoted in Ryan, *Forerunners of the All Blacks,* 44–45.

45. Brendan Hokowhitu, "'Physical Beings': Stereotypes, Sports, and the 'Physical Education' of New Zealand Maori," in *Ethnicity, Sport, Identity: Struggles for Status,* ed. J. A. Mangan and A. Ritchie (London: Frank Cass, 2004), 192–218, 211; *The Times,* 28 September 1888; the cartoon is reprinted in Ryan, *Forerunner of the All Blacks,* 53.

46. *The Times,* 6 May 1889.

47. Ryan, *Forerunners of the All Blacks,* 56, 94, 141–42.

48. Nicholas Black Elk, *Black Elk Speaks: Being the Life Story of a Holy Man of the Oglala Sioux* (Lincoln: University of Nebraska Press, 1993), 226–27. The dream actually took place in Paris.

49. Kate Flint, *The Transatlantic Indian, 1776–1930* (Princeton: Princeton University Press, 2008), 230.

50. Bobby Bridger, *Buffalo Bill and Sitting Bull: Inventing the Wild West* (Austin: University of Texas Press, 2002), 336; Paul Reddin, *Wild West Shows* (Urbana: University of Illinois Press, 1999), 86.

51. Bridger, *Buffalo Bill and Sitting Bull,* 336–37.

52. L. G. Moses, *Wild West Shows and the Images of American Indians* (Albuquerque: University of New Mexico Press, 1996), 52–54.

53. For a list of early-twentieth-century tour dates, see Charles Eldridge Griffin, *Four Years in Europe with Buffalo Bill* (Lincoln: University of Nebraska Press, 2010), 137–53.

54. *Western Mail,* 5 May 1887.

55. Sam A. Maddra, *Hostiles? The Lakota Ghost Dance and Buffalo Bill's Wild West* (Norman: University of Oklahoma Press, 2006), 129–32; Reddin, *Wild West Shows,* 94.

56. Joy Kasson, *Buffalo Bill's Wild West: Celebrity, Memory, and Popular History* (Vancouver: Douglas and McIntyre, 2000), 65–69, 77–79; Louis Warren, "Buffalo Bill Meets Dracula: William F. Cody, Bram Stoker, and the Frontiers of Social Decay," *American Historical Review* 107:4 (October 2002), 1135–37.

57. Reddin, *Wild West Shows,* 87; Warren, "Buffalo Bill Meets Dracula," 1146; *Sunday Chronicle,* 17 October 1887; Bridger, *Buffalo Bill and Sitting Bull,* 325.

58. Bridger, *Buffalo Bill and Sitting Bull,* 329–30; Reddin, *Wild West Shows,* 87.

59. Luther Standing Bear, *My People the Sioux* (New York: Houghton Mifflin, 1928), 256; *The Era,* 27 August 1887; Warren, "Buffalo Bill Meets Dracula,"

1133–34; Moses, *Wild West Shows,* 46; Kasson, *Buffalo Bill's Wild West,* 188–90.

60. Alan Gallop, *Buffalo Bill's British Wild West* (Stroud: Sutton, 2001), 49.

61. For a historiographical discussion, see Stephen Howe, ed., *The New Imperial Histories Reader* (London: Routledge, 2009).

62. Official guide to White City Exhibition, Kiralfy Archive, accession 82.232, box 8.2, Museum of London archives.

INTERLUDE SIX: A NOTEBOOK

1. The life of Anthony M. Fernando is chronicled in Fiona Paisley, *The Lone Protestor: A. M. Fernando in Australia and Europe* (Canberra, Australia: Aboriginal Studies Press, 2012). Fernando's notebooks are held at the Australian Institute of Aboriginal and Torres Strait Islander Studies.

CHAPTER 7. THE CITY OF LONG MEMORY

Epigraphs: Sir Alexander Cuming, "Journal of Sir Alexander Cuming (1730)," in *Early Travels in the Tennessee Country, 1540–1800,* ed. Samuel Cole Williams (Johnson City, Tenn.: Watauga, 1928), 142; Jodi Byrd, *The Transit of Empire: Indigenous Critiques of Colonialism* (Minneapolis: University of Minnesota Press, 2011), xiv.

1. The return of Long Wolf had begun in 1991 with the work of Worcestershire resident Elizabeth Knight and the U.K.-based American Indian Support Group. In addition to Long Wolf, the grave in question contained the remains of his seventeen-month-old daughter Star Ghost Dog, although this part of the story is subdued or avoided altogether in press coverage. See "Chief Long Wolf Goes Home, 105 Years Late," www.cnn.com/WORLD/9709/25/chief.long.wolf/, 25 September 1997, accessed 14 June 2013; "London to Wounded Knee: Custer's Conqueror Goes Home," *The Independent,* 23 September 1997; "Family Seeks New Burial Ground for Chief Who Died in London," *The Times,* 31 January 1995; "After 121 Years, Long Wolf Will Be Buried at Wounded Knee," *The Times,* 23 September 1997; and "Chief Returns to Beloved Black Hills," *The Times,* 26 September 1997.

2. Quoted in Antoinette Burton, "Rules of Thumb: British History and 'Imperial Culture' in Nineteenth- and Twentieth-Century Britain," *New Imperial Histories Reader,* ed. Stephen Howe (London: Routledge, 2009), 43.

3. John M. MacKenzie, "The Persistence of Empire in Metropolitan Culture," in *New Imperial Histories Reader,* 274; Wendy Webster, "The Empire Comes Home: Commonwealth Migration to Britain," in *Britain's Experience of Empire in the Twentieth Century,* ed. Andrew Thompson (Oxford: Oxford University Press, 2012), 287.

4. Stuart Ward, "Introduction," *British Culture and the End of Empire,* ed. Stuart Ward (Manchester, U.K.: Manchester University Press, 2001), 12; Thompson, "Introduction," *Britain's Experience of Empire,* 1–32; Jodi Burkett, *Constructing Post-Imperial Britain: Britishness, "Race" and the Radical Left in the 1960s* (Basingstoke, U.K.: Palgrave MacMillan, 2013), 158; Krishnan Kumar, "Empire, Nation, and National Identities," in *Britain's Experience of Empire,* 298–329; J. E. Wilson, "Niall Ferguson's Imperial Passion," *History Workshop Journal* 56:1 (2003), 175–83; Bill Schwarz, *Memories of Empire,* vol. 1: *The White Man's World* (Oxford: Oxford University Press, 2011), 6, 12.

5. John M. MacKenzie, general editor's introduction, in *British Culture and the End of Empire,* ed. Stuart Ward (Manchester, U.K.: Manchester University Press, 2001), vi.

6. John Darwin, *The Empire Project: The Rise and Fall of the British World-System, 1830–1970* (Cambridge: Cambridge University Press, 2011), 648.

7. For a discussion of the trip, see "The Constitution and the Trip to England," *National Indian* 2:5 (January 1979), 6–7; "Chiefs Visit England," *National Indian* 2:10 (July 1979), 2; and "Business Suits Replace Moccasins for Chiefs' Constitution Message," *Globe and Mail,* 11 July 1979, repr. in *National Indian* 2:10 (July 1979), 6–7. For a general history of the fractious debates surrounding patriation, see Fréderic Bastien, *The Battle of London: Trudeau, Thatcher, and the Fight for Canada's Constitution* (Toronto: Dundurn, 2014).

8. "Faulkner Says Chiefs' U.K. Jaunt 'Theatre,'" *National Indian* 2:10 (July 1979), 5; "Extraordinary Lobby," *House Magazine,* n.d., repr. in *National Indian* 2:10 (July 1979), 14; and "Business Suits Replace Moccasins," 6–7.

9. "Constitutional Update," *Indian News* 22:8 (November 1981), 8.

10. Keith Banting and Richard Simeon, eds., *And No One Cheered: Federalism, Democracy, and the Constitution Act* (Toronto: Methuen, 1983), 305.

11. Byron Rogers, "Mohawk Girl Appeals to Fair Play," *The Times,* 20 May 1969, 6.

12. J. R. Miller, "Petitioning the Great White Mother: First Nations' Organizations and Lobbying in London," in *Canada and the End of Empire,* ed. Phillip Buckner (Vancouver: UBC Press, 2005), 299–318; Cecilia Morgan,

"Wigwam to Westminster: Performing Mohawk Identity in Imperial Britain, 1890s–1990s," *Gender and History* 15:2 (2003), 319–41.

13. For the context of the Proclamation of 1763, see Colin G. Calloway, *The Scratch of a Pen: 1763 and the Transformation of North America* (Oxford: Oxford University Press, 2006).

14. Delegation documents in author's collection.

15. Marlene J. Norst, *Burnum Burnum: A Warrior for Peace* (Sydney: Kangaroo, 1999), frontispiece.

16. Ibid., 132–38.

17. Ashley Mallett, *Black Lords of Summer: The Story of the 1868 Aboriginal Tour of England and Beyond* (Brisbane: University of Queensland Press, 2002), 141.

18. See "Aboriginal Cricketer Not Forgotten," *Daily Telegraph* (Sydney), 15 July 1996; "Plaque Restores Memory of Aboriginal Cricketer," *The Advertiser*, 15 July 1996.

19. Mallett, *The Black Lords*, 143–46; see also "About Cricket," *Daily Telegraph*, 1 September 2001.

20. For the broader political and legal context of Mahomet Weyonomon's journey, see Paul Grant-Costa, "The Last Indian War in New England: The Mohegan Indians v. the Governour and Company of the Colony of Connecticut, 1703–1774" (Ph.D. diss., Yale University, 2008).

21. "Marriages & Deaths &c. in August," *Gentleman's Magazine* 6:487, 1736; *Grub Street Journal* 346 (12 August 1736).

22. "Wigwam Ma'am," *The Sun*, 23 November 2006; Caroline Davies, "Queen Buries Hatchet with a Host of the Mohegans," *Daily Telegraph*, 23 November 2006, 5; and "Me Big Chief Elizabeth," *Daily Mail*, 23 November 2006, 11. More neutral coverage of the event included Rebecca English, "Queen Honours the Lost of the Mohegans," *Daily Mail*, 18 November 2006, 3; "Court Circular," *The Times*, 23 November 2006, 82; "Queen Accepts Pipe of Peace," *The Times*, 23 November 2006, 26; "News in Brief," *Evening Standard*, 23 November 2006, 6. Parts of the event were also broadcast on television programs around the world, including the *Today* show in the United States. For the Mohegan take on the event, see the Mohegan Tribe's official newsletter, *Ni Ya Yo* 3:7 (Wolf Moon 2007), 1, 6–7.

23. The Mohegan Tribe, "Our Vision," http://www.mohegan.nsn.us/our_vision.htm, accessed 11 February 2012.

24. Alden Vaughan, *Transatlantic Encounters: American Indians in Great Britain, 1500–1776* (Cambridge: Cambridge University Press, 2007), 4–9.

25. Susan Rowley, "Frobisher Miksanut: Inuit Accounts of the Frobisher Voyages," in *The Archaeology of the Frobisher Voyages*, ed. William W. Fitzhugh and Jacqueline S. Olin (Washington, D.C.: Smithsonian Institution Press, 1993), 31–32.

26. Artist's statement at www.firstvisionart.com/tania/peter.html, accessed January 16, 2015.

27. E-mail from Peter Morin to the author, 3 March 2015. Used by permission.

28. Ibid.

29. *St. Olave's Hart Street* (London: n.p., 1933), 1, 11.

30. A. A. Gill, "My London, and Welcome To It," *New York Times*, 27 April 2012.

31. For further discussion, see Felicity Barnes, *New Zealand's London: A Colony and Its Metropolis* (Auckland: Auckland University Press, 2012), 2.

32. For Papakura, see http://www.teara.govt.nz/en/biographies/3p5/papakura-makereti, accessed 14 March 2015. For the soldiers, see Alan Gallop, *The House with the Golden Eyes* (Sunbury-on-Thames, U.K.: Running Horse, 1998), 110.

33. Interview with Esther Jessop and Maia Nuku, 14 April 2014. Used by permission.

34. Ibid.

35. For the history of Hinemihi, see Gallop, *The House with the Golden Eyes;* and Dean Sully, ed., *Decolonizing Conservation: Caring for Maori Meeting Houses Outside New Zealand* (Walnut Creek, Calif.: Left Coast, 2007).

36. Karl Burrows, "Hinemihi and the London Māori Community," in *Decolonizing Conservation*, Sully, ed., 161–63, 167.

37. Interview with Jessop and Nuku; Conal McCarthy, *Exhibiting Maori: A History of Colonial Cultures of Display* (London: Berg, 2007), 120; and Amiria Henare, *Museums, Anthropology, and Imperial Exchange* (Cambridge: Cambridge University Press, 2005), 3.

38. For a discussion of the exhibit out of which *The Connection with London* emerged, see Briar Wood, Amiria J. M. Henare, Maureen Lander, and Kahu Te Kanawa, "Visiting the House of Gifts: The 1998 'Maori' Exhibition at the British Museum," *Journal of New Zealand Literature* 21 (2003), 83–101.

39. See www.parishoftyendinaga.org/chapelroyal.htm.

40. For local accounts of Tomochichi and his relationship to Savannah's history, see Helen Todd, *Tomochichi: Indian Friend of the Georgia Colony* (Atlanta: Cherokee, 1977), and C. C. Jones, Jr., *Historical Sketch of Tomochichi, Mico of the Yamacraws* (Savannah: C. C. Jones, 1868).

41. Personal communication with Gordon Handcock, professor emeritus of geography, Memorial University of Newfoundland, 18 and 21 September 2013. According to Handcock, the Inuit communities of Labrador were not consulted in this renaming.

42. For documents and narratives related to Bennelong's story in Sydney, see findingbennelong.com.

43. See, for example, Kamanamaikalani Beamer, *No Mākou Ka Mana: Liberating the Nation* (Honolulu: Kamehameha, 2014), in which the author writes, "From my perspective, Liholiho's voyage is a strategic accomplishment for the preservation of the Hawaiian kingdom. Liholiho and his dying companions can be considered martyrs for Hawaiian independence—possessors of daring spirits—reminiscent of early ali'i . . . who navigated vast oceans seeking good fortune and meeting with foreigners in their own lands" (p. 100).

44. Jocelyn Hackforth-Jones, *Between Worlds: Voyagers to Britain, 1700–1850* (London: National Portrait Gallery, 2007), 22–35, 56–77.

45. "Native of the Capital," *Evening Standard*, 23 October 1995, p. 54.

46. According to the one newspaper account, a clipping in the church's records pointed to the remains belonging to a woman named Ah-mik-waw-begum-o-je (Beaver or Diving Mouse), who died in 1835 after being christened Antoinette. I have found no other reference to this person. See *The Times*, 24 November 1932, p. 9.

47. "Pocahontas Musical Next Month," *The Times*, 19 September 1963, p. 16; "Princess Pocahontas," *The Times*, 24 October 1963, p. 15; "Jumping the Boxing Day Gun: Lyric Theatre, Pocahontas," *The Times*, 15 November 1963, p. 17; "Patricia Cornwell Offers New Window on Pocahontas Row," *Sunday Telegraph*, 29 April 2001, p. 7; "Shattered: Patricia's Window Vow," *Daily Mail*, 9 December 2005, p. 47; "Pocahontas's Historic Earrings Return to U.K.," *Western Daily Press*, 13 June 2005, p. 9.

48. *The Times*, personal ads, 26 August 2006, p. 71; "For a Different View of London, Get Off the Beaten Railway Track," *The Times*, 21 July 2007, Features p. 4; *Evening Standard*, 25 November 1995, p. 45.

49. John Darwin, *The Empire Project: The Rise and Fall of the British World System, 1830–1970* (Cambridge: Cambridge University Press, 2009), 546; Jodi Burkett, *Constructing Post-Imperial Britain: Britishness, "Race" and the Radical Left in the 1960s* (Basingstoke, U.K.: Palgrave MacMillan, 2013), 68, 72; John Eade, *Placing London: From Imperial Capital to Global City* (New York: Berghahn, 2000), 179.

50. Jean M. O'Brien, *Firsting and Lasting: Writing Indians Out of Existence in New England* (Minneapolis: University of Minnesota Press, 2011). See also Coll Thrush and Colleen Boyd, eds., *Phantom Past, Indigenous Presence: Native Ghosts in North American History and Culture* (Lincoln: University of Nebraska Press, 2011).

51. Iain Sinclair, *Downriver* (London: Penguin, 1991), 11, 469–72.

52. Mike Bannister, *Pocahontas in Ludgate* (Durham, U.K.: Arrowhead, 2007).

53. The Monacan were not originally part of the Powhatan polity, but in recent centuries they have become allied with other Virginia tribes.

54. Virginia Indian Festival program brochure, 2006, copy in author's possession. The Pamunkey Indian Tribe obtained federal recognition in the summer of 2015.

55. Linwood "Little Bear" Custalow and Angela L. "Silver Star" Daniel, *The True Story of Pocahontas: The Other Side of History* (Golden, Colo.: Fulcrum, 2007), 79–88; Paula Gunn Allen, *Pocahontas: Medicine Woman, Spy, Entrepreneur, Diplomat* (New York: HarperOne, 2004).

EPILOGUE

1. "The City of Dreadful Night" first appeared as a serial in *The National Reformer* on 22 March, 12 and 26 April, and 27 May 1874.

2. James Thomson, "Sundays at Hampstead," in *London: A History in Verse* (Cambridge: Harvard University Press, 2012), 418.

3. Rudyard Kipling, "In the Neolithic Age," in *The Seven Seas* (London: Methuen, 1896), 399–400; and "The River's Tale," in *London: A History in Verse*, 471–72.

4. The writings by Evaristo and Rosen are untitled and appeared on the walls of the "London Before London" exhibition in 2013 at the Museum of London. Evaristo's poem is used with her permission.

5. Jonathan Cotton, personal communication with the author.

6. Worthington G. Smith, *Man the Primeval Savage: His Haunts and Relics from the Hill-Tops of Bedfordshire to Blackwall* (London: Edward Stanford, 1894), 45–59.

7. Will Self, *Psychogeography* (London: Bloomsbury, 2007), 138.

Index

Page numbers in italic type refer to illustrations